DATE DUE

Legislators and Politicians: Iowa's Women Lawmakers

Legislators and Politicians: Iowa's Women Lawmakers

SUZANNE O'DEA SCHENKEN

8 September 1996

Suzanne O'Dea Schenken

IOWA STATE UNIVERSITY PRESS / AMES

Suzanne O'Dea Schenken, a former floor clerk in the Iowa House of Representatives, columnist, and lobbyist, received her PhD in history from Iowa State University. She is presently an independent researcher and writer, currently writing a book-length biography.

♾ Printed on acid-free paper in the United States of America

First edition, 1995

Library of Congress Cataloging-in-Publication Data

Schenken, Suzanne O'Dea
Legislators and politicians: Iowa's women lawmakers / Suzanne O'Dea Schenken.
p. cm.
Includes bibliographical references and index.
ISBN 0-8138-2277-7
1. Women in politics—Iowa. 2. Women legislators—Iowa. I. Title
HQ1236.5.U6S34 1993
328.777'0082—dc20 95-14434

CONTENTS

ACKNOWLEDGMENTS

Several individuals and corporations contributed to making this book possible. The first among them is Minnette Doderer, who had the idea for an oral history of the women who had and were serving in the Iowa General Assembly. The research from that project led to further efforts that resulted in this work.

More than sixty women legislators, in addition to the family members and friends of deceased lawmakers, spent hours narrating the stories of women lawmakers. They also read the transcriptions of the interviews and edited them. These people have made significant contributions to Iowa history and women's history. The stories that they told have given life to this work that could come only from the legislators themselves or the people who knew them. The forthrightness with which they described the experiences permitted interpretations that otherwise would not have been possible. These women and men had the courage to tell the stories without the cloak of anonymity. I hope that I have honored their trust.

Professor Richard S. Kirkendall defended the oral history project when its validity was questioned. Through his explanations of its significance, he prevented its premature death. When Kirkendall left Iowa State University, Professor John Dobson kindly accepted its oversight. Dobson read early interview transcripts and made helpful and constructive suggestions. When I was trying to turn the research into a dissertation, Dobson patiently helped me through numerous attempts to organize the material I had gathered. In addition to his scholarly talents, his goodwill would well serve any graduate student's adventures.

In addition, two friends read all or part of the manuscript in various stages. Katy Gammack, a lobbyist for several years, offered constructive and thoughtful comments that helped eliminate some tiresome repetitiousness. Dr. Judith Fabry, a graduate school colleague, graciously took time from her own work to apply her pencil to some chapters and clarified otherwise murky areas.

My thanks to Bonnie Trede who labored over the tape recordings to transcribe them. Her professional standards and her patience have made the transcripts useful tools.

My thanks also to Vernon Tyler at the Iowa State Historical Society Library. He is a congenial and helpful guide to the library's many resources.

Another kind of contribution to this project came in the form of financial support for the oral history portion of the research. Judith Conlin, lobbyist Joe Kelly, and State Representatives Minnette Doderer, Dorothy Carpenter, Johnie Hammond, Mary Lundby, and Kathleen Chapman raised the funds that paid for transcribing the interviews and for travel expenses. Several individuals, associations, and corporations responded to their requests. While the list of contributors is too long to be included in full here, some large donors deserve recognition, including Cobbs Manufacturing, Maytag Corporation, MCI Telecommunications, Northwestern Bell, Philip Morris, Rockwell International, Dorothy Carpenter, Minnette Doderer, Joe Kelly, and The Principal Financial Group.

When reading acknowledgments in other works, I have wondered why authors thanked their family members for their support. Now I know. A person who is preoccupied with a subject, who monopolizes dinner conversation with stories about the day's research, and who really wants to get back to the chapter on the computer screen can become a tiresome household companion. Thank you to my husband John for the days you stayed home from your work so that I could continue mine and for the hundreds of other ways you have demonstrated your respect for my endeavors. Thanks to my daughter Maggie and my son Bill who have shared my enthusiasm for a life of learning.

INTRODUCTION

"The state senator from Taylor County is expert at making meat loaf."

"The representative from Webster County put up 51 quarts of blueberries this year."

"A Wapello County representative is happy to get the kids off to school every morning so the dishes can be washed" is the way *Des Moines Register* reporter George Mills began a 1946 article describing the women who would serve in the 1947 session of the Iowa General Assembly. He continued, "The Iowa legislature has gone feminine to a limited extent. Three women will leave their kitchens in January and come to Des Moines to help cook up more laws for the state of Iowa."[1]

In the 1990s some might object to the lead sentences that Mills chose. Other attributes of these women might be more agreeable. For example:

"The state senator from Taylor County is a basketball coach."

"The representative from Webster County is a leader in the Farm Bureau."

"A Wapello County representative sold advertising for the *Des Moines Register*."

All of which would be equally true. Kathlyn Wick coached a basketball team and was the "expert at making meat loaf." Amy Bloom was a Farm Bureau leader and "put up" blueberries. Edna Lawrence had two young children and had sold newspaper advertising.

Mills points out that only four women had served in the legislature before these three and that: "Three women among 158 members isn't much representation."[2] In many ways, Mills's article summarizes the characteristics of women in the Iowa legislature. They have included mothers with young children, retirees, and middle-aged women, all of whom have had varied interests in their personal and public lives. They have been few in number. And, his lead implies something unusual has happened, something out of the ordinary has occurred: women do not fit expectations of what a politician is. That may be changing.

In *Megatrends for Women*, Patricia Aburdene and John Naisbitt argue that women have "established [a] political power base at the state and local levels" and that, combined with a number of other factors, will contribute to the election of more women to higher office. Aburdene and Naisbitt forecast: "By 2008, U.S. women will hold at least 35 percent of governorships. A woman will be electable, or already elected, as U.S. president."[3] There are reasons to consider the predictions as real possibilities. While the growth in the number of women in elected offices has been neither steady nor even, over the past two decades the number of women has doubled in some positions and tripled in others. For example, in 1971 there were two women in the U.S. Senate and in 1994, before that year's elections, there were seven. For the same years, the number of women in the U.S. House grew from 13 to 48, in state legislatures nationally from 344 to 1,523, and in the Iowa legislature from 8 to 23.[4]

Until the 1970s, only scattered interest in political women existed in either the popular or scholarly press. The few articles that appeared in the years after women gained the vote in 1920 generally fell into two categories. Some warned women to avoid the dirtiness of politics and instead to monitor and clean it up, and others profiled the few women officeholders, depicting them as oddities. Perhaps they were. With the emergence of the feminist movement in the 1960s and 1970s, especially with the organization of groups like the National Women's Political Caucus, sustained efforts to elect women to public offices have been evident and sometimes successful. As the number of successful female candidates has increased, so has the research on them.

This book is one of stories about political women. Some of the stories have been told by the woman whose story it is, some told through newspaper articles. Many of them are stories of courage, some are those of challenging the status quo, some are told in humor, others in frustration, others forthrightly and directly. These stories describe the entrance of one group of women into politics, traditionally a world that men had held as their exclusive domain.[5]

The notion that politics has historically been the province of men does not qualify as a novel thought. In fact, it is not even the result of scholarly research or the product of feminist theorists. Rather, the men who drafted the United States and Iowa Constitutions specified their exclusive access to the voting booth. It was only with the passage of the Nineteenth Amendment to the United States Constitution in 1920 that Iowa women became voters in general elections.[6]

Another obstacle prevented women from full political participation. As in several other states, the men who drafted the 1857 Iowa Constitution clarified their stake on the territory by specifying that only men could qualify for membership in the Iowa House of Representatives. It was probably only an oversight on their part when they failed to make the same restriction for election to the Iowa Senate. A constitutional amendment in 1926 removed the limitation.[7]

Although these limits existed, Iowa women served in elective offices in the nineteenth century. In 1869, Julie C. Addington was first appointed and subsequently elected to serve as the Mitchell County Superintendent of Schools. When questions arose about the legality of the election, the state attorney general decided in favor of it. Even though other women had won election to the office, Elizabeth S. Cook's 1875 election to county superintendent of schools triggered a state supreme court case. Before the court offered a decision, the legislature enacted a law specifically allowing women to serve in any school office. With that clarification already made, the court's opinion dealt with other issues, stating that the legislature could allow women to serve in any office not prohibited by the Constitution. Notably, the first woman to serve in the Iowa General Assembly had been a county superintendent of schools in the 1910s. Another elective office opened to women in 1880 when the legislature made them eligible for election as county recorders.[8]

Women began seeking and winning statewide races in the 1920s. In 1922 May E. Francis of Waverly won her race for State Superintendent of Public Schools. She lost her office in 1926 to Agnes Samuelson in that year's Republican primary. Samuelson won the 1926 general election and was repeatedly reelected until she left the office for other pursuits.[9]

In the area of legislative races, some women did not wait for the amending process and made the decision to run despite the constitutional restriction. In 1920 Lilly B. Gibbons of Greene County ran unopposed in the Democratic primary, but lost in the general election. When leaders of the Iowa League of Women Voters discovered Republican Bess Ross of Audubon and Democrat Jennie Herbster of Arnolds Park on the list of primary candidates in 1922, they asked the women to withdraw. The League argued that the clarity of the constitutional prohibition would prevent the women, if they won, from taking their seats. The League's president also worried that the women's candidacies would become jokes. The candidates refused the League's request. Bessie Farnsworth had intended to run for a House seat, but after the state attorney general told her that women were not eligible for the seat, the League encouraged her to run for the Senate seat representing Louisa and Muscatine counties, which she did. None of the women won, nor did the women who ran in 1924 and 1926. It would be 1928 before a woman would win a seat in Iowa General Assembly.[10]

In other states, women had begun winning legislative races in the 1890s. Colorado voters elected three women to their House of Representatives in 1894. Utah elected a woman to that state's Senate and two women to its House of Representatives in 1896; in the same year Colorado elected four women to its House of Representatives. In 1921, thirty-one women served in state legislatures; the number had grown to 153 in 1929 when Carolyn Campbell Pendray began representing Jackson County in the Iowa House of Representatives.[11]

In addition to this historical background, a brief overview of the structure of the Iowa General Assembly will help in understanding the contributions of the state's women legislators. The Iowa General Assembly works under provisions of the state constitution, state laws, court decisions, joint rules of the House and Senate, and the rules of each chamber. In addition, tradition and unwritten rules influence the ways the chambers conduct their business.

Iowans elect their state representatives and senators in even numbered years, representatives for two year terms and senators for four year terms. Sessions begin on the second Monday of January after the general elections. The legislature met only in odd-numbered years until voters approved a state constitutional amendment providing for annual sessions in 1968. The number of members has varied over the years from the high of 124 in the House and 61 in the Senate to the current 100 House members and 50 Senate members. Until the 1970s, candidates ran for at-large seats in multi-member districts but since have represented single member districts. Until the late 1960s, counties defined the legislative districts, but those created since then have not conformed to county lines, taking on more creative shapes reflecting population distributions and attempts to meet the standards established in U.S. and Iowa Supreme Court decisions.

While some aspects of the Iowa General Assembly have changed over the years, much of the overall framework has remained the same and shares characteristics with other state legislatures, excepting Nebraska which has a unicameral legislature. The presiding officer of the House is the Speaker, who is elected from and by the body. Until a constitutional change in 1988, the lieutenant governor served as the presiding officer of the Senate, but with the change the President of the Senate, like the Speaker of the House, is elected from and by the body. Next in line after these officers are the pro tempore (temporary) President of the Senate and Speaker of the House. Except in some very unusual circumstance, these officers will all be members of the majority party.

Both chambers have majority and minority leaders and assistant leaders, who are elected by their party caucuses. According to a 1980 description:

> The majority floor leader in each house is particularly influential in light of the important responsibilities that accompany the position, including: presiding over party caucus meetings; serving as the primary spokesperson for the party; establishing the daily work schedule of the house in accordance with house rules; and working closely with party leaders and committee chairpersons to ensure that priority bills are introduced, debated, and passed.[12]

In other words, the majority floor leader holds a great deal of power. The minority floor leader presides over that party's caucus, but seldom has the opportunity to direct the chamber's agenda, although some minority leaders have demonstrated great agility at frustrating the majority party's goals. The amount of power and influence exerted by these leaders depends upon many factors, including the relative strength of each party in the chamber, the political strength of the leader, and the amount of loyalty and discipline the leader has developed.

Leaders in both parties also have assistants (usually four). The leadership generally meets on a daily basis to raise questions or concerns presented to them by other members and to discuss strategies for upcoming bills. Theirs is a job that requires consistent party discipline and loyalty.

The party caucuses serve several purposes, which include helping new members learn the procedures, electing their leaders, identifying legislative priorities, developing cohesiveness, and sometimes cajoling and sometimes demanding members' allegiance and discipline. Often closed to the public and the press, caucus meetings allow members to argue, debate, negotiate, and sometimes resolve differences in strategies, amendments, bills, and, on occasion, personalities. Depending upon the leadership's style, caucuses can become loud and angry or may be more subdued in character. More than one person has left a caucus spitting and sputtering in frustration, although that is less frequent than more congenial resolutions. Regardless, the leadership attempts to bring all of the members to a united position on any given topic.

The committee system provides another structure within the chambers. Each chamber has its own set of standing committees that can initiate bills, as well as act on the bills assigned to it by the presiding officer of the chamber. The committee chair, awarded based on leadership, appoints subcommittees (frequently three people) to investigate and report on a bill. If the subcommittee reports favorably on the bill, the committee then acts on it, and again with a favorable recommendation, it moves to the full chamber for action. After passage in one chamber, the bill begins the same process in the second. With passage in both chambers, it moves on for the governor's signature. Admittedly, this is a very simplified explanation of the process, as anyone who has tried to get a piece of legislation passed would assert. Amendments, scheduling delays, the burial committee (an unfavorable subcommittee that refuses to act on a bill), and dozens of other obstacles complicate the process. This brief description does highlight the central role committees play in the legislative process. Depending upon the inclination of the committee chair and the leadership, a bill can be placed on a fast track to passage or deeply buried in a legislator's desk. Some of these possibilities will be described more fully in later chapters.

Two groups of research staffs assist legislators as they sort their ways through the hundreds of bills introduced each session. As a result of the increasing professionalization of legislative bodies in the 1960s and 1970s, partisan and nonpartisan specialists were added to the structure. The nonpartisan Legislative Service Bureau (LSB) and the Legislative Fiscal Bureau (LFB) serve the general membership and committee chairs. In response to legislators' requests, the LSB drafts bills and amendments, assists in committee meetings, and provides research, such as examples of comparable legislation in other states. The LFB estimates how much a proposed piece of legislation will cost (for example, a new education program), how much revenue a bill will generate (for example, a lottery bill), and forecasts the state's income and the state's expenses to help with budget matters, along with other financial estimates and forecasts.

In addition, the majority and minority parties in both chambers employ caucus staffs. While the LSB and LFB presumably offer nonpartisan assistance, the caucus staffs seek out and articulate a frankly partisan bias on legislation. Caucus staffs provide members with information that might be useful in drafting legislation, arguing it in committee, or debating it on the floor. Often, the trust with which members invest these staffs grants them significant influence.

A discussion of the General Assembly demands at least brief mention of lobbyists. The number of organizations, corporations, state agencies and individuals with representatives at the legislature has increased over the years, now numbering in the hundreds. On behalf of those they represent, lobbyists have wined, dined and entertained legislators over the years. Currently, however, there exists a limit of a few dollars that can be spent on those activities. Campaign contributions have become a far more significant financial outlet in recent years. The ethics and worthiness of these financial connections, while important, are beyond the scope of this book. On the other hand, legislators have conceded the importance of lobbyists as sources of information. While the staffs described above provide legislators with research, some lawmakers find it inadequate, a gap lobbyists help fill. Lawmakers acknowledge that lobbyists offer information that is intended to reflect favorably on their clients' positions but say they know that and take it into consideration and that it is too valuable a resource to ignore or shun.

Another resource and influence is the press. Many members receive their hometown (or several, if theirs is a rural district) newspaper. If a person were in the gallery as legislators arrive in the chambers in the morning, one of the first things they would hear is the sound of newsprint rustling as members scan their papers. Most members would have already read the *Des Moines Register* before they arrived, looking for the reports of the previous day's activities. They might criticize the interpretation given to an event or might smile because they found themselves quoted in a way they favored. The degree to which the press influences legislators again lies beyond the scope of this book, but the responses it generates suggest that at least it is a factor.

This brief overview of the Iowa General Assembly only offers in broad strokes a picture with hundreds of shadings and colors. It suggests something stable and consistent, predictable and static, which the legislature in its daily dealings is not. When a person works or serves in the legislature, during the months it is in session it feels like the bill currently in focus is the only thing in the world, and for that moment it may well be, to the person trying to get it passed or buried. But in reality, the world acts on the legislature as much as the legislature works on bills. The economy, federal legislation, a flood, a plant closing or opening, a leaking underground gas storage tank, an election year, a personal crisis, and dozens of other events and situations, some of them seemingly invisible, can influence the dynamics of a legislative session. Even more intimately, the personalities in the Statehouse, whether those of elected officials or those of the hundreds of others involved, create and influence the dynamics of the institution. A strong Speaker or a feisty minority leader, an emerging leader or a woman with a new perspective give the process excitement and life.

The reader is asked to remember that this work deals with the 86 women who have served in the Iowa General Assembly and is not a history of Iowa politics or even of the legislature. (See Table I.1.) For that reason, many significant events in the legislature's history have not been included. Several issues that undoubtedly would be discussed in a history of the Iowa legislature have received little or no attention. A primary example is the state's long battle for reapportionment. While some comments refer to events surrounding reapportionment, this work does not provide an examination of it, instead maintaining a narrow focus on those events in which women played primary roles.

With this narrow focus and with so few people involved, the reader may wonder what purpose this book serves. Imagine two societies that had regular contact with each other and that had amiable relationships among themselves, but that had different building shapes. One society could only build things with right angles. The other could only use circular forms. Both societies generally managed very well, especially considering their limitations. One day, the two groups were working together to move a large object. The right-angle society built a box and together the two groups loaded the object into the box and began shoving it with great effort. Discouraged with the poor progress being made, they sat down and tried to figure out a way to move it more easily. The circular society, familiar with the many uses of their objects, opined that perhaps they could use their forms in a way to solve the problem. With wheels in place, the cart easily moved the object.

It was the combination of perspectives and the combination of forms that solved the problem. So it appears to be with policymaking. The more ideas, resources, experiences, and perspectives contributed to solving a problem, the more innovative and creative the solutions. Women have brought an additional perspective and an additional set of experiences to solving problems facing the state. When women repeatedly held their opinions and ideas up for examination, their proposals often found supporters. The means by which women have come to the position of demanding attention for their ideas, and the results of their efforts demonstrate the ways in which adding women to the Iowa General Assembly has made a difference in state policy.

Making the uncommon decision to run for public office marks the place this story begins.

Table I.1. Iowa women legislators, their party, and their term(s)

Last Name	First Name	Party	Years in House	Years in Senate
Adams	Janet	D	1987-1992	
Baxter	Elaine	D	1982-1986	
Beatty	Linda	D	1985-1994	
Bloom	Amy	R	1947-1948	
Bock	Lenabelle	R	1961-1964	
Boettger	Nancy	R		1995-
Bogenrief	Mattie	D	1965-1966	
Boggess	Effie Lee	R	1995-	
Boyd[a]	Nancy Shimanek	R	1977-1982	
Brandt	Diane	D	1975-1982	
Buhr	Florence	D	1983-1990	1991-1994
Burnett	Cecilia	D	1995-	
Carl	Janet	D	1981-1986	
Carpenter	Dorothy	R	1981-1994	
Chapman	Kathleen	D	1983-1992	
Clark	Betty Jean	R	1977-1990	
Cohen	Gertrude	D	1965-1966	
Conklin	Charlene	R	1967-1968	1969-1972
Corning	Joy	R		1985-1990
Crabb	Helen	D	1949-1952	
Doderer	Minnette	D	1964-1968 1981-	1969-1978

[a]Nancy Shimanek Boyd married after her service in the legislature. In state documents, her surname is Shimanek, in this work it is Boyd.

Table I.1. (*cont'd*)

Last Name	First Name	Party	Years in House	Years in Senate
Douglas	Joann	R		1995-
Duitscher	Lucille	D	1970	
Egenes	Sonja	R	1971-1982	
Elliott	Isabel	D	1937-1940	
Franklin	June	D	1967-1972	
Freeman[b]	Mary Lou	R		1994-
Garman	Teresa	R	1987-	
Garner	Ada	D	1933-1934	
Gentleman	Julia	R	1975-1978	1979-1990
Glanton	Willie	D	1965-1966	
Gregerson	Mary Pat	D	1965-1966	
Greiner	Sandra	R	1993-	
Gruhn	Josephine	D	1983-1992	
Grundberg	Betty	R	1993-	
Hakes	Frances	R	1961-1964	
Hammitt	Donna M.	R	1995-	
Hammond	Johnie	D	1983-1994	1995-
Hannon	Beverly	D		1985-1992
Harper	Mattie	D	1973-1977	
Harper	Patricia	D	1987-1990 1993-	
Hester	Joan	R	1985-1994	
Hoffman-Bright	Betty	R	1977-1984	
Jacobs	Libby	R	1995-	
Jochum	Pam	D	1993-	
Judge	Patty	D		1993-
Kiser	Emma Jean	R	1973-1974	

[b]Mary Lou Freeman was elected in a special election in 1994.

Table I.1. *(cont'd)*

Last Name	First Name	Party	Years in House	Years in Senate
Kramer	Mary	R		1991-
Larsen	Sonja	R	1979-80	
Laughlin[c]	Janis	D	1983-1986	
Lawrence	Edna	R	1947-1950	
Lipsky	Joan	R	1967-1978	
Lloyd-Jones	Jean	D	1979-1986	1987-1994
Lonergan	Joyce	D	1975-1986	
Lundby	Mary	R	1987-	
Lynch	Mae	D	1943-1946	
Mann	Karen	R	1981-1982	
Martin	Mona	R	1993-	
Mascher	Mary	D	1995-	
McElroy	Lillian	R	1971-1976	
McKee[d]	Vera	R		1963-1964
Mertz	Dolores	D	1989-	
Metcalf	Janet	R	1985-	
Metz	Katheryn	R	1949-1952	
Miller	Elizabeth	R	1969-1972	1973-1980
Miller	Opal	D	1975-1978	
Mullins	Sue	R	1979-1988	
Nelson	Beverly	R	1995-	
Nelson	Gladys	R	1951-1956	
Nelson	Linda	D	1993-	
Neuhauser	Mary	D	1987-1994	1995-
Nielsen	Joyce	D	1989-1992	

[c]Janis Laughlin married after her service in the legislature. In state documents her surname is Torrence, in this work it is Laughlin.

[d]Vera McKee married after her service in the legislature. In state documents her surname is Shivvers, in this work it is McKee.

Table I.1. (*cont'd*)

Last Name	First Name	Party	Years in House	Years in Senate
O'Halloran	Mary	D	1973-1978	
Orr	Jo Ann	D		1970 1973-1980
Peick	Doris	D	1983-1986	
Pendray	Carolyn	D	1929-1932	1933-1936
Poffenberger	Virginia	R	1979-1982	
Sargisson	Hallie	D	1971-1972	
Shaw	Elizabeth	R	1967-1972	1973-1978
Smith	Jo	R	1981-1982	
Svoboda	Jane	D	1987-1992	
Svoboda	Linda	D	1975-1978	
Szymoniak	Elaine	D		1989-
Teaford	Jane	D	1985-1992	
Thompson	Patricia	R	1977-1980	
Tinsman	Maggie	R		1989-
Trucano	JoAnn	R	1981-1982	
Van Alstine	Percie	R	1961-1964	
Walter	Marcia	D	1981-1982	
Wick[e]	Kathlyn	R	1947-1948	
Wolcott	Olga	D	1965-1966	
Yenger	Sue	R		1979-1982
Zastrow[f]	Katherine	D	1959-1964	
Zimmerman	Jo Ann	D	1983-1986	

[e]Kathlyn Wick married after her service in the legislature. In state documents her surname is Kirketeg, in this work it is Wick.

[f]Katherine Zastrow married after her service in the legislature. In state documents her surname is Falvey, in this work it is Zastrow.

Legislators and Politicians: Iowa's Women Lawmakers

CHAPTER 1

Candidacy: The Pioneers

The typical state legislator—and the typical Iowa legislator—is well-educated, involved in a profession, business, or agriculture, middle or upper class, white, middle-aged, and male. He uses the business and personal relationships he has developed as the base of his campaign for office. As a community leader in civic, business, political, and professional groups, he has come to the attention of party recruiters or others interested in finding candidates. In Iowa, interest groups, party leaders, and other community leaders fill the role of recruiting potential candidates for more or less promising legislative seats. Often, men are the members of these groups or are the leaders and they look to the people they have worked with or known.[1]

The typical female legislator, in Iowa and in other states, with the notable exception of her gender, shares all but one of the characteristics listed above. She has a different occupational background. Homemaker and housewife are the words most women have used to describe their occupations. The words carry connotations of cookies in the oven, children coming home from school, church and volunteer meetings, and friends and neighbors visiting. The images of homemakers do not include the power of public office or the drive of political ambition. Cleaning closets and developing campaign strategies for winning an election do not seem to belong in the same picture. Yet they do. Many women nurtured their gardens and cultivated voters. Like her neighbors and friends, and like women legislators in other parts of the country, she probably had years of service on library boards and school boards, participated in Farm Bureau activities, and held offices in the local Women's Club, P.E.O., Order of Eastern Star, and other traditional women's groups. Like her friends and neighbors, she has probably led a traditional woman's life. Unlike her female friends and neighbors, she converted her homemaking and volunteer skills into political ones and her social relationships into political networks and votes.[2]

While women are not generally considered part of what political scientists call the "eligible pool" of candidates, other factors have opened doors for them. Finding candidates to fill the ticket occasionally challenges Iowa party officials who want to offer voters a full slate of candidates and who do not want the opposition party to win by default. Both women and men have demonstrated their party loyalty by becoming the proverbial sacrificial lambs and have run for a seat that could only be won with extraordinary labor or with the influence of factors on the state or national level, such as President Franklin D. Roosevelt's election in 1932.[3]

For Iowa women legislators, filling the party ticket in those years of unusual circumstances considerably benefited their candidacies, particularly before the mid-1960s. These women did not necessarily seek to become candidates. As faithful and loyal members of the Republican or Democratic Women's Clubs, they attempted to recruit candidates to fill the ticket. It was after men had declined that other partisan club members or other party leaders recruited these women to help the party by becoming a candidate. In most situations the odds that they would succeed were minimal. Winning sometimes even came as a surprise. After the mid-1960s, women continued to run to fill the ticket and for other reasons, as will be seen in Chapter 2.[4]

Adding a woman's perspective to the legislature clearly has not been an adequate reason for electing women in voters' minds. More than 400 women have run for seats in the Iowa legislature. About one-half ran before the mid-1960s and the others in the years since. Of the approximately 200 women who ran before the mid-1960s, less than 10 percent of them won their legislative races. In more recent years, the percentage has hovered around 45 percent.[5]

One might expect that many of the women who had developed political skills in the suffrage campaigns would have used their political acumen and become legislative candidates. Instead, suffrage leaders did not consider political office as the next challenge. If Iowa suffragists ran for the legislature, they did not win. Instead, the winning candidates came from kitchens and women's clubs. They saw themselves as good citizens answering their parties' calls to fill the ticket, campaigned, won, and assumed their new responsibilities in a new environment.[6]

The fifteen women elected between 1928 and 1963 offer an interesting paradox. As might be expected in a rural state, thirteen of the fifteen farmed, owned a farm, or lived in a rural area as defined by the United States Census Bureau.[7] Some women ran farms, while others had less active roles in farm management and decision making. Two studies of rural Iowa women point out the paradox. Anthropologist Deborah Fink characterized rural Iowa women as excluded "from the public nonfamily world of business and politics."[8] In addition, historian Dorothy Schwieder found that farm women had too much work to do to leave the farm, even to attend extension classes relating to their farm labors. If farm women did find time for outside interests, their husbands resisted their participation in nonfarm activities. The culture that kept many women out of politics and at home also provided the network for other women's successful candidacies.[9]

The independence that these women exhibited may have its roots in another area of rural life and women's culture, the rural school. In a pattern similar to that found in other states, fourteen of the fifteen early women legislators taught in public schools, generally one-room rural facilities. Teaching may have prepared these women for public office in ways that other professions open to women such as nursing and secretarial work did not. Nurses and secretaries usually work under the direct supervision of others, while teachers manage their own classrooms more independently, especially in one-room schools. The speaking, decision making, and organizational skills used in the classroom are among those needed to run a successful campaign. Even though these women generally had taught before they married, and several years before they became candidates, their classroom experiences may have helped them develop campaign skills and contributed to their ability to perceive of themselves as candidates.[10]

Another dimension of the independence of seven of these fifteen legislators' lives may have been that they had greater freedom than their neighbors because they did not have children. Acquaintances of these women have noted that without the obligations and responsibilities related to raising children, they had more time and freedom than mothers.[11]

The women and men who ran before the mid-1960s, the period considered here, conducted their campaigns in a somewhat different atmosphere than the current one. Some candidates mailed postcards asking for support, but they did not compare with today's elaborate mass mailings. Instead of the $100,000 legislative campaigns that now appear occasionally, a few hundred dollars would pay for printing costs and newspaper advertising.

Iowa newspapers served as more than vehicles for paid political advertising; many times they directly supported candidates in their news stories. In 1947, for example, Iowa had over 500 mostly weekly, but also more frequently published, newspapers. Well over half of the papers had a partisan allegiance, and 80 percent of those were Republican. While the papers were not evenly distributed across the counties, some simple math suggests that each of Iowa's 99 counties had an average of almost three partisan newspapers. Some newspapers took their partisanship seriously, without subtlety or elegance. Often publishers and editors energetically entered political campaigns with loyalty and vigor.[12]

These generalizations about candidates and campaigns provide a rough sketch of women's backgrounds and some of the elements involved in legislative races. The candidacies of a few women illustrate some of the circumstances of their decisions to run for the legislature. While not every candidate or campaign is described, those included illustrate aspects of all these women and their political races.

The first woman elected to the Iowa General Assembly came from a political family and had held elective office before running for the legislature. Carolyn Pendray's mother had been a suffragist and her father had been a state representative. Pendray recollected that: "For my part I grew up in a political environment and I knew as much about that as teaching school and keeping house."[13] After teaching in Henry County and Des Moines, Pendray became a candidate for Henry County superintendent of schools in 1910, but failed to campaign and lost. Two years later she campaigned for a second attempt and won. She continued to serve as Henry County superintendent until 1920, when she married William Pendray of Oskaloosa. After living in Ottumwa, the couple moved to Maquoketa in 1923 where William was a retail merchant.[14]

In her new home, Pendray participated in the community's political and social life, providing leadership in various volunteer and church organizations. She chaired the Jackson County Democratic central committee and, in the summer of 1928, became a member of the state central committee. When the county party organization did not have candidates for either the House or Senate races, Pendray saw an opportunity, claimed it, and became the House candidate at the county convention. The same convention named George W. Tabor its Senatorial candidate.[15]

The issue of gender arose in the last month of the campaign when the Republican candidate, J.L. Kinley, tried to use his gender and property to his advantage. The Jackson County Republican newspaper argued that the county needed a man to deal with the other men in the legislature, that a man would receive respect, and that a man was a safe choice. By implication, a woman would not have good judgment, would not become part of the legislative decision-making process, and would be a risk. Property taxes also became an issue when Kinley told voters that Pendray would be unsuitable as a state representative because she did not pay them.[16]

Jackson County's Democratic newspaper countered the arguments by reminding voters of her tenure as Henry County superintendent of schools and her volunteer work in Maquoketa. In addition, the newspaper almost gleefully pointed out that Pendray owned a farm on which she paid property taxes. The newspaper steadfastly stood by its candidate, rebutting every charge against Pendray and asserting her ability at every opportunity.[17]

Pendray won the race, the first Democratic state representative from Jackson County in more than a decade. Her friends and supporters hosted parties celebrating Pendray's victory and the election of the first woman state representative in Iowa. She served two terms in the House of Representatives and one term in the Senate before she retired in 1936, the longest any woman would serve until Minnette Doderer (Democrat, Johnson), who began her political career in 1964, surpassed Pendray's record.

In 1932, the year that Pendray was elected to the Iowa Senate, Democrat Ada Garner from Butler County won a seat in the Iowa House of Representatives. One of the few women to run a campaign on clearly stated issues, Garner stands alone among the successful women candidates in the power of her rhetoric. Emphasizing her agricultural background and her gender, Garner campaigned as a farmer's wife. She ran for the legislature to represent rural concerns, believing that city lawyers in the legislature scoffed at bills to modernize farms and rural life.[18]

Garner's campaign speeches addressed problems Iowa farmers had faced since the 1920s. In some parts of the state, the economic difficulties confronting farmers had triggered violence and farm strikes. Many of the economic problems required national policy changes for their remedy, but Iowa farmers believed the state could assist them through greater economy in state government.[19] Calling herself "a plodding farmer's wife" who knew "the ills from which the farmer is suffering," she sympathized with problems facing agriculture:

> The farmer of today has so many injustices flung at him that it is making him see red, but he is not "too damned dumb to understand." If I am elected, I shall use all of my power to help enact laws that will be of relief to the farmer and to reduce government operating expenses in general. I stand for true economy and to keep expenditures within the limits of the income.[20]

Campaigning in Shell Rock, Garner argued that Butler county farmers had "plenty of taxation without representation." She reminded the audience that, in addition to the state's position as the nation's highest producer of corn, horses, and poultry, Iowa also led the nation in farm mortgages. She called for a long-term refinancing plan for farm mortgages with low interest rates. In another speech, Garner used Henry Wallace's statement that the farmers of Iowa had more to revolt against than the colonists of pre-revolutionary times.[21] Garner accused the University of Iowa and Iowa State College of wasting taxpayers' money by duplicating courses. She criticized the proportion (over 50 percent) of the state's education appropriation that went to the three state colleges and wanted more of that money to be used in public schools. She ended one speech declaring: "Agricultural prosperity is the most vital issue of this election—as when the farmer is prosperous and contented, everybody else is also."[22] Once in the legislature Garner worked with colleagues to find new uses for corn. After failing to convince the House that corn alcohol could be added to gasoline to fuel cars and trucks, she and other legislators passed legislation allowing the manufacture and distribution of industrial alcohol from grain.[23]

Garner's campaign was among the most clearly issue-oriented campaigns of the successful women legislators. Newspapers have reported few issues in legislative campaigns, and women legislators only seldom recollect contests based on issues. An incumbent's actions may have prompted a woman to seek to replace her or him, but she based her campaign on her experiences and abilities, rarely raising the issues of which she disapproved. Generally, women candidates worked to convince the electorate that they would work hard, study the issues and listen to constituents, then pointed to their community activities as evidence of their leadership ability.

In addition to her strongly issue-oriented campaign, Garner differs from other successful women candidates in her use of her gender and marital status. Unlike Pendray, who attempted to overcome the presumed political disadvantage of her gender by demonstrating that she shared taxpaying responsibility with men, Garner emphasized her gender and marital relationship by calling herself a farmer's wife. She used her marriage to convince voters that she intimately knew the problems confronting farmers, knowledge that equipped her to represent their interests in the legislature. Garner alone used this strategy so publicly or successfully. With her rhetoric establishing her knowledge, she identified herself with other women and with a role men understood. Although a friend identifies her as a member of the feminist National Women's Party, she did not argue the validity of her candidacy based on women's political ability. Instead, she presented herself in the traditional women's roles and images.[24]

Garner's success, however, may have been more directly related to the larger political drama than her style. In both Iowa and the nation, Democrats won their races with the help of Franklin Delano Roosevelt's victory. Garner was the only Democrat to represent Butler County between 1888 and 1970, a clear indication that the nationwide Democratic landslide in 1932 significantly contributed to her victory. For several other Iowa women legislators, voters' preference for one political party or another in a specific election cycle greatly influenced the outcome of their races.

While Garner became a candidate for clear, issue-oriented reasons and campaigned aggressively, other women ran for less politically well-defined reasons. In 1936 Isabel Elliott (Democrat, Woodbury) ran for a House seat after her husband died. Elliott believed: "A woman's place is in the home. She'll be happier there. If she has a good husband, a home, children to bring up—that's the finest thing any woman can hope for." At the same time, she believed that women had an obligation to find a place for themselves "even in the legislature." In a straightforward manner, she explained her successful campaign: "The friends I've been making all my life elected me."[25] Elliott's reference to the importance of home, family, and friends emphasizes traditional values. Only after her children were raised and her husband had died did she look for something to do with her days and a place to be, through seeking a public office.

Another widow entered the legislature in 1947. Kathlyn Kirketeg Wick (Republican, Bedford and Taylor) was the first woman to fill a vacancy created by her husband's death. O. J. Kirketeg, Wick's first husband, had completed one session of a two-session term in the Senate before he died. Recruited by the local League of Women Voters to run for the balance of Kirketeg's term, Wick had no opposition in the primary or general elections. She did not run for reelection because the legislature paid poorly. Instead, she returned to teaching. Republican women had run for legislative seats since 1922, but none succeeded until Wick and two other women, Amy Bloom of Dayton and Edna Lawrence of Ottumwa won their seats for the 1947 session.[26]

Serendipity sometimes contributed to a woman's decision to become a candidate. Helen Crabb (Democrat, Guthrie) had been active in the local and county Women's Clubs and in the Order of Eastern Star, as well as other community groups. In 1948 a neighbor asked Crabb to run for the legislature not because of her experience or demonstrated leadership but because it would help him get a better job. As she told the story:

> There was a young man [Ed McDermott] in Jamaica who was a postmaster, a Democrat postmaster, and he wanted the rural mail carrier job, and he went down to Des Moines to see Jake More [the State Democratic Chairman] to see what he could do about it, and Jake said, "If you can get somebody to run for the House of Representatives, I may consider it." And so Ed McDermott . . . came to the house and I was ironing . . . and told me that they just wanted a name on the ticket. That was all they really cared about, if I just let them put my name on the ticket . . . And, you know, I almost laughed in his face, I thought it was so funny. I was only 31, you know, and here were all these guys in the legislature, old fuddy-duddies I thought. And I stood there a few minutes, and I thought, well, what the heck, I don't have to do anything. . . . And so I said yes; I didn't even consult my husband.[27]

During the summer Crabb decided to campaign, not wanting her Republican opponent to win the race by default. Jake More sent fifty dollars for her campaign, which she used to buy penny postcards. She recollects that she may have spent a few additional dollars for business-sized cards and for newspaper advertising, but that the biggest portion of her campaign budget was More's contribution. McDermott and his wife helped Crabb print the postcards on a hand-turned press, and her bridge club, instead of playing cards, helped her address the postcards.[28] She did not make any speeches during her campaign, explaining: "You might call it a silent campaign."[29]

Crabb campaigned by going door to door in residential areas. She looked for opportunities to shake hands and introduce herself in businesses, but that did not always work out well. After stopping in a machine shop and being treated coldly, she became intimidated when entering men's territory to campaign. She remembers another occasion:

> I drove up to a sale barn one time . . . to pass out my cards, and I got there and those pickup trucks were lined up, I suppose, two miles at that sale

> barn. And I drove up to the entrance and stopped the car and I looked around and I thought, Helen Crabb, what are you doing here? And I just turned around and left. I just couldn't face it. I thought those men wouldn't want to talk to me.[30]

Crabb's intimidation by the sale barns and machine shops contrasts with her campaign assertion that she "intended to show that a woman can handle responsibilities in our state government without apology."[31] The sentiments, however, do not contradict each other. Crabb decided to become a candidate while she performed a domestic task and in response to a neighbor's request for help. Active in the community, Crabb did not seek office to further some goal emerging from her volunteer work, nor did McDermott ask her to run to remedy a local problem, other than his employment. After making the choice, however, Crabb acted on it and campaigned for the office. Her traditional domestic and volunteer work defined her status and limited her access to men's gathering places. Seeking ways around the barriers by using a less personal medium to contact voters, she decided to send postcards.

In 1948 Democrats Harry S. Truman, U.S. Senator Guy Gillette, and Crabb won in Guthrie County. A Democrat had not represented Guthrie County in the Iowa House since 1917. As in any election, several factors contribute to the outcome. Crabb's work with the women's club was important and the *Bagley Gazette* credited her with running a strong campaign. In addition, Guthrie County considered itself dry, but Crabb's incumbent opponent had voted to ease liquor restrictions during the 1947 session, alienating many voters. Crabb believes that her victory came on Truman's coattails.[32]

In 1951 Gladys Nelson (Republican, Jasper) joined Helen Crabb in the Iowa House of Representatives. The first woman to enter the legislature by way of the League of Women Voters, she served as state president from 1937-1939 and continued to serve on League boards after that. In 1950 she was vice-chair of the Jasper County Republican Party when Ennis McCall, chair of the group, asked her to run for the position of state representative. The Democratic incumbent worked for a local newspaper and had union support, so he appeared to have the race won before it began, an assumption that discouraged Republican men from running. Nelson ran to fill the ticket and because of her husband, Ed. When Ed came home for lunch, Nelson told him about the inquiry, adding that of course she would not run. He challenged her by questioning the truth of the things she had said about women becoming active in politics and running for public office. Nelson changed her mind and decided to run.[33]

In addition to using traditional campaign tools, Nelson had another resource available to her: pictures from a summer trip to Alaska. Various groups, such as rural churches, invited the Nelsons to give slide presentations; Nelson narrated the slide show while her husband ran the projector. Nelson could meet, greet, and chat with voters while not appearing to campaign actively, which she perceived as an advantage.[34]

Some women who campaigned with and for their husbands had personal experience asking for support and appear to have been more comfortable doing the same for themselves. An example is Katherine Falvey Zastrow (Democrat, Monroe) who was recruited by party leaders after her husband Lawrence Falvey died. Zastrow enjoyed speaking and other aspects of campaigning. A partner in several family businesses, she regularly rode in the companies' trucks as they made deliveries, campaigning at the various stops. This process solved another problem for Zastrow: she did not drive.[35]

When Zastrow began campaigning for herself, she started with a firm base of activism in the community, but she was aware of ways she differed from others in the county. Monroe County was one of the two poorest in the state, but Zastrow's partnerships in a lumberyard, a bank, and a farm gave her considerable financial resources. She tried to minimize the differences between herself and her constituency, but they still appeared, sometimes in strange ways. For example, Zastrow was a small woman who ate very little at campaign events if the after-dinner agenda included her making a speech. Her strategy was to play with the food heaped on her plate until she once heard someone say: "She's just too darn pernicky to eat our food."[36] After that she cleaned her plate.

Like Zastrow the women elected in 1960 became candidates to fill their parties' tickets. Two of the women came from political families, which helped them decide in favor of running. Republican Percie Van Alstine's mother had been a suffragist and mayor of Gilmore City; her father had been a state senator. She knew that some voters would not support a woman, but decided to run anyway.[37] Her family's political activism led to Van Alstine's political involvement. "The only reason I probably was even president of Republican Women," she confessed, "was because of my mother–she was a political animal and so was my dad."[38] She was the first single woman elected to the Iowa General Assembly.

As a legislator, Van Alstine gained national publicity for her efforts to find uses for the state's overabundance of corn. To bring attention to the problem, she convinced the Statehouse cafeteria's manager to include corn muffins on the menu. Explaining the request, she asked: "Good night, why shouldn't we serve corn muffins or corn bread in our State Capitol? It is ridiculous not to be using corn, our greatest Iowa product."[39] *The Christian Science Monitor* lauded Van Alstine's efforts to get corn bread served in the Statehouse and in any other place.[40]

Like Van Alstine, another woman elected in 1960, had a political heritage. Frances Hakes's (Republican, Pocahontas) father, Fred Gilchrist, had served in the Iowa House and Senate and in the U.S. House of Representatives. Hakes enjoyed saying that she grew up on politics and then explaining that she had used the *Code of Iowa* for a booster seat as a child. When no Republican men appeared willing to challenge the Democratic incumbent, friends asked Hakes to declare her candidacy at the last possible moment. She hesitated for half an hour and missed the filing deadline and had to run as a write-in candidate in the primary. The candidacies of Van Alstine, Hakes, and Lenabelle Bock (Republican, Hancock), who was also elected in 1960, answered a party need. As legislators they joked about it. Running for the legislature to be helpful—one of women's roles—was an honorable calling for them.[41]

After 1963, urban women outnumbered rural women by a ratio of two to one in the legislature. Reapportionment accounts for much of the change. Large urban areas, dramatically underrepresented before redistricting in 1964, had large populations from which to recruit candidates. In contrast, rural districts contained a much smaller pool of hopefuls, so that women were more often sought to fill the party ticket. After reapportionment, each district had approximately the same number of people. In the new and relatively smaller urban districts, women's chances for success increased.

The women who first ran in the 1964 general election also became candidates to fill the ticket. A temporary reapportionment plan passed earlier in the year created several new seats in the state's more populous counties. Filling the new seats posed problems for political leaders. The 1964 reapportionment plan increased Polk County's House representation from two to eleven and its Senate members from one to three. According to a *Des Moines Register* article: "Some political observers hold that perhaps not enough qualified men can spare several months every two years from their businesses, jobs, or professions. Many fine women, these watchers say, don't have this kind of problem."[42] To find candidates, Republican and Democratic leaders expressed interest in attracting women for the legislature. They would not have needed to worry because a record number of candidates filed in 1964. In previous years, about 300 people had filed nomination papers, but in 1964, 420 candidates ran in the primary election, 18 of them women.[43]

Twenty-six women ran in the 1964 primary and general elections across the state, fourteen more than in 1962. Three Republican and two Democratic women survived the Polk County primary; the two Democrats won House seats in Polk County's general election. Polk County voters had chosen Mattie Bogenrief and Willie Glanton to be part of the delegation. Bogenrief and her husband Carl had long been active in the county's Democratic Party. Glanton and her husband Luther had been active in Des Moines' African-American community and in the civil rights movement. Both women ran in the spirit of reform that enveloped much of the state and nation in the 1960s.

In other parts of the state, three women won their races. Democrat Olga Wolcott from Cerro Gordo County, a Roman Catholic, ran because her bishop encouraged her.[44] Mary Pat Gregerson (Democrat, Pottawattomie) was recruited by a legislator who believed that her father's political connections, her Scandinavian married name, and her Roman Catholic religion would help her win. A teacher, Gregerson decided to run because she "wanted to leave the world a better place."[45] Gertrude Cohen ran for the experience, not expecting to win. Family members pointed to three reasons she could not expect a victory: her political inexperience, her gender, and her Jewish religion.[46]

Not one of the five women first elected in 1964 included filling the party tickets as their reason for running. Party recruiters may not have presented the idea to them that way. However, every successful woman that election year ran in a district that had one or more new seats.[47]

The Democratic landslide in 1964 cannot be overlooked as a reason for these women's successes. Every woman who won in 1964 was a Democrat. The three Republican women who had served the two previous terms and had run in 1964 were defeated. Even though they campaigned hard, Gregerson and Cohen believed they won because of the Democratic Party's state and national successes, a valid appraisal for all five of these women. Being a member of the winning party in that election cycle clearly benefited these candidates, as it had for others before them.[48]

From the 1928 through the 1964 general elections, 21 women had been elected to the Iowa General Assembly. The six women who served in 1965 were the largest group of women to serve at one time and would be until 1970 when eight women would serve. Eleven Democrats had been elected to serve an aggregate of eighteen sessions, and ten Republicans to seventeen sessions. Until the 1964 special and general elections, which reflect the Democratic landslide in that year, only five Democratic women had been elected. The party affiliations of the fifteen women elected before 1964 (ten Republicans and five Democrats) reflect Iowa's historic Republican heritage. It suggests that while women ran to fill their party tickets, they were not necessarily sacrificial lambs in the sense that they had entered races that could not be won. The winners in these years may well indicate that a few districts with a strong potential for Republican success simply did not have men interested in becoming candidates. To put this in perspective, however, almost 200 women had run in those years and fifteen of them won seats, suggesting that a substantial number of sacrificial lambs had entered races. (See Table 1.1.)

Nationally, the number of women serving in state legislatures had also grown. In 1921, thirty-one served: seven Democrats, twenty-three Republicans, and one Independent. A little over forty years later, in 1963/1964, 351 women served: 206 Republicans, 141 Democrats, and 4 Independents. The number of women serving in 1963/1964 had increased eleven times over the number in 1921.

Perhaps the most interesting sidebar to the partisan affiliations of women legislators, both in Iowa and in other states, is that the Democratic Party had far more aggressively courted women's participation. For example, the Democratic National Committee added the position of national committeewoman for each state, with full voting rights, in 1920, eight years before the Republican Party would do the same. In addition, the Democratic Party had several strong women leaders. Emily Newell Blair, Democratic Party vice-chairman in the 1920s, regularly and consistently provided a clear and effective voice for the inclusion of women in the party. Then, during the 1930s and 1940s, Eleanor Roosevelt and her associates created avenues for women's participation in the Democratic Party. The Republican Party far more reluctantly included women in its affairs and did not have women in leadership positions comparable to those that women held in the Democratic Party. The inconsistencies between women's relative levels of inclusion in their parties and in state legislatures, however, must remain unresolved for this study.[49]

After the early 1960s, friends, party leaders, and others continued to recruit women to run for the legislature. Filling the ticket, however, became only one of the many reasons that women considered when making the decisions to become candidates. The proportion of women who became legislative candidates because they believed they could make contributions to the policy making process grew after the mid-1960s.

Table 1.1. Number of women serving in each session of the General Assembly by party and by chamber

Year	House Republicans		House Democrats		Senate Republicans		Senate Democrats		Total	% of legislature
1929			Carolyn Pendray	1					1	0.6[a]
1931			Carolyn Pendray	1					1	.6
1933			Ada Garner	1			Carolyn Pendray	1	2	1.3
1935							Carolyn Pendray	1	1	.6
1937			Isabel Elliott	1					1	.6
1939			Isabel Elliott	1					1	.6
1941									0	0
1943			Mae Lynch	1					1	.6
1945			Mae Lynch	1					1	.6
1947	Amy Bloom Edna Lawrence	2			Kathlyn Wick	1			3	1.9
1949	Edna Lawrence Katheryn Metz	2	Helen Crabb	1					3	1.9

[a]From 1907 until 1964, the legislature had 158 members, in 1965 it had 183 members, from 1967 to 1970 it had 185 members, and from 1971 to the present it has had 150 members.

1951	Katheryn Metz Gladys Nelson	2	Helen Crabb	1					3	1.9
1953	Gladys Nelson	1							1	.6
1955	Gladys Nelson	1							1	.6
1957									0	0
1959			Katherine Zastrow	1					1	.6
1961	Lenabelle Bock Frances Hakes Percie Van Alstine	3	Katherine Zastrow	1					4	2.5
1963	Lenabelle Bock Frances Hakes Percie Van Alstine	3	Katherine Zastrow	1	Vera McKee	1			5	3.2
1964	Lenabelle Bock Frances Hakes Percie Van Alstine	3	Minnette Doderer[b]	1	Vera McKee	1			5	3.2

[b]Doderer was elected in a special election for an extraordinary session. Zastrow married before the special session and was not allowed to serve in the extraordinary because she moved to another district.

Table 1.1. (*Cont'd*)

Year	House Republicans		House Democrats		Senate Republicans		Senate Democrats		Total	% of legislature
1965			Mattie Bogenrief Gertrude Cohen Minnette Doderer Willie Glanton Mary Pat Gregerson Olga Wolcott	6					6	3.3
1967	Charlene Conklin Joan Lipsky Elizabeth Shaw	3	Minnette Doderer June Franklin	2					5	2.7
1969	Joan Lipsky Elizabeth Miller Elizabeth Shaw	3	June Franklin	1	Charlene Conklin	1	Minnette Doderer	1	6	3.2
1970	Joan Lipsky Elizabeth Miller Elizabeth Shaw	3	Lucille Duitscher[c] June Franklin	2	Charlene Conklin	1	Minnette Doderer Jo Ann Orr[d]	2	8	4.3
1971	Sonja Egenes Joan Lipsky Lillian McElroy Elizabeth Miller Elizabeth Shaw	4	June Franklin Hallie Sargisson	2	Charlene Conklin	1	Minnette Doderer	1	8	5.3

[c]Duitscher was elected in a special election.

[d]Orr was elected in a special election.

1973	Sonja Egenes Emma Jean Kiser Joan Lipsky Lillian McElroy	4	Mattie Harper Mary O'Halloran	2	Elizabeth Miller Elizabeth Shaw	2	Minnette Doderer Jo Ann Orr	2	10	6.7
1975	Sonja Egenes Julia Gentleman Joan Lipsky Lillian McElroy	4	Diane Brandt Mattie Harper Joyce Lonergan Opal Miller Mary O'Halloran Linda Svoboda	6	Elizabeth Miller Elizabeth Shaw	2	Minnette Doderer Jo Ann Orr	2	14	9.3
1977	Nancy Shimanek Boyd[e] Betty Jean Clark Sonja Egenes Julia Gentleman Betty Hoffman-Bright Joan Lipsky Patricia Thompson	7	Diane Brandt Mattie Harper Joyce Lonergan Opal Miller Mary O'Halloran Linda Svoboda	5	Elizabeth Miller Elizabeth Shaw	2	Minnette Doderer Jo Ann Orr	2	16	10.7

[e]Nancy Shimanek Boyd married after serving in the legislature. In state documents, her name is Shimanek. In this work, her name is Shimanek Boyd.

Table 1.1. (*Cont'd*)

Year	House Republicans		House Democrats		Senate Republicans		Senate Democrats		Total	% of legislature
1979	Nancy Shimanek Boyd Betty Jean Clark Sonja Egenes Betty Hoffman-Bright Sonja Larsen Sue Mullins Virginia Poffenberger Patricia Thompson	8	Diane Brandt Jean Lloyd-Jones Joyce Lonergan	3	Julia Gentleman Elizabeth Miller Sue Yenger	3	Jo Ann Orr	1	15	10.0
1981	Nancy Shimanek Boyd Dorothy Carpenter Betty Jean Clark Sonja Egenes Betty Hoffman-Bright Karen Mann Sue Mullins Virginia Poffenberger Jo Smith JoAnn Trucano	10	Diane Brandt Janet Carl Minnette Doderer Jean Lloyd-Jones Joyce Lonergan Marcia Walter	6	Julia Gentleman Sue Yenger	2			18	12.0

1982	Nancy Shimanek Boyd Dorothy Carpenter Betty Jean Clark Sonja Egenes Betty Hoffman-Bright Karen Mann Sue Mullins Virginia Poffenberger Jo Smith JoAnn Trucano	10	Elaine Baxter[f] Diane Brandt Janet Carl Minnette Doderer Jean Lloyd-Jones Joyce Lonergan Marcia Walter	7	Julia Gentleman Sue Yenger	2			19	12.7
1983	Dorothy Carpenter Betty Jean Clark Betty Hoffman-Bright Janis Laughlin[g] Sue Mullins	5	Elaine Baxter Florence Buhr Janet Carl Kathleen Chapman Minnette Doderer Josephine Gruhn Johnie Hammond Jean Lloyd-Jones Joyce Lonergan Doris Peick Jo Ann Zimmerman	11	Julia Gentleman	1			17	11.3

[f]Baxter was elected in a special election.

[g]Janis Torrence Laughlin married after serving in the legislature. Her name in state documents is Janis Torrence. In this work, she will be referred to as Janis Laughlin.

Table 1.1. (*Cont'd*)

Year	House Republicans		House Democrats		Senate Republicans		Senate Democrats		Total	% of legislature
1985	Dorothy Carpenter Betty Jean Clark Joan Hester Janis Laughlin Janet Metcalf Sue Mullins	6	Elaine Baxter Linda Beatty Florence Buhr Janet Carl Kathleen Chapman Minnette Doderer Josephine Gruhn Johnie Hammond Jean Lloyd-Jones Joyce Lonergan Doris Peick Jane Teaford Jo Ann Zimmerman	13	Joy Corning Julia Gentleman	2	Beverly Hannon	1	22	14.7
1987	Dorothy Carpenter Betty Jean Clark Teresa Garman Joan Hester Mary Lundby Janet Metcalf Sue Mullins	7	Janet Adams Linda Beatty Florence Buhr Kathleen Chapman Minnette Doderer Josephine Gruhn Johnie Hammond Patricia Harper Mary Neuhauser Jane Svoboda Jane Teaford	11	Joy Corning Julia Gentleman	2	Beverly Hannon Jean Lloyd-Jones	2	22	14.7

1989	Dorothy Carpenter Betty Jean Clark Teresa Garman Joan Hester Mary Lundby Janet Metcalf	6	Janet Adams Linda Beatty Florence Buhr Kathleen Chapman Minnette Doderer Josephine Gruhn Johnie Hammond Pat Harper Dolores Mertz Mary Neuhauser Joyce Nielsen Jane Svoboda Jane Teaford	13	Joy Corning Julia Gentleman Maggie Tinsman	3	Beverly Hannon Jean Lloyd-Jones Elaine Szymoniak	3	25	16.7
1991	Dorothy Carpenter Teresa Garman Joan Hester Mary Lundby Janet Metcalf	5	Janet Adams Linda Beatty Kathleen Chapman Minnette Doderer Josephine Gruhn Johnie Hammond Dolores Mertz Mary Neuhauser Joyce Nielsen Jane Svoboda Jane Teaford	11	Mary Kramer Maggie Tinsman	2	Florence Buhr Beverly Hannon Jean Lloyd-Jones Elaine Szymoniak	4	22	14.7

Table 1.1. (*Cont'd*)

Year	House Republicans		House Democrats		Senate Republicans		Senate Democrats		Total	% of legislature
1993	Dorothy Carpenter Teresa Garman Sandra Greiner Betty Grundberg Joan Hester Mary Lundby Mona Martin Janet Metcalf	8	Linda Beatty Minnette Doderer Johnie Hammond Patricia Harper Pam Jochum Dolores Mertz Linda Nelson Mary Neuhauser	8	Mary Kramer Maggie Tinsman	2	Florence Buhr Patty Judge Jean Lloyd-Jones Elaine Szymoniak	4	22	14.7
1994	Dorothy Carpenter Teresa Garman Sandra Greiner Betty Grundberg Joan Hester Mary Lundby Mona Martin Janet Metcalf	8	Linda Beatty Minnette Doderer Johnie Hammond Patricia Harper Pam Jochum Dolores Mertz Linda Nelson Mary Neuhauser	8	Mary Lou Freeman[h] Mary Kramer Maggie Tinsman	3	Florence Buhr Patty Judge Jean Lloyd-Jones Elaine Szymoniak	4	23	15.3
Total		118		130		34		31	272	

[h]Freeman was elected in a special election.

CHAPTER 2

Candidacy: The Mid-1960s and After

In 1963, Betty Friedan's *The Feminine Mystique* appeared in bookstores and changed many women's perceptions of themselves, their roles, and their ambitions. Although Friedan had called it "The Problem with No Name," her book had indeed identified a conflict between women's constricted social roles and the human need for full participation in life. The same year, the President's Commission on the Status of Women submitted its report of the legal inequalities, economic discrimination, and other barriers that hobbled American women's attempts to gain power and provided further definition of the limits placed on women.[1]

Congress began to act by passing the Pay Equity Act of 1963, which made it illegal for private employers to pay women and men differently for the same job. The next year Congress passed the 1964 Civil Rights Act which prohibited discrimination on the basis of race, creed, national origin, and sex. The Equal Employment Opportunity Commission (EEOC), created by the Civil Rights Act, however, appeared unable or unwilling to respond to the mountains of complaints women brought to it. In frustration, Friedan and others in her network of women activists formed the National Organization for Women in 1966 to provide women with a new political presence in the nation. In 1971, Friedan and U.S. Representatives Bella Abzug and Shirley Chisolm formed the National Women's Political Caucus to help women become more visible in politics. With the problem identified, a study providing additional evidence of it, laws attempting to begin remedying a part of it, and organizations for articulating further needs and goals, groups of women began to seek ways to change their lives and their society. The modern feminist movement had appeared.[2]

Events in Iowa reflected those on the national scene. In 1963, Governor Harold Hughes created the Iowa Committee on the Status of Women, which issued a report the next year. In 1965, the Iowa Committee sponsored a conference on the status of women. In 1971, women organized a NOW chapter in Des Moines. In 1972, Iowa labor leader Betty Talkington organized a conference of union women and the Iowa legislature ratified the federal Equal Rights Amendment only a few days after Congress passed it. In 1973, Roxanne Conlin organized the Iowa Women's Political Caucus (IWPC); planners for the organization's first convention, held that fall, had prepared for 200 attendees but almost one thousand attended. As a song of the era noted, the times were changing.[3]

The effects of modern feminism did not appear in the number of women elected to state legislatures for almost a decade. In Iowa, the number of women legislators increased from five in 1963 to ten in 1973 and twenty-five in 1989. In 1991 and 1993 twenty-two women served. (See Table 1.1.) To put the increase in Iowa women legislators in perspective consider these examples: in 1971, 5.3 percent of Iowa legislators were women and 4.5 percent of all state legislators were women; in 1981, 12.0 percent of Iowa legislators were women and 12.1 percent of all women legislators were women; and in 1989, 16.7 percent of Iowa legislators were women and 17 percent of all state legislators were women. In 1993, women were 14.7 percent of Iowa legislators and 20.5 percent nationally. In both Iowa and nationally, more women have served in the lower chambers than the upper. To add another perspective, in 1984, Louisiana, Mississippi, Texas, and Virginia did not have any women in their state senates.[4]

In addition to the increasing percentage of women serving in the Iowa General Assembly roughly paralleling the national growth, the successful candidates in both groups shared several common views and perspectives. Instead of emerging from groups like the National Women's Political Caucus, they more likely had belonged to and been leaders in the League of Women Voters, and they generally pointed to League experiences as a reason for becoming candidates. The influence of the League appears significantly greater after the mid-1960s than before it. While some women found the League's approach to politics conservative and ponderous, they credited the

League with introducing them to political activity and often with providing them with a political education. One Iowa woman noted that a campaign workshop sponsored by the Iowa Women's Political Caucus (IWPC) gave her the tools she needed to conduct her campaign but that it was her years of membership and leadership in the League that motivated her to become a candidate. More specifically, Iowa's women legislators of this era do not point to the feminist movement as a reason for their candidacies. In addition, they did not want to be identified on the basis of their gender, that is, they did not want to be the woman candidate. They wanted to simply be the candidate. Whether women ran in Iowa or in other states, very few (only one woman in Iowa has been identified) advertised their feminist beliefs in their campaign materials or speeches or campaigned on the themes that the movement espoused.[5]

The reasons women resisted conducting campaigns based on increased rights for women include straightforward political considerations and personal perceptions. Several women believed that they would lose their races if they focused on feminist issues, even if they did not label themselves feminists. In addition, most women who have served in the legislature have not considered themselves feminists until after they began serving in the body, and then they found themselves having greater understanding of the messages of the feminist movement. Their experiences in the legislature sometimes made them into feminists.

For these women, the motivation for running was not to change the world or Iowa for women. Instead, it came from a belief in themselves and their abilities to effectively assume the responsibilities of the office they sought. They became candidates for reasons that reflected the changing times and the greater power women sought in many aspects of their lives. Women legislators recruited other women. Legislative secretaries decided that they could perform the duties of the office. It may seem contradictory that women did not run as feminists and then that women's candidacies reflected the changing social opinion of women, but it is not. A significant difference separates one woman deciding to become a candidate because she felt capable from the woman deciding to run for office specifically to enact a feminist agenda. Women pointed to their law practices, their professional volunteer work, and their business or farm enterprises as their credentials, not their gender.

Minnette Doderer's (Democrat, Iowa City) introduction to politics came through the League of Women Voters, which she joined "because I just thought it was the greatest organization with all those smart women in it."[6]

Through the League, Doderer became an advocate for state reapportionment and then secretary of and a speaker for the Citizens' Committee for Constitutional Convention, a group that advocated a convention to write a new constitution as a means to reapportion the state.[7] The effort failed in 1960. After that year's election, Governor Herschel Loveless appointed her to the Commission for Fair Representation, which continued to advocate reapportionment.[8]

An active Democrat, Doderer was vice-chair of the Johnson County Democratic Party and did many of the chair's tasks, such as organizing meetings and preparing agendas. When the chair's position became available, she wanted it, telling the group: "I'm running. I want to be chairman, I've been doing all of the work for these three years."[9] When she lost the election, she had her first acknowledged experience of being discriminated against for her gender.

With Governor Harold Hughes's call for a special legislative session to design a reapportionment plan in 1964, Doderer saw an opportunity. Incumbent Johnson County State Representative Scott Swisher was in prison for federal income tax evasion.[10] After he resigned, Doderer worked to win the Democratic county committee's nomination for the special election. Like Ada Garner, Doderer believed she had developed expertise in an area and that she should be allowed to use it in direct ways. She also had paid her political dues by working for the party and helping other candidates in their campaigns. The time had come for her to move beyond preparing the meetings someone else would chair and beyond working on campaigns someone else would win. She asked committee members for support, counted the votes, and believed she had the position, until a man told her he had it. She recollects:

> A farmer ran against me, and I had counted 27 votes. We were both nominated—my friend Bob Burns nominated me—and somebody else nominated Bernard Campion. We both then had to go out to the hall in the courthouse while they did the voting. And he said, "Well, I'm not worried about this one, but I'm sure worried about the fall." . . . And I thought, my God, I thought I had the votes. It never occurred to me to doubt what he was talking about. . . . So I thought, well, he's right, he's counted the votes too. Well, it turned out that I did get my votes, and I was nominated.[11]

Doderer experienced the same kind of unsureness that kept Helen Crabb out of the sale barn, the self-doubt that women discover as they enter new territory. Unlike the women discussed earlier who ran to help their party and coincidentally became political, Doderer had a political goal and asked the party to help her. The likelihood that the Democratic candidate would win was great. In a district that had generally elected Democrats since 1927, gaining the committee's nomination was tantamount to winning the seat.

Unlike most women legislators, Doderer entered the political arena while she and her husband still had children living at home. For women with children at home, conflicts regularly appeared between traditional motherly duties and the candidate's commitments to campaign and then reside in the state capital. During campaigns, voters often questioned whether the candidate had adequately provided for the children's needs. Doderer considered her family responsibilities, but because the special session was expected to last only three weeks, she explains: "I rationalized that if I was a wealthy woman, I could go off to the Bahamas for three weeks." When voters asked what would happen to her husband and children, she told them that the children would be fine and "Fred's [her husband] all grown up."[12] She believed that people talked more to each other about her family responsibilities than to her. Doderer's responses to voters' concerns about her family differ from those of most women candidates with children at home. Earlier women explained the arrangements that had been made with grandmothers or others to prepare meals and provide child care. Doderer believed that she and Fred had made adequate provisions and that only they could judge that. While her responses may appear flip, through them she turned attention away from her personal life and focused it on the campaign.[13]

Her purpose in running was explicit: she wanted to help shape the reapportionment plan that she had advocated for so long. She does not recollect having any long-term political ambitions at the time, but her experience was quite different. In the following twenty-eight years, Doderer served in the House and in the Senate, ran unsuccessfully for lieutenant governor in the 1970 general election and in the 1978 primary, and returned to the House in 1981 where she continues to serve at this writing.[14]

For some women local and county offices preceded their campaigns for the legislature. Virginia Poffenberger (Republican, Perry) began by challenging a decision made by the Perry city council and then running for a seat on it. The story began when the woman who had been on the city council resigned. Believing that it was important to continue having a woman on the council, Poffenberger called council members and suggested a woman they might appoint to complete the term. Poffenberger received affirmative responses to her suggestion, but when the city council met, it chose a man.

Poffenberger was "furious." She asked to be on the next meeting's agenda, intending to express her anger over the decision.[15]

The next city council meeting was scheduled for the same time that Poffenberger was to present the program for her church circle. Poffenberger explained the conflict to her circle chair, who decided that the city council meeting would be the program. When the group of women filed into the council chamber, the council's curiosity about the women was clear. Recollecting that night, Poffenberger described a hole in the middle of the council table where members stared when confronted with a problem, and which held every member's attention as she spoke. Although she addressed her questions to the council, the city attorney responded until Poffenberger challenged a council member to answer. As she describes it: ". . . one of the council members swivelled around in his chair and looked at me and said, 'Virginia, you have to understand one thing. Women aren't fit to be on the council.'" When she asked him to explain the reasons, the council member responded: "They don't understand sewers."[16] Angered by the council meeting, Poffenberger ran for the city council with her circle serving as her campaign committee. She won and served two terms.[17]

In 1976 a friend told Poffenberger that the district's House member, Andrew Varley (Republican, Stuart), intended to retire and that she should run for his seat. A law student at the time, Poffenberger could not see any way to do both. Varley visited her and offered to stay another term if Poffenberger would run in 1978. She agreed. During her campaign, Poffenberger realized that some voters did not want a woman to represent them. However, she felt that after she had served one term, voters accepted her candidacy more readily. She describes the change as: "It was, hey, she's okay, she went down and didn't make an ass out of herself, you know, she did some good things for us. So they were okay the second time, but I had to prove myself over and beyond what a man would have to do."[18]

For two women, Mary O'Halloran (Democrat, Cedar Falls) and Betty Jean Clark (Republican, Cerro Gordo), the decision to become politically active meant making a choice between that and pursuing a religious vocation. As a young woman, O'Halloran joined a teaching order of Roman Catholic nuns, but when she wanted to become active in Robert Kennedy's presidential campaign, her order discouraged her. In 1970 O'Halloran decided in favor of politics as her preferred route to serve people. Teaching in Cedar Falls two years later, she attended her precinct caucus where others encouraged her to run for the legislature. She remembers: "I worked very hard to get elected, even knocked on four thousand doors. And in the end,

I think I ran harder to get elected because I wanted to encourage the women who had encouraged me."[19]

A Methodist minister's daughter, Betty Jean Clark's personal and professional life had centered on the Methodist church. In the 1970s she studied to become a lay preacher in the church, the culmination of a life of ministry. But in 1972 Clark began to wonder if she had a calling to serve in the legislature. Believing that the Watergate scandal was keeping good people out of politics, Clark worried that the problems would get worse. But also believing that a person could misinterpret divine messages, Clark hesitated.[20]

When a Methodist leader told Clark that he intended to nominate her to be a delegate to the General Conference of the United Methodist Church, she confronted the conflict between her goals of activism in the church and in politics. She consulted with her bishop, explaining that she had completed one year of the program for a license to preach, that she wanted to run for the legislature, and that she could not do both. The bishop told her that serving in the legislature could be her ministry. Clark remembers: "I walked out of there like I'd had papal dispensation. . . . That was just the thing that decided it for me." She describes it as a religious decision and says: "Now it's almost embarrassing to say that, because when most of the people you hear about going into politics from a religious decision, they are people going into it in order to try to force everybody into their beliefs. That wasn't what I was trying to do."[21]

Two years before she became a candidate, Clark subscribed to a legislative newsletter in order to become familiar with the issues before the General Assembly. Discovering that she knew little about many of the issues debated, she researched them at the Mason City library and asked people familiar with specific issues for guidance and sources of information. Her preparation helped her win the election and helped her when she entered the House in 1975. Through the research she gained a realistic impression of the legislature, its organization, and the lawmaking process.[22]

Clark's and Poffenberger's candidacies introduce another aspect of women's entrance into politics. They planned for it for two years, carefully arranging their personal and professional lives in preparation for it. While many women made thoughtful decisions to run, Clark and Poffenberger stand out for making commitments to run so far in advance of an election. In Poffenberger's case, the incumbent made what would appear to be a significant personal sacrifice and a commitment to her candidacy by staying in the legislature two more years than he desired. Clark's two years of research suggest her dedication to winning and her intent to be effective.

Incumbent women have served as examples to other women that winning is possible. The presence of women on boards, commissions, city councils, and in legislatures has given some women the courage to take the risks involved in running for public office. More directly, women have recruited other women, offering them campaign assistance and advice, a practice considered critical to increasing the number of women in elective offices by some. The Des Moines suburbs provide an example of women recruiting other women, a chain of recruitments that began with a man.[23]

Patricia Thompson (Republican, West Des Moines) continues the early tradition of women serving on the local school board before entering the legislature. While she was grocery shopping one day, a school principal stopped Thompson and asked her to consider running for the school board. They knew each other through Thompson's work as the school's PTA president and other volunteer activities. During her school board campaign, Thompson called for community education programs and an expansion of the adult education programs, efforts she would continue in the legislature.[24]

After serving on the school board, Thompson was also recruited for her next public office. Even though two Republicans had already entered the House primary in 1976, retiring incumbent Edgar Bittle (Republican, West Des Moines) asked Thompson to become a candidate. Surprised at the suggestion, she initially had little interest in running until Bittle invited her to visit the House and observe. The visit convinced her that she wanted to become part of the body. Thompson believes that her name recognition from serving on the school board and her volunteer activities contributed to her success at the polls.[25]

When Thompson decided to retire from the legislature four years later, she began looking for her replacement. She and Bittle encouraged Dorothy Carpenter (Republican, West Des Moines) to run for the House seat Thompson was leaving. In addition to being an active member of the League of Women Voters and a former president of the local Planned Parenthood affiliate, Carpenter had been Valley High School's band uniform mother-volunteer for four years. She smiles as she recollects how that humble task helped her meet hundreds of students and their parents and, she believes, ultimately helped her win her seat.[26] When Carpenter decided to retire after serving fourteen years in the legislature, she recruited Libby Jacobs to run for her seat.

Carpenter had earlier recruited Janet Metcalf (Republican, Windsor Heights) to run for a neighboring district. Intimidated by the prospect, Metcalf initially resisted the idea. Carpenter and others convinced Metcalf that she could make a difference, especially in the area of abortion rights, a commitment the women shared. Carpenter also told Metcalf that she would find the legislature challenging and interesting. Metcalf decided to become a candidate in order to advocate pro-choice issues in the legislature.[27]

Like many candidates, Metcalf walked door to door asking for voters' support. Some people who answer the door share their ideas and concerns with candidates, while others give the candidate only a moment or two to make their pitches. Metcalf describes her attempts to tailor her comments to the person who opened the door:

> If it was an older man and he looked like a business person, I would say, "I own my own business." If it was an older woman, I'd say, "I think more women need to be in the legislature," or I would say, "I have elderly parents and I'm really concerned about elderly people." If it was a younger woman, I'd say, "I think that government needs to stay out of people's lives," which was the buzz word for the pro-choice thing, if I sensed that she would be acceptable to that. Or I would simply pound on the fact, "You know, there aren't many women in the legislature. I think we need to be represented, too." I said that to one woman who was about 40 years old. She opened up her screen door and jumped out on the porch and said, "Go for it!"[28]

Metcalf's use of her gender as a reason for voters to consider supporting her stands in contrast to some earlier and some contemporary women. While her campaign literature did not solicit support on the basis of her sex, and instead emphasized her business experience and volunteer activities, she came to believe that for some voters gender was an important and positive factor.

On a much lighter side, Metcalf describes the ways she motivated herself to keep knocking on doors:

> At about 7 o'clock [P.M.], when I'd been walking since 4:30 [P.M.] and was just beat, I'd say, "If I go and get a chocolate malt, I bet I can go one more half hour." So I'd go to the Dairy Queen and get a chocolate malt, and I'd go and walk till dark. Or I'd play a little game with myself. I'd be at the end of the street and there would be maybe four houses and then a couple of vacant lots and one house way down at the end. I'd say, "That house way down there is the one vote. I'm going to win by one vote, and that's it."[29]

Metcalf's description suggests the discipline required to get the winning vote. It also illustrates a difference between state legislative campaigns and statewide or congressional races where the media is so important. Iowa legislative candidates seldom use radio or television in their campaigns; the expense prohibits it and the audience cannot be adequately targeted. More important than those factors, though, legislators point to specific advantages of going door to door. They have an opportunity to meet constituents and hear their concerns, and in the process develop a familiarity with their constituencies that helps them as legislators. Urban candidates who have compact districts have an easier time door knocking than do rural legislators who have large districts spanning parts of several counties.

Janet Carl's (Democrat, Grinnell) candidacy contrasts with those in which lengthy preparation and deliberation preceded the decision to run for office. In 1980, the House seat in Carl's district was open and two Democrats had entered the primary race. When the son of one candidate was convicted of murder and bank robbery, the candidate's political future began to evaporate. The other candidate, Mary Hartnett, was a graduating senior at Grinnell College, but she withdrew after receiving a law school scholarship. Three weeks before the primary election Hartnett asked Carl to run, but Carl points out "I wasn't really a very likely candidate. I was not associated with the county party. I had never worked for a candidate."[30]

The next morning, Carl remembers: "I woke up with this huge amount of energy, and I sort of bounded out of bed, and I said, 'I'm going to do it.'"[31] An administrator at Grinnell College, she talked to her boss, who first hesitated and then later agreed that she could run without jeopardizing her job. Carl began a write-in campaign, because the filing deadline had passed. Hartnett publicly withdrew from the race and encouraged voters to support Carl, but Hartnett's name remained on the ballot.

Carl began calling key Democratic leaders in her area. Her innocence of political issues appeared in a telephone conversation with the local United Auto Workers contact, Greg Johnson. Nervous before making any of the calls to key Democrats, Carl began by explaining her eagerness to serve and her willingness to learn and work hard. When Johnson asked her about her position on labor issues such as the right to work, Carl answered: "Well of course I support the right to work." Carl did not know the significance of the words to labor. Under the "right to work law" in Iowa, employees do not have to belong to a union to get a job covered by a union contract. Labor generally opposes the right to work law. Carl describes her response as a "faux pas." To Johnson's credit he listened to her and helped her.[32]

Carl lost the primary and Hartnett, who had withdrawn, won. The task of choosing a candidate went to the county convention. Having become more sophisticated, Carl began calling convention delegates and asking them for their support. When the convention met in July, Carl became the candidate and won her race.[33]

The same year that Carl won, 1980, JoAnn Trucano (Republican, Des Moines) waged an aggressive campaign against a popular but frequently absent incumbent, Norman Jesse (Democrat, Des Moines). Trucano maintained that Jesse missed almost one-third of the House's roll call votes and argued that Jesse's job as head of the Polk County attorney's civil division kept him away from his legislative duties. Jesse countered that he took a leave from his job and worked on an hourly basis for the county attorney during the session. A twelve-year House veteran, Jesse said: "I could get things done she couldn't begin to, even as a minority party member."[34] After Trucano defeated him, Jesse did not take it gracefully and accused her of being "dumber than a post."[35] The first day of the 1981 session, Trucano carried a wooden post into the House chamber. She called it "a listening post."[36]

A different kind of absenteeism played an important role in a 1984 race in western Iowa. Incumbent Laverne Schroeder (Republican, McClelland), who had served eighteen years in the House, divorced his wife, remarried, and moved out of his district to Waukee in central Iowa. Joan Hester (Republican, Honey Creek), a woman who felt legislators should live in the districts they represented, was certain no one else would challenge Schroeder in the primary and decided to take on the job. She brought experience running legislative campaigns to her own. She had run her husband's Senate races and she had worked as her husband Jack's Senate secretary. After Hester had defeated him in the primary, Schroeder entered the general election as an independent but Hester easily defeated him and the Democratic candidate. When Hester won the race, she and her husband became the first married couple to serve together in the Iowa General Assembly, she in the House, he in the Senate.[37]

Financing campaigns has often been perceived as a particular barrier to women entering politics. Three factors appear to make it more difficult for women to raise money for their campaigns than men. Women do not like asking for money; even experienced politicians have expressed their distaste for asking for money for themselves, in spite of the fact that they may have raised money for other causes or candidates. Secondly, women tend not to belong to the informal networks that provide access to contributions such as Rotary and Kiwanis. And last, PACs tend to favor incumbents as recipients of their benevolence and obviously men tend to be the incumbents. In one study, women legislators in other parts of the country ranked raising money as the primary problem in their campaigns. Another study of selected Oklahoma legislative races in 1978 and 1980 contradicts this view. In that study women raised more money than men, including those races between incumbent men and the women who challenged them.[38]

Iowa women candidates also challenge the belief that women have less success raising campaign money than men, but that does not mean they enjoyed the task. Iowa women have generally expressed few problems raising money, but they expect to work for the contributions. They have used entertaining and neighborly fundraisers such as hog roasts, backyard picnics, and dinners in their homes. These forms of fundraising point back to traditional women's skills: cooking food and feeding guests. While Iowa's women candidates send fundraising letters, they focus on family-centered events for their campaigns. In Iowa, women on the average spent more for their campaigns in 1988 than men and less than men in 1992. (See Table 2.1.) The inability to attract money may have doomed some women's campaigns in the past, but that does not now appear to be the situation. The greater problem may be that women find the task of raising significant amounts of money for a legislative campaign overwhelming. While comparable data are not available for earlier years, the costs of conducting a legislative campaign have increased dramatically, even in the years between 1984 when an average House campaign cost $6,237 and 1992 when it cost $13,234. Senate campaigns increased from $12,566 in 1984 to $25,436 in 1992.[39]

Table 2.1. Summary of campaign expenditures for 1988 and 1992 House and Senate races by sex

	House, 1988	House, 1992	Senate, 1988	Senate, 1992
Women	$10,792	$13,371	$23,563	$25,371
Men	$10,570	$13,495	$18,516	$25,449

Sources: "A Report on Campaign Finance in Iowa, 1988," Common Cause of Iowa, 1989, n.p.; "A Report on Legislative Election Campaign Finance in Iowa, 1992," Common Cause/Iowa, p. 18-19.

For some women, the realization that they, and not the party or anyone else, held the responsibility for raising the money for their campaigns came as a surprise. In 1984, a Statehouse staff member had recruited Beverly

Hannon (Democrat, Anamosa), who had made the decision after some trepidation. Hannon describes the next step:

> As soon as I signed the declaration of candidacy, I was told, "Fine, now all you have to do is come up with about $20,000." I yelled, "What? What do you mean I have to come up with $20,000; I thought the party raised the money." The answer was they'd help, they'd tell me how to raise it. The last thing in the world I ever wanted to do was to raise money. I hate doing that. They suggested I get my Christmas card list, look over my relatives, neighbors, club colleagues. . . . When I complained about hating to do that, they impressed on me if I can't ask people for money to support me, then I don't have much confidence in myself, and why should anyone else? I did it and hated every minute of it. Asking friends was the hardest. I had a hog roast, bake sales, letter appeal for money; I raised about $11,000. Some advised me to borrow money for more advertising. I refused. My husband and I had agreed, no borrowing. I'd spend every dime I collected, but I wouldn't go into debt. We knew if I lost, people would be reluctant to contribute to a loser after the election.[40]

In 1988, Hannon had an interesting race. Her opponent, Hurley Hall, was an incumbent in another district, then before the election moved to Hannon's district, ran from his new district, and changed his party affiliation from Democrat to Republican. Hall outspent Hannon $41,256 to $34,749. Hannon won in 1988. She ran for re-election in 1992, this time under the new reapportionment plan, which placed her in the same district as incumbent Jack Rife (Republican, Moscow). In 1992, Hannon spent $48,351, but Rife spent $68,907, making their race the most expensive legislative contest in the state that year. Rife won.[41]

One last route to the Statehouse deserves attention. A few women worked as legislative secretaries before they became candidates. Each member of the Iowa House and Senate has a secretary for answering correspondence, keeping bill and committee books current, and related tasks. The secretaries work on the House and Senate floors, sitting next to their legislators. As they do their daily tasks, secretaries can listen to debate (although some prefer not) and observe the process. After listening to her state representative in debate and watching him work, one woman who served in the 1970s decided that he did not represent her views and that she could do a better job. Other secretaries also believed that they understood the legislative process, knew the issues, and could use their knowledge to serve the state. These observers who became legislators brought a familiarity with the legislature that only a few other women enjoyed before entering the body.[42]

One reason for candidacy, lifelong political ambition, stands out precisely because only two women, Mary O'Halloran (Democrat, Cedar Falls), and

Mary Lundby (Republican, Marion) even mentioned childhood interests in the more than sixty interviews done as part of the research for this project. O'Halloran recollects political debates being served along with family dinners. She credits those lively discussions as being the source of her interest in political activism.[43] Only Lundby expressed childhood dreams to be a politician holding public office, being a policymaker, or having power. As a teenager, Lundby had visited the Statehouse with a friend whose father was a state legislator. She recollected that: "I knew when I sat up in that gallery [of the House] I was coming back."[44] Some women introduced the topic in their interviews, saying they had never expected to run for office. Indeed, some initially laughed at the idea when they were asked to become candidates. Few women had professional aspirations beyond teaching. Several women had participated in or listened to dinner-time political discussion but did not imagine themselves in elective office. Political ambitions did not enter their lives until much later, and then usually after marrying and raising their children. When offered the opportunity to dream bigger dreams, however, these women and others worked to make those dreams a reality. By 1994, eighty-six Iowa women made the transformation.

Many women believed that some voters would not support a woman's candidacy. Lenabelle Bock noted that: "You [as a candidate] were just sort of out there all alone as a woman, and a woman has to work *twice* as hard as a *man* to get elected, that's absolutely true."[45] The questions of how many voters made their decisions based upon the candidates' gender and the number of women who lost their races because of it remain for another project. Women who lost their races may attribute that outcome to sexism.

The roles women have played in other women's candidacies included recruiting the candidate, working on her campaign, listening to the problems in the campaign, and providing advice and guidance. Candidates regularly mention a friend or a neighbor who contributed time, energy, and resources to the effort. Only infrequently are men's names included among the primary activists in a woman's campaign. A reasonable explanation, beyond sexism, includes the differences between the social and volunteer organizations men and women join.

The likelihood of a woman winning her race has increased since the 1972 general elections. The success rates of the women candidates in the 1972 and 1992 general elections are shown in Table 2.2. In 1972 eight women ran for the Senate, and four won (50 percent); twenty-one women ran for House seats and six won (28.5 percent), an overall percentage of 34.4 percent. In 1992, nine women ran for the Senate and four won (44.4 percent); thirty-three women ran for the House and sixteen won (48.4 percent), an overall percentage of 47.6 percent.[46] The different success rates for women between 1972 and 1992 may be related to some combination of the campaigns

Table 2.2. Women Candidates for Iowa House and Senate by party for 1972 and 1992 general elections

Year	House Republicans	House Democrats	Won	Lost	Senate Republicans	Senate Democrats	Won	Lost
1972	10	11	4 (R) 2 (D)	6 (R) 9 (D)	2	6	2 (R) 2 (D)	0 (R) 4 (D)
1992	16	17	10 (R) 6 (D)	8 (R) 9 (R)	4	5	3 (R) 1 (D)	2 (R) 3 (D)

Sources: *Iowa Official Register, 1973–1974,* pp. 174–178; *Iowa Official Register, 1993–1994,* pp. 431–448.

conducted by the candidates, the sophistication of the candidates, an increased number of female incumbents, and an increasing willingness of voters to choose women.

Women's abilities to raise money and to win have developed while the candidates themselves have not changed significantly. They continue to be mothers, wives, PTA presidents, LWV members, and active church members, possessing many of the characteristics found in women elected in the decades before the feminist movement. They remain a generally conservative group of women—women like those who live next door. They still do not belong to that group that political scientists define as the eligible pool. It may be that these women and those serving in other state legislatures have begun to redefine the eligible pool of candidates. The time for women to believe that their candidacies would be a condemned effort because of their gender has passed. As women discover that increasing numbers of contributors will consider their candidacies on grounds other than that of gender and that they have close to even odds of winning compared to men, more women may decide to enter legislative races.

CHAPTER 3

Women in a Men's Club

Running their state legislative campaigns provided many women with their first experiences in crossing into traditional men's territory. When they entered those exclusive men's clubs, the legislatures, they encountered further evidence that they had endeavored to do something unusual for women. There they found traditions, practices and protocols different from those in the League of Women Voters, the PTA, and the Federation of Women's Clubs. A fundamental difference separates these groups from the legislature. Power resides at the center of the legislature. Obtaining power, using it, asserting it, and maintaining it posed several conflicts for women lawmakers, and they responded to it, theirs and others, in a wide spectrum of ways. Depending upon the woman and the situation, she may have refused it, acquiesced hers to other people, fought for it and won, or fought and lost.

Women made these encounters with power in a decidedly male-dominated culture. Legislatures have been described as having "the *macho* culture of the locker room, the smoker, the barracks [emphasis in original]," and as "male clubs."[1] It is an atmosphere that has left women even with decades of legislative service feeling excluded from its membership. For example, Massachusetts legislator Mary Fonseca, at the time minority whip, had been in the Senate for twenty-eight years, but said she had "never been a member of the club," a sentiment echoed by veteran Iowa legislator Minnette Doderer.[2] Rather than being members, women have been described as "political immigrants," "outsiders," and "intruders."[3] Some women accepted the limitations implied in those words, but women who had political agendas or who had spent years on bills they had nurtured came to find the restraints unacceptable. One woman described it as becoming politicized and another as becoming a feminist. Regardless, they had encountered attempts to stifle their efforts, identified the power they had, and used it.

For many people, power and women are not words that go together, especially until recent decades. The authors of *Women in Power* explain that: "The old-fashioned spectrum of femininity typically encompasses attributes such as affectionate, sympathetic, sensitive to the needs of others, understanding, compassionate, warm, tender, fond of children, gentle, yielding, cheerful, shy, responsive to flattery, loyal, soft-spoken, gullible, or even childlike. There is no room in the traditional female stereotype for powerful. Femininity doesn't imply tough, strong, or decisive."[4] Again from *Women in Power*: "As our society defines power, one can't be powerful without being tough."[5] Powerful and tough have not generally been the descriptions that women have wanted for themselves. Iowa women legislators and those in other states have generally viewed themselves as traditional women and have fulfilled women's traditional roles, as their volunteer work, husbands, and families attest. In addition, they are a relatively conservative group of women.[6] Even some of Iowa's most powerful women legislators have been dismayed when they have read newspaper articles portraying them as tough. Contemporary women in politics have acknowledged that even when they had power, they were not "conscious" of having it and did not think of themselves as powerful. Jo Ann Zimmerman, former Iowa House member and lieutenant governor said: "I never thought that I had power until I realized that other people were telling me that I did."[7] Yet, power is what many of them sought. They wanted the power to have their voices heard, their ideas considered, their proposals debated, and their word trusted; and they wanted to work with their male colleagues on an equal basis. Regardless of women's interpretations of their power, as legislators they found other legislators, leaders, and lobbyists both familiar with and accustomed to using power.

Just as women were unfamiliar with the uses of power that they found in the legislature, male legislators were uncertain about having women among their colleagues. Male legislator's responses to the women joining them ranged from amusing to hostile. For example, in 1929, after Carolyn

Pendray's (Democrat, Jackson) election, some legislators wondered if she would mind if they smoked and offered a reporter a box of candy to find the answer.[8] Pendray explained she "was reared on smoke," and did not care if the members smoked, adding: "And besides, I want to be one of the 108 and I'm making no bids for favors on the grounds of femininity."[9]

Other examples of men's attitudes toward women come in many forms and from almost every decade that women have served in the General Assembly. Helen Crabb (Democrat, Guthrie) felt that men had not adjusted to women's presence in the chamber when she served in the 1940s.[10] Gertrude Cohen (Democrat, Waterloo), who served in the 1960s, believed that men perceived the legislature as their province and wanted to keep it that way.[11] In praising Gladys Nelson's political career in the 1950s, a *Des Moines Register* editorial explained that her sex had not "impaired her effectiveness."[12] The *Newton Daily News* wrote that despite the "disdain" held for political women, Nelson continually "held her own."[13] A state senator told Nelson that men in the legislature did not like working with women, but, she recalled: "He had never heard one complaint against me. I took that as a compliment."[14] In the 1960s, Joan Lipsky (Republican, Cedar Rapids) encountered a legislator who considered "women absolutely brainless and totally incompetent to deal with something like figures and money."[15] Male legislators told Sonja Larsen (Republican, Ottumwa), who served in the 1970s, that they believed that women should not be in the legislature and that a woman's place was at home. In the 1980s, Janet Adams (Democrat, Webster) described the problem as poor vision on the part of men: they either did not see her or they looked over her. Because legislatures differ from men's clubs in that they do not have the power to reject duly elected members, the men who objected to women's presence could only express their opinions and demonstrate their objections by their actions.[16]

When women describe their relationships with their male colleagues, they repeatedly assert their beliefs that their male colleagues respect them, but one might question the nature of that respect, because they also describe demeaning words and actions. Examples include the evening Jo Ann Orr (Democrat, Grinnell) sat next to a colleague at a legislative dinner and felt his hand on her thigh, which she told him to remove if he did not "want real trouble." She also disliked George Kinley's (Democrat, Polk) habit of calling her "dear," which he stopped using after she called him "darling." In addition, she recounted the afternoon she had taken a nap in the Senate's private lounge and later heard that senators said that they had slept with her. She did not use the lounge again. Other Iowa women privately described similar experiences but felt that having them discussed in a published work would not serve their political interests. In other words, they needed to be able to get along with their colleagues and accusing them of offensive behavior could isolate them from the offenders as well as other men in the legislature.[17]

Sometimes male legislators focused their attentions on their female colleagues in ways that appeared to be benign but that conveyed the clear message that the women were different. In *Political Woman*, Jeane K. Kirkpatrick describes the actions as "symbolic putdown[s]" that she categorizes as "killing with kindness." She points out that: "The 'Sweetheart' or 'darling of the house' is *not* (emphasis in original) an equal participant."[18] Examples of women being given Valentines or flowers extend from Mississippi to Minnesota, and include Iowa, but not all women took offense, and some women reciprocated.[19] For example, the House gave Carolyn Pendray (Democrat, Jackson) a bouquet in memory of all Iowa women.[20] In 1943 the House gave Mae Lynch (Democrat, Pocahontas) a bouquet and declared her the chamber's Valentine, a gesture she returned two years later when she gave each member of the House a rose. She told the assembly: "This morning, with the consent of the wives and sweethearts, I am asking the 107 true and stalwart men to be my valentines. . . ."[21] In the 1960s, the four women in the House gave each man a carnation in appreciation of "the kindness of the men in allowing a woman the floor every now and then."[22] The charming sentiment reveals the sense of separateness these women felt. A group of male legislators would not have reason to thank their colleagues for opportunities to exercise their rights or fulfill their responsibilities.

In the 1980s, attention to women took a different form. During Women's History Week, female legislators used points of personal privilege (comments that are not part of the formal debate on the chamber floor) to describe women's accomplishments or aspects of women's lives. For example, Diane Brandt (Democrat, Cedar Falls) once read a passage that described women's labors in the nineteenth century; other women described the accomplishments of notable females. Acknowledging activists' achievements carries a different message than making a legislator the chamber's Valentine.

Until the mid-1960s, most women adhered to the old adage that silence is golden. U.S. Senator Margaret Chase Smith, who classified herself as "one of the Senate's five least talkative members," refrained from speaking to prove that women did not talk unnecessarily.[23] Women in state legislatures have described themselves as speaking only rarely. Those Iowa women who made conscious decisions to be generally silent have pointed to it as an attribute that contributed to their credibility. Speaking readily on every bill and amendment during debate does not gain the good will of one's colleagues, whether the legislator is male or female, but few men would perceive their silence as any particular virtue. One could speculate that these women used their silence to avoid confrontations or in an effort to assume the role they believed their colleagues had assigned them: the powerlessness of invisibility.[24]

Other women legislators have certainly found their voices, but some of that burden to be invisible still remains. Jean Lloyd-Jones (Democrat, Iowa City) described her observations in 1989:

> Well, one thing I noticed early was the difference in the way men and women just acted when they walked in the morning. For example, the women would tend to go straight to their desks and sit down and start to work, or start to read the mail, or start to do something just right there. Almost as if our greatest need was to run for cover, just get out of sight, not be conspicuous, as soon as possible. I noticed that so many men would just kind of roam around the chamber, saying hello, greeting people, slapping each other on the back, and things like that. Men seem to want to take as much space as they could.[25]

Lloyd-Jones also noted that when women gathered in the chambers, men became suspicious:

> I remember one day, some of us women—I remember Beje Clark and two or three others and myself—happened to be standing in the middle aisle in the House, and I think it was just after lunch period before we took up again, and some of the men began to kind of come around and want to know what we were doing. They would say afterwards, "What were you all talking about?" Just drove them crazy to think that there we were, and when we realized how nervous it made them, we did it often! We filled the aisle. But it was not a comfortable place for us to stand. We did not feel real comfortable there, but we made it a point after that to just go and take up some space.[26]

Other women have used their personal resources and abilities to find useful and comfortable strategies. Afraid of the microphones used during floor debate, Helen Crabb made her points in committee meetings.[27] Lillian McElroy believed that in order to gain men's cooperation on some issues, women lawmakers had to "sort of hold back on some subjects."[28] Joan Lipsky disagreed, saying: "Women have always been taught that to be nice is the way to go—but to get anywhere a person must function from a position of strength. Just being right isn't enough—women must be ready to do battle."[29] Janet Metcalf and others tried to play the game as members of the team, which also permitted them to cast some independent votes. Josephine Gruhn presented complex bills in the simplest, most direct terms that she could, avoiding unnecessary elaboration during her remarks.[30]

Betty Jean Clark, fondly known as Beje, used her abilities as a humorist and a poet when the occasion allowed. As a freshman, Clark had wanted to use her microphone for something inconsequential the first time, and a bill for a state poet laureate provided the opportunity. Clark found the idea nonsensical, made fun of it by telling the chamber she would perform the service gratis, offered a sample of her work, and added that the price reflected the quality. She read:

> Oh hail to Iowa, the state of tall corn.
> Oh hail to all efforts to rid her of porn.
> Oh hail to Bob Ray, her untiring chief
> whose photogeneity defies belief.
> Oh hail to this House with its wisdom sublime.
> And hail to the Senate, if you have extra time.
> Oh hail to our staff, our pages, our clerks,
> without whom we'd all end up looking like jerks.
> Oh hail![31]

Through her poetry, an approach available to those with rhythm and rhyme, Clark took gentle jabs at some of the legislature's antics and effectively made her points for more than a decade.

Iowa's women legislators have regarded themselves, their responsibilities, and their roles in a number of ways. Lenabelle Bock (Republican, Hancock) described herself as a concerned legislator and denied being a politician. Minnette Doderer (Democrat, Iowa City) listed her occupation as politician. The difference between a legislator and a politician may appear to only be a matter of word choice, but it is more important than that. It indicates the levels of activism and leadership a legislator anticipates for herself. Some women consigned themselves to roles as observers while others more fully engaged in the power struggles of the assembly.[32]

Iowa's first woman lawmaker, Carolyn Pendray (Democrat, Jackson) took an active role in the political life of the General Assembly by organizing her partisan colleagues into a caucus during the first days of her freshman year in the House. Democrats had not organized as a caucus since some time around the 1900s, when Pendray's father had served in the General Assembly. She organized the caucus to help strengthen the party in the state. She believed that by identifying issues with the Democratic Party it would give Democratic candidates campaign issues, both in the form of bills passed and those defeated. Acknowledging that few issues in the legislature were partisan, Pendray saw political opportunities for her party if it identified distinctions between Democrats and Republicans. With only fifteen Democrats out of 158 members in the General Assembly, she recognized that her partisan colleagues did not constitute a strong voting bloc.[33]

Even though Pendray was a loyal party member, she did not always acquiesce to the demands of her caucus. As a member of the Senate in 1935 Pendray refused to bow to her party's pressure when the Senate considered an investigation of the liquor control commission in the 1930s.[34] When her caucus needed one more vote to bury the investigation, the leadership tried "to whip Mrs. Pendray into line." She explained: "I was asked to change my vote for the good of the party, but I claim the best thing the party can do is to sponsor a thorough investigation." She justified her decision, saying: "And while I was under fire I couldn't help remembering that I was a Democrat before it got to be popular. I was a party worker a good many years before some Democrats now in the Senate had decided they weren't Republicans."[35] The leadership made a compromise with other members that alleviated the need for Pendray's vote.

In the 1940s, another woman, Edna Lawrence (Republican, Wapello), objected to her leadership's rejection of Republican Governor Robert D. Blue's proposals to solve problems at a state institution without allowing the House to debate them.[36] Lawrence accused the Republican leadership of placing a "gag" on the discussion of bills. She objected more to the process used than the outcome, saying: "I am not willing to represent my county and the state in a process in which just a few men draw up the legislation. I might just as well have stayed home."[37] House majority leader Arch W. McFarlane (Republican, Black Hawk) responded: "It's just one of those things that happens sometimes," an explanation Lawrence did not accept.[38]

Perhaps it was "those things" referred to by McFarlane that prompted Lawrence, Amy Bloom (Republican, Webster) and others to form the '52 Club' (for 52nd General Assembly) at the end of the session. While some of the members told a reporter the group had a social purpose, others suggested a different agenda. Many new members had felt that they had not been included in the decision-making process during the session. To remedy the problem, they organized a legislative school for the class of 1948, enabling the newly elected legislators to understand the process and procedures from the beginning of the session.[39]

Some women who have not bowed to party leadership have later found it unwilling to defend their districts during reapportionment battles. After the final district lines were drawn, these women were left with districts in which party registrations or other factors made races in the new districts unusually unfavorable to them. June Franklin (Democrat, Polk) and Gertrude Cohen (Democrat, Black Hawk) include themselves in this group. A freshman, Cohen introduced a work-release bill for county jail inmates, an idea favored by her party. According to Cohen, she made an unforgivable error—she had a Republican sponsor, Francis L. Messerly, also from Black Hawk County, for the companion bill in the Senate. The House Democratic leadership explained to Cohen that having a Republican sponsor for the bill would allow that party to get credit for the idea, and the Democrats wanted to keep it for themselves. They wanted her to let her bill die, and then the judiciary committee would introduce the same bill under its sponsorship.[40]

Cohen refused, the House debated her bill, and her partisan colleagues badgered her during debate. One lawmaker grilled her, asking her to define felonies and indictable misdemeanors and to explain the difference between them, attempting to destroy her credibility. Cohen remembered: "I couldn't answer the questions. After about fifteen minutes of . . . examining me . . . I quoted something from our Bible, when a good daughter of her people realizes she is defeated, she admits it. . . . They killed the bill. I felt naked. . . . I felt exposed."[41] After the debate a House member chided other members of the body: "The lady from Black Hawk [Cohen] has been exposed to some terrible things in this House this morning," and described them as "despicable."[42] She felt that the bill's defeat and her humiliation came as a direct result of her perceived disloyalty to the party: "I mean, loyalty to the party is very important. It's an important aspect of political life. But somehow or other, something in my personality wouldn't allow for me to admit that perhaps it would have been wiser to let the bill die."[43] Later in the session, the House Judiciary Committee produced a bill with the same purpose and passed it.[44]

The same year, the legislature passed one of its many reapportionment plans. Cohen, who had worked on the issue during her years in the League of Women Voters, contended that leaders protected some legislators' seats as they developed that year's plan, but she believed that she did not receive the same consideration, saying: "I think as far as the party was concerned, I was expendable, because I had not cooperated as fully as I should have. I had a lot of differences with the party. I think the county chairman knew that, I think the state Democratic chairman knew that."[45] The party gave her a Republican district but later could not find a candidate for the Senate seat. They convinced Cohen to run for that seat, but 1966 was a Republican year and Cohen lost. After another reapportionment plan, Cohen ran for the Iowa House in 1968 but again lost.[46]

Another form of legislative bargaining, trading votes, offended some women. In *Sex Roles in the State House*, Irene Diamond asserts that: "There is very little in the traditional training for women that is readily transferrable to the give-and-take of politics."[47] Lenabelle Bock (Republican, Hancock) never traded her vote in her two terms. For her it was a moral issue.[48] Gertrude Cohen also refused to trade her vote and acknowledged the cost: "A person can have too much integrity in politics, and it doesn't work. You cannot have integrity in politics; it's a bargaining agency. I mean, you scrub my back and I'll scrub your back, and you'll do this for me and I'll do that for you, and that's the way you deal. . . . I can't deal that way."[49]

In a story that almost sounds like a morality play, Joyce Lonergan (Democrat, Boone) described her decision to bargain with her party leadership and the consequences. She no longer remembers the issue, but clearly recalls the events. She had told lobbyists, her caucus, and her constituents how she intended to vote, but the leadership took her in a back room and convinced her to participate in a charade. She recollects: "They said just put in your vote until we get 52 votes, then withdraw yours, and then we'll sucker in enough Republicans on the vote so that it won't be one-sided and then you will just change your vote and it will be okay." The man who happened to be in the Speaker's chair at the time of the vote did not know about the agreement, and after 51 votes appeared for the bill, he turned off the voting machine. Lonergan continues: "It was in the afternoon and I just left the chamber and came home. I was so upset, I could not deal with it. I thought your word is your bond." She feared that she would not be trusted again. Leadership explained what had happened to the lobbyist, and Lonergan apologized. He told her that she was not a "very good game player." She decided to never put herself in that situation again.[50]

Jean Lloyd-Jones described her experience with leadership:

> Every freshman has this problem with the leadership tell[ing] you what to do, and whether you should do it, and most women are so intimidated in this setting that when the leadership says, now we need you to vote this way,

> and you've got to do this, they'll do it. I do not remember what was the first thing that I disagreed with him [one of the leaders] and decided not to follow the leadership, but it was very agonizing for me not to go along with him, but when I did vote what I wanted—I went my own way—I learned immediately that they respect you more, that they don't run over you, they have to stop and see what you're going to do. . . . So this thing about well, the leadership, if you want to get along then you have to go along—that is total nonsense. If you want them to respect you and take into account your views, then you definitely do not go along with them. [51]

In dealing with pressure to change their votes, women like Josephine Gruhn (Democrat, Spirit Lake) believed that making a decision, especially in controversial issues, and then staying with it benefited her. When leadership understood that a legislator could not be harassed into changing her vote, they left her alone and looked for more pliable lawmakers. Several women explained that a willingness to negotiate and compromise on specific items within bills was an essential aspect of the legislative process but it did not extend to those votes that carried moral implications, as in the many gambling bills. In other situations, the legislators believed that the sentiment in their district regarding some issues was so strong that they had a responsibility to respect public opinion. Few Iowa women held the adamant position expressed by Lenabelle Bock, who never traded a vote, and few portrayed themselves as readily trading their votes. Most placed themselves someplace in the middle.[52]

In addition to the leadership, committee chairs hold both influence and power. In contrast to some women's experiences in other states, Iowa women legislators have regularly received the committee assignments they requested and they have held committee chairs since the 1930s. This acknowledgment of their ability did not consistently carry with it the members' cooperation. For example, when Edna Lawrence, chair of the House Social Security Committee in 1949, could not persuade her committee members to meet, she used humor and the carrot approach to getting what she wanted. Unable to get a quorum of her committee together to make changes in workmen's compensation, she passed out gum and cigars to entice members to the meeting. The scenario is rather cute, and it demonstrates Lawrence's resourcefulness, but it also indicates the lengths women had to travel to gain their colleagues' cooperation in fulfilling their responsibilities. With a direct use of power beyond her reach, she found a way to gain the committee members' cooperation.[53]

A mental health bill in the 1970s provides other examples of the culture in which women worked and the resistance to believing in women's credibility. Betty Jean Clark (Republican, Rockwell) and others had worked for years to make substantive changes in Iowa's mental health programs. After dozens of committee meetings, interim studies, consultations with mental health experts, and seemingly endless negotiations, Clark's committee had a bill ready for debate and passage. As chair of the committee, Clark had the responsibility to lead her caucus's discussion of it. The caucus scheduled a lunchtime meeting, and Clark stopped on her way to buy a sandwich from a vending machine. When she got to the caucus, she discovered the members had begun debating the mental health bill without her. She put her name on the list of speakers waiting their turns.[54]

When Majority Leader Roger Halvorson (Republican, Monona) called her name, Clark told the group: "I want you folks to know that I am absolutely, positively furious! You have no business talking about the most important bill that was put in my committee when I wasn't here. You would not do that with Del Stromer on an education bill, you would not do that with [Larry] Pope on an unemployment bill, and you will not do that to me again!"[55] Then she began discussing the points that others had raised.

Later, when the bill did not appear on the debate calendar, Clark asked Halvorson when he intended to bring it up. He explained that some caucus members objected to the way she had voted on some bills, and might resist her bill in retaliation. Clark told him: "That's a bunch of bull. They don't mind the way I have been voting, because I have been with the caucus almost 100 percent. What they mind is sometimes in caucus when I tell them it's stupid." He stalled, and Clark told him that the longer he waited the harder it would be to fight the caucus members. This woman, who wears a pin on her shoulder that is a replica of an angel and who used poetry to gently jibe her colleagues, remembers: "I saw I wasn't getting anywhere, and so I shook my finger in his face, and you should never do that to a man, especially one shorter than you are, and I said, 'I want you to know this. If that mental health bill doesn't come to the floor, and soon, I'm going to go to the press, and I'll tell them that in our caucus we're having a battle between the political hacks and the statesmen, and the hacks have been winning all the rounds.'" After Halvorson finished swearing, he and Clark parted. In a short time, Halvorson returned to tell Clark the bill would be on the calendar, but it would be when they could schedule the six hours of debate he anticipated. He pointed to the number of amendments on the bill and questioned whether the bill had enough votes for passage. Clark countered that she could finish the bill in three hours, that she had negotiated with sponsors of the amendments, and that she had the votes. When the House completed debate in less than three hours and passed with more than 90 votes, Clark returned to Halvorson and said: "'Rog, the next time I tell you I've got the votes, I've got the votes.' He didn't like it much. I really got my dander up; that's when I became political."[56]

Some women, like Gertrude Cohen and Lenabelle Bock did not ever become political in the way Clark described. They did not become part of the "smoke-filled room" decision-making process and although Bock was content that "they [leadership] kept us [women legislators] pretty well informed about what was going to be done," it also kept them out of the process.[57] Another Iowa woman's recollections of her legislative service in the 1970s helps cast light on some women's relationship to power. During an interview in the 1980s, she was asked if she had sought a leadership position. Angrily, the former legislator said that she had been treated the same as men, that she was not a feminist, and that she had not held a leadership position. At the end of the interview, the legislator returned to the topic of leadership. She said that at the time, she had not thought that she knew enough to be a leader, but upon reflection she realized that men, who had been freshmen with her and who had no more ability than she, had been elected to leadership. She wondered why she had not been asked, still not understanding the quest for power.

Other women believed that unless they became part of the power structure they could not effectively make a difference in the legislature. Joan Lipsky (Republican, Cedar Rapids) ran for assistant leader in 1977 because she wanted the recognition as a leader and wanted to influence leadership decisions. She explains: "Women have always exercised influence in ways that are not from clearly occupying positions of leadership. Believe me, much of what I did was never reported in the papers, and much of what I did came from getting others to do things."[58] Mary O'Halloran (Democrat, Cedar Falls) echoed the sentiment: "You either deal with the struggle for power, or you watch the parade go by."[59] Elizabeth Shaw (Republican, Davenport) felt that she and Lipsky "should have been in the leadership long before" they were. She added: "I do feel it took us a long time, longer than it should have in terms of the amount of work that we did and the amount that we all accomplished in the legislature, to come into the leadership."[60] But she did not feel that they were discriminated against.

Women legislators in Iowa and elsewhere reinforce Shaw's statements that it may have taken them longer to become leaders and that men resisted women holding that power. They have expressed their frustrations at the slow pace at which they have progressed through the power structure. As Jeane J. Kirkpatrick has pointed out, however, women did win enough male support to hold the formal positions of leadership. While men resisted choosing the women among them for leadership, at the same time they supported those women willing to challenge the status quo.[61]

In 1974, women legislators in one study concluded that the higher leadership slots probably were beyond their reach, and men concurred, but nationally in 1983, women held 7 of the top 279 jobs, as house speaker, president of the senate, or majority or minority leader. As a percentage (2.5 percent of the leadership positions were held by women, in 1983, 13.3 percent of all legislators were women), it is unremarkable, but as an indicator of changing attitudes and the implication that women had sufficient seniority to hold those powerful jobs, it is significant. It suggests that women do indeed seek the positions and have developed the necessary credibility to win them.[62]

Women have noted several reasons for and benefits of being in leadership. Betty Hoffman-Bright (Republican, Muscatine) sought and won a leadership position because she believed that men "sometimes forget that there are two sides to an issue"—a male side and a female side.[63] As a member of leadership, Dorothy Carpenter (Republican, West Des Moines) realized several benefits from holding a leadership position. She learned about more issues and in greater depth from the leadership meetings than from her regular committee work and from debate. As a member of leadership she participated in weekly meetings with the governor. Frequently the only woman in those meetings, she had the opportunity to provide perspectives and insight that her male colleagues did not have. In addition, she points to her years as an assistant minority leader as helping her become a more effective and disciplined legislator, explaining that: "When you're in leadership you vote the way the party is supposed to vote. You have to set an example for the rest."[64]

In the 1980s, several women recruited Florence Buhr (Democrat, Des Moines) to run for assistant majority leader because they felt that leadership needed at least one woman member. Later, Kathleen Chapman (Democrat, Cedar Rapids) wanted to run for one of the four assistant majority leader positions. When Chapman asked colleagues for their support, they perceived it as Chapman running against Buhr for the "woman's spot" in leadership and Chapman dropped out. Eventually, Chapman felt that the sentiment had changed enough that the members would support having two women in leadership. The year she ran, 1989, Buhr did also and both women won.[65]

June Franklin (Democrat, Des Moines), the first African-American legislator in America to win a leadership position in either party, had other motives for seeking to become a member.[66] She saw "the Black woman legislator as having a very important role. In the first place a woman is in the minority in the Legislature and as a Black woman legislator I run into many difficulties. Therefore, I feel it is my role to try to be a part of the leadership, to create an image for other women legislators all over the country."[67] Franklin ran for minority whip for the 1969 session because: "I knew I couldn't be the floor leader or the assistant floor leader, because I knew they wouldn't let me do that, so I said, well I'll be number three." Describing her winning strategy, she said: "It was funny how I got elected. I decided I wanted to run for whip, so I needed 18 votes. So I just got on the phone and called 18 people and told them that I had 17 and theirs was the winning vote. When I got there, I was elected unanimously when we had our caucus." Franklin felt that one benefit of being in leadership was: "They couldn't leave me out of their meetings, their little caucuses. It really gave me insight to what was going on, better than just wandering out there as a member of the caucus."[68]

In 1967, Minnette Doderer (Democrat, Johnson) had become Iowa's first woman in a leadership position. She had wanted to run for minority leader, but told her caucus:

> I have an announcement to make. I am a woman!! Funny? Voters of Johnson County don't know this yet, and I would appreciate it if we could agree that this information doesn't leave this room. Consequently, because I am a woman, and have been told by several of you great white fathers that I am, therefore, ineligible to be considered for minority leader of the Democratic party in the 62nd G.A. [General Assembly], I am withdrawing my candidacy. Don't misunderstand, I was, am, and will be always aware that I am a woman. I like it. Now that I have poked a bit of fun at all of you, and I trust you will accept a bit of well meant razzing, I'll tell the honest reason that my name will not be in the balloting for leader. The reason is—I'm not ready for it as a legislator—one and one-half session which is the extent of my legislative experience is not enough.[69]

Instead, she became minority whip for the session.

A few years later, Doderer was the center of contest for power that began after the 1974 general elections and continued through the first week of the 1975 session. Control of both chambers had passed from Republicans to Democrats, giving Democrats the pleasant task of organizing the chambers. With her party holding the majority, Doderer decided to run for Senate President Pro Tempore. Before the organizational caucus that followed the general election, she lobbied caucus members for their support, which she won and which all but guaranteed that she would become Senate President Pro Tempore when the legislature convened.[70]

Before the session began, newly elected Senate Majority Leader George Kinley told her that he wanted her and other leaders to monitor the standing committee meetings. Doderer agreed, but wanted the activity to be called something else, because: "The word [monitor] just strikes me wrong."[71] Kinley threatened her, saying that she would perform the task or he would not give her the customary appointment as an appropriations subcommittee chair. Not taking him seriously, she held firm. So did Kinley who did not give her a subcommittee to chair, but offered her the position of ranking member of the State Government Committee. She refused it.

In the days before the session began, Doderer accused Kinley of sex discrimination for the way he treated her: leaving her out of leadership meetings, making committee appointments, organizing the Senate, and hiring staff without consulting her. She accused him of reducing the power allotted to the position of Senate President Pro Tempore and wanted it restored. She added a threat to her demand: she would vote against her party on the Senate rules unless he recognized the traditional power of the Senate President Pro Tempore. Kinley replied that Doderer had isolated herself by refusing to join other Democratic leaders in monitoring committees, which two other leaders had agreed to do. At odds with the Senate Democratic caucus, Doderer said: "I am not content with having this position [pro tempore] downgraded because there is a woman in it. Evidently male members of the Democratic caucus have encouraged Kinley to do it. I base this on the fact that Kinley told me what other members of the caucus think of me. So I have to think that, because they have downgraded me, he has taken the license to treat me this way."[72]

When the session opened in January 1975, Doderer broke party discipline by voting against the leadership in a procedural vote on temporary rules, just as she had promised. She insisted that the rules gave the majority leader too much power and continued to object to monitoring committees. The number of Republicans (24) and of Democrats (26) became significant when Doderer voted against her party, because it tied the vote 25-25. The Republican lieutenant governor broke the tie with his partisan vote, defeating the majority leader's proposed rules. After Doderer voted against him on the rules vote, Kinley "took her to the woodshed," a legislative term meaning just what it implies. The person is scolded for her or his transgression and is supposed to emerge chastised and prepared to be more cooperative. Doderer, however, refused to change her vote, and the Senate did not organize itself that day.[73]

The second day of the session, pressure mounted as the state Democratic Party chairman, the state's national party committeeman, and Senate colleagues tried to convince Doderer of the error of her ways. In an attempt to end the standoff, Richard Norpel (Democrat, Bellevue) offered to give Doderer his appropriations subcommittee to chair in what a reporter called a "touching and emotional period" of the caucus. Doderer thanked Norpel, but "graciously" declined, saying the time for that had passed, her greater concern focused on the division of power. Doderer held the power at that time. Only a senator voting on the prevailing side can file a motion to reconsider, which would allow the Senate to vote again on the rules. It was unlikely that any Republican would rescue the Democrats by filing the motion. The only Democrat who could file the motion was Doderer who had voted with the prevailing side.[74]

On the third day, William Palmer (Democrat, Des Moines) entered as negotiator. He offered a compromise in which the four leaders (pro tempore, majority leader, and assistant leaders) would share the power to assign bills to committees and to name conference committees and the steering committee. After Lieutenant Governor Art Neu told Doderer that another deal had been developed in which Joseph Coleman (Democrat, Clare) would vote with the Republicans and a Republican would win the position, Doderer agreed to Palmer's compromise. She filed the motion to reconsider, and the legislature continued with its organizational tasks. With the problems solved, Doderer asked to delay her nomination for President Pro Tempore because women in the House wanted to hear her nomination and they had gone home for the day. Her request was granted.[75]

The vote on her nomination was delayed on the fourth day because Kinley had to convince two Senate Democrats to continue supporting Doderer, but later that morning all of the problems were resolved. In her acceptance speech, Doderer acknowledged the tradition that had been broken: for the first time in the state's history a woman held the position. She told the body: "I'd like to commend not only the members of my party, but the Senate as a whole, for entrusting a woman with the responsibilities of this office—the third highest in the state."[76] She expressed her pride in having the position and added that she would have been equally proud if another woman had been elected. She announced that: "The Iowa Senate has advanced the cause of all women by its choice for president pro tempore. I sincerely thank you."[77] Three hours later she presided over the inaugural ceremonies for the new governor and lieutenant governor. She described it as the biggest week of her political career.

Senate Minority Leader Clifton Lamborn (Republican, Maquoketa) praised Doderer's use of power. Describing the power battle as "gutsy" he said: "Minnette's got the power and the skill to use it," adding "she's carrying the big stick and she'll use it."[78] Doderer's female colleagues gave her power play mixed reviews, some clearly supporting her, others questioning if she handled it in the best way. Jo Ann Orr (Democrat, Grinnell) wondered whether the conflict really had anything to do with sex discrimination. Mary O'Halloran (Democrat, Cedar Falls) found "hers was an extraordinary act of political courage." Casting Doderer's actions in a larger frame, O'Halloran continued: "She exhibited a great deal of consistency and integrity in wanting to maintain those duties and responsibilities for whoever comes after her, male or female, for now and for ten to 25 years from now." O'Halloran also pointed out that: "On the woman's side, it shows how hard a time women have getting to the higher echelons of power."[79] Sonja Egenes (Republican, Story City) thought that women in the legislature and both men and women in the state hoped for her success, adding: "Minnette showed that with her total grasp of the political process and knowledge of the political tools she could legitimately reach her goal."[80] Another supporter, Joan Lipsky (Republican, Cedar Rapids), pointed to Doderer's demonstrated legislative ability and questioned the political wisdom of Kinley offending a member of his caucus.

When the Senate organized in 1976, Doderer lost her leadership position to Joe Coleman (Democrat, Clare). In some ways, Coleman's success signified the end of Doderer's ascending power in the Senate. The Senate fight became part of Doderer's reputation as a scrappy fighter, a master of legislative politics, and an occasional political outsider from her party. Doderer believes that she "made senators mad at me so they made sure I didn't get the nomination for lieutenant governor in '78" and as will be seen later, Doderer's challenges haunted her in other political endeavors.[81]

One route to leadership involves recruiting candidates, advising them on campaign strategy, and helping them win. It involves driving hundreds of miles, talking to dozens of people, and spending hours convincing potential candidates that they can do the job and are needed. During the campaign season it means spending precious energy on someone else's campaign helping them recruit volunteers and raise money. For four years, Mary

Lundby (Republican, Marion) performed these tasks as Legislative Campaign Committee Chair for the Republican Party of Iowa and some of her recruits won.[82] When Republicans gained control of the House in the 1992 general elections, at least in part due to Lundby, her reward for her labors and success should have been the Speaker's chair. After the 1992 elections, she sought it. Before the caucus met, she knew that she faced barriers to the election, saying that: "One person made the comment that Iowa is not ready for a woman Speaker yet. So I think there's part of the Old Guard that that's a serious consideration for them."[83] She was right. Her opponent, a 63-year-old male farmer became Speaker. She became House Speaker Pro Tempore.

Since 1977, at least one woman has held a leadership position in one of the chambers in every session. In addition to Doderer, Jean Lloyd-Jones (Democrat, Iowa City) was elected Senate President Pro Tempore in 1991. From 1987 through 1990, Jo Ann Zimmerman was Senate President as part of her duties as lieutenant governor. No woman has been a majority or minority leader, or Speaker. Iowa's political equivalent of the glass ceiling may be that a woman can be an assistant leader or a temporary presiding officer but not the leader.[84]

Legislative service has convinced some women that the General Assembly's priorities are not what they should be. One way to change the legislature has been suggested since the 1950s: elect more women. Joan Lipsky believed that would change the body's priorities. In a fighting spirit after losing a battle over licensing day care centers, she announced: "I'm going to tell women all over the state to run for the legislature, that we're not going to have women's issues considered as long as the men—and the men still run the legislature—won't consider them. It's just this plain: Some men don't think licensing of day care centers is important."[85] Women in other state legislatures found they had the same problem: men ran the bodies and did not place the same priority on women's, children's, and family issues as they did. The slow progress in achieving that goal has already been noted.

Beginning in the late 1970s, women developed a new approach to setting the agenda. They began forming legislative caucuses, and by 1987 eleven states had them. These bi-partisan groups generally establish an agenda and meet weekly during the session to provide each other with updates on the progress of bills through the committee system and to develop strategies for their priorities. With women in the minority in every state legislature in the country, none of these groups has the power to pass their priorities without the votes of their male colleagues, but by transcending party lines, caucus leaders can present their issues independent of party and focus on their importance to good state policy. Leadership, however, does not favor rump caucuses that can hinder its power. Caucuses have met with a spectrum of responses: in one state the formation of a caucus met with "laughter and derision," in another it saved a prenatal care bill, and in still others leadership has consulted with it.[86]

Once again, the diversity of women serving in legislatures appears in their opinions of legislative caucuses. A South Dakota state senator felt that working with men was more important that the isolation she believed would result from forming a caucus. South Carolina women legislators expressed the concern more strongly, saying that they did not want to "alienate their male colleagues." Even though they believed that a caucus could be beneficial, they did not want to visibly present themselves as feminists, which they felt would be the result if they formed one. Feminists there worked quietly behind the scenes with informal networks.[87]

In Iowa, the initial awareness of the potential of this power tool came in the late 1970s from a tragedy in the legislature involving one of the high school seniors hired to work as a page during the session. Recollections of the specific events vary, but the stories generally concur that a young male legislator dated one of the high school students who worked in the legislature as a page and a pregnancy resulted from the relationship. The leadership dealt with the offending member and asked women legislators to meet with the female pages to explain what is now known as sexual harassment, as well as appropriate behavior between legislators and pages, and the limits that pages could place on legislators' behavior. The women organized a dinner in one of their apartments, discussed being female with the girl pages, and offered to intercede if any of the girls had problems with men. That evening the women discovered that they had more legislative interests in common than they had thought and began meeting informally. While women had worked together on the Equal Rights Amendment, juvenile justice, rape legislation, and other issues, they began to solidify their mutual support as a result of that evening.[88]

In 1981, Minnette Doderer (Democrat, Iowa City) and Sue Mullins (Republican, Corwith) began to organize a more formal caucus. During that year and into the next, they held their weekly meetings surreptitiously. Doderer's clerk prepared meeting notices and reserved meeting rooms under protective guises. The women did not want the men to know that they were organizing themselves because they did not want their discussions public. They wanted to speak freely, bargain among themselves, and present seemingly spontaneous unity on issues. Within a couple of years, the caucus began having open meetings and inviting speakers and observers to its meetings.[89]

Some women chose not to participate in the caucus, and among those who did the level of commitment varied. Conservative Karen Mann (Republican, Scranton) did not have the same legislative agenda that the caucus espoused. Philosophically, she differed from many of the other women, including perceptions of women's status. Jo Ann Trucano (Republican, Des Moines) opposed the idea of a women's caucus, believing it created divisions that did not otherwise exist. Some women resolutely reserved the meeting time; others had other priorities.

The caucuses serve as networks and clearinghouses for information, ideas, and support. They bring women together so they can meet each other across party lines and become acquainted with their female colleagues' priorities and share their expertise. Veteran legislators have shared knowledge and background on issues and protocols, giving advice and counsel to the novices. Regularly, they have told new members to do one, simple, but essential thing: ask. Ask for committees, ask for bills, ask for help, ask for leadership's attention, and ask for inclusion in planning meetings and political assignments. Understanding that the response may be a refusal, veteran legislators tell freshmen that they will get nothing without asking. Mullins told one group: "Everything you get is because you asked for it."[90]

In addition to advising freshmen women, caucus members keep each other informed about the progress of legislation. They monitor bills and work to keep priority bills moving through the committee system, alerting their colleagues when a bill needs attention from leadership to keep it on track. Women in leadership also use their influence to that end. Caucus members also identify male colleagues with whom they can discuss specific bills in the pursuit of support for them.[91]

The women's caucus has also helped alleviate some of the isolation they have experienced. Knowing that others will join in debate on controversial issues has helped women, who might otherwise remain silent, raise their microphone and contribute their words and ideas. While the legislature remains a male domain, the caucus has helped women carve a territory in it for themselves. It has given women a place within the larger body to belong.

Caucus support for an idea also gives its leaders negotiating power with the leadership. When a group of Republican women representing the women's caucus in 1982 told the Speaker that their partisans needed to "support funding of the AFDC-UP (Aid to Families with Dependent

Children-Unemployed Parent) because their party should not endorse the breakup of the family by forcing husbands to leave their wives and children," the leadership began taking an active role in crafting the reinstatement of the program.[92]

Later, when Democrats gained the majority, Don Avenson became Speaker of the House for eight years in the 1980s. He and Minnette Doderer appeared to have reached agreements on priority issues on several occasions. As a caucus leader, Doderer met with Avenson, explained the issues, found ways to reach agreements with him, and obtained his support. With Avenson's backing, Doderer and other Democratic women could more easily gain the Democratic caucus's approval of their proposals.

Women in the caucus carefully choose their issues. They settled on topics that focus on women, children, employment, and marriage and divorce. Comparable worth emerged as an early priority and the caucus provided much of the momentum behind its passage. The caucus has avoided abortion because members held differing opinions about it. Ideas for legislation came from a number of sources, such as other states, constituents, and women's advocates.

Other ideas originated among the members. For example, Johnie Hammond (Democrat, Ames) and Sue Mullins (Republican, Corwith) led the caucus's advocacy for remodeling the College of Home Economics building at Iowa State University. The building did not have adequate classroom space, adequate wiring or other physical features. The Board of Regents had discussed remodeling the building for several years, but it had been regularly postponed in deference to other projects. Hammond believed that: "To some extent it (the delay) is a stereotyped view of home economics of women cooking and sewing so they can become wives."[93] Hammond and Mullins met with Governor Terry Branstad and others, activated lobbying networks outside the legislature, and used the pressure of the women in the caucus to obtain appropriations to begin planning and then to remodel the building. The caucus also provided advocacy for women in prison, questioning policies and passing legislation that benefited them. Through coalescing on these issues they gave the proposals greater credibility and improved their chances for consideration and passage.

In the early 1980s, the women's legislative caucus added another dimension to its activities, a biennial fishing trip without the fishing. Don Avenson (Democrat, Oelwein), Speaker of the House at the time, and several other male legislators regularly took a fishing trip at the end of the session. Stories about the good times and the big fish they caught and the camaraderie they shared became part of the folklore in the legislature. As Jean Lloyd-Jones explained: "Well, it [the women's fishing trip] started out because we sort of resented Don Avenson taking the men off on a fishing trip, and we decided we'd have our own fishing trip."[94] The women went to Lloyd-Jones's cabin on one of the state's lakes. True to their stereotype of being hard and diligent workers, the women took a facilitator with them to work on improving their political skills. Lloyd-Jones believes that the women gained "a new appreciation for each other" and "began to support each other better in the legislature."[95]

Any discussion of power in legislatures almost demands consideration of powerful lobbyists with their expense accounts for wining and dining lawmakers who support their issues and those who could be convinced to do so. Images of back rooms and bargaining and votes bought and sold come to mind. Readers who now eagerly await scandalous tales are doomed to disappointment. Iowa has remarkably clean politics and no stories of a legislator, female or male, selling her or his vote for some financial or other favor have emerged.

In *Sex Roles in the State House*, Irene Diamond explains women have the same inexperience with lobbyists that they have with the give and take of political bargaining. She found that women legislators and lobbyists had little communication because women were not interested in talking to lobbyists, lobbyists sought out legislators with power and that did not include women, and that women did not serve on the committees in which lobbyists had an interest. In the years since Diamond's work some things have changed, at least in Iowa. Women have chaired the ways and means, small business, economic development and trade, transportation, and state government committees, all of which deal with issues of interest to lobbyists.[96]

Iowa women legislators would generally concur with Diamond's point that many women legislators do not focus their interests on issues that have wealthy or powerful constituencies that employ professional lobbyists. Instead, they more likely find themselves battling those groups. For example, Johnie Hammond (Democrat, Ames) has worked to create no smoking environments (unpopular with the tobacco industry) and to provide medical coverage for all Iowans (unpopular with business and other groups). Sue Mullins (Republican, Corwith), Dorothy Carpenter (Republican, West Des Moines), Jo Ann Zimmerman (Democrat, Waukee), and others spent years changing provisions in the state indigent patient program at the University of Iowa (disliked by the university and many of the physicians who trained there). Mullins devoted years to advocating issues concerning children, generally a group for whom only a few volunteer lobbyists work.[97]

None of the recent women legislators expressed the distaste and contempt for lobbyists that Carolyn Pendray (Democrat, Jackson) repeatedly displayed, nor have they conducted campaigns to limit lobbyists' activities as Pendray did. Pendray's hostility toward lobbyists began to appear during her second term in the House, 1931, and continued through the balance of her legislative career. She objected to the "third degree lobbying tactics" they used and to lobbyists sitting next to legislators, coaching them on how to vote. Over the years, she used parliamentary maneuvers, House rules, and the press to crusade against lobbyists and their influence.[98] Pendray received support from a newspaper editorial which described lobbyists "swarm[ing]" around the House, disrupting its "dignity" and allowing "high pressure methods" to promote the acceptance or defeat of legislation.[99]

Pendray continued her crusade against lobbyists when she went to the Senate. After unsuccessful attempts to keep lobbyists off the Senate floor, Pendray and a Senate colleague persuaded the body to place a rope barrier in the back of the chamber. While lobbyists could still be on the Senate floor, they could no longer sit or stand next to senators at their desks. Corralling lobbyists in the back of the chamber at least limited the intense pressure of having them breathing on the legislators as they cast their votes.[100]

Pendray's crusades against lobbyists and her independence from her caucus may be clues to another aspect of her political career. Toward the end of her Senate term, she considered running for governor. Instead, she retired from politics. No reasons for her decisions have been found. It may be that her criticisms of her colleagues' acceptance of lobbying practices and her occasional unwillingness to cooperate with leadership isolated her from her party and it responded by withholding its support for her candidacy. Her fights for her convictions may have alienated the centers of power needed for a viable campaign.[101]

After Pendray had corralled lobbyists behind the rope barrier, legislators in later sessions restricted lobbyists to the benches on the back and sides of the chamber. From these positions, lobbyists continued to monitor lawmakers' votes and directed the votes by signaling to members on the floor. Eventually, the House and Senate floors became restricted to members, clerks, and staff from one-half hour before the day's session began until one-half hour after the day's adjournment. Lobbyists and others wanting to talk to legislators could send notes to members and meet with them in other areas of the Statehouse.[102]

One of the more vexing problems for women has been the after-hours social life of legislatures. It has taken a variety of forms, including evening events sponsored by associations and those sponsored by lobbyists. The evening cocktail parties or dinners sponsored by associations, like the Farm Bureau, Chamber of Commerce, or professional associations, became virtually extinct in 1993 after the legislature passed a bill limiting gifts to $3.00 per day per lawmaker, but they had been a source of conflict for some women who believed that they should pay for their own meals from their legislative expense allowance. For several years, Diane Brandt (Democrat, Cedar Falls) paid for her own meals, but after a divorce, she found that she could no longer afford to pay for dinners with constituent groups. A conflict between her commitments arose. She felt an obligation to meet with those members who were her constituents, so refusal became difficult. Brandt eventually decided to accept the free meals, but it made her uncomfortable because some constituents did not have the same avenue for meeting and socializing with lawmakers. Brandt's changed situation substantiates an observation made by women in other parts of the country: their freedom from dependence on lobbyists for meals was a by-product of the economic independence they had because their spouses provided the family income. Jo Ann Orr (Democrat, Grinnell) also believed that the expense money she received for her meals should be used for that purpose and refused gift dinners or entertainment. A friend told her that her choice would be unpopular with her colleagues because it impugned their motives, but she felt she made the appropriate choice. Orr and other women appreciated the time in the late 1970s when lawmakers could not accept anything from lobbyists, no matter how small, because they felt it created a more comfortable relationship between lawmakers and lobbyists.[103]

In contrast, Kathlyn Wick (Republican, Taylor County) had joined her husband in Des Moines when he had served in the Senate. When she became the legislator in the 1940s, she arrived familiar and comfortable with the practice of organizations paying for her meals. She appreciated the explanations of legislative priorities presented at the dinners and enjoyed the meals and social life that accompanied them.[104] Elizabeth Shaw (Republican, Davenport) quoted another lawmaker to describe one perspective on the relationship between legislators and lobbyists: "If you can't eat their [lobbyists'] food and drink their wine (and he was cruder than this) and sleep with their women and look them in the eye and vote no, you don't belong here."[105]

Another kind of socializing took place in the evening when a lobbyist would take a legislator to dinner. Joan Lipsky (Republican, Cedar Rapids) once explained: "The professional lobbyists were really floored by women. They were accustomed to forming a social relationship with legislators. They really didn't know exactly how to handle us, and they ignored us."[106] The seven women in the General Assembly in 1970 all said they received few dinner invitations from lobbyists, but none of them complained. They felt that constituent events consumed enough of their evenings, and they looked forward to having some free time to study bills or take care of other obligations. They also believed that for a male lobbyist to take a female legislator out for dinner created an awkward situation. A lobbyist agreed with that assessment, implying that a romantic or sexual connotation existed. Some women have believed that they had to be cautious about the appearance of their activities in order to protect their reputations. Remarkably little has changed in twenty years; lobbyists tend not to take women lawmakers to dinner, except occasionally in groups, and women tend not to mind.[107]

Legislators have told a story about an evening in the late 1980s when six women lawmakers decided to go to a local bar and restaurant for dinner, a place where legislators regularly gathered. When the group walked into the restaurant, other legislators asked them what they were doing. Beverly Hannon (Democrat, Anamosa) tells the rest of the story:

> The majority leader, Bill Hutchins, came over after we were seated to ask what was going on, "What's the occasion?" We told him we just decided to go out for dinner together. He was amazed. "Hell, why don't you get a lobbyist to take you out?" He was genuinely stunned to think there were six women buying their own dinner and going out together without a lobbyist. Apparently some legislators never buy their own meals! Without any rehearsal, we said one by one, that lobbyists don't usually invite us out for dinner. If they do, it's generally in a larger group of women; occasionally they mix male and female legislators.[108]

After Hutchins left, the women discussed lobbyists and discovered that none of them could remember when a male lobbyist had taken one of them out alone for a meal, as they did with male legislators. They conjectured that lobbyists were afraid to be seen with just one of them or perhaps they feared the women. A footnote to the story is that after Hutchins left, one of the lobbyists hosting the Hutchins group approached the women and offered to pay for their meals. The legislators refused the offer, and said that they would accept it when they were having dinner with the lobbyist.[109]

Another dilemma women faced involved the extent to which they would become "one of the boys." Again, it usually involved socializing at the end of the day. Women legislators have repeatedly explained that they avoided the appearance of doing anything that would raise questions about their morals or ethics. In particular they did not want to do anything that would suggest that they were involved in any sort of sexual affairs. Some women went to movies together, many studied bills. Some men gathered to play poker or drink. They became better acquainted and brokered legislative deals. Some women found that avoiding the evening gatherings denied them opportunities to meet with their colleagues on an informal basis and to be part of the deal making, others have found it less important.[110] One South Carolina legislator explained: "The difficult thing is figuring out how to be one of the boys without being one of the boys. You can't share a cigar with them. . . ."[111]

The Iowa versions have taken a number of forms. Early in the 1960s, before legalized liquor by the drink (mid-1960s), a group of women legislators accompanied the Des Moines police on a series of late night raids on illegal drinking establishments, where they saw some of their colleagues drinking and socializing, which one of the women found shocking. Later in the 1960s, a group of lobbyists hosted a regular by-invitation-only hospitality room, called the Wigwam, and the invitation list did not ever include women. At least one woman objected to the deals made during those hours, but she did not want an invitation. By the 1980s, a weekly poker game sponsored by a lobbyist had become something of a tradition, deals were made there, and women were included.[112]

An annual social event, the Gridiron Dinner sponsored by the Advertising Club of Iowa, became the occasion for a mean-spirited attack on one of Iowa's legislators, which led to the involvement of other women legislators, and finally to a change in the club's policies. The Gridiron Dinner, a stag event, featured reportedly funny, political skits that had state and local celebrities as their targets. When Minnette Doderer received an invitation to the dinner in 1969, she sent a check for tickets for herself and her husband, but an Advertising Club secretary returned it, explaining that, because she was a woman, Doderer could not attend. Doderer responded by publicizing the snub with a news release and distributing a description of it to Senate members. (See Appendix A.) The Women's Advertising Club of Des Moines defended the Advertising Club saying that: "We feel we have taken our rightful places. . . ."[113] Doderer believed that her rightful place was with other legislators at the dinner.

The Advertising Club's insults to Doderer continued in 1970, when the organization's publication included an ad for the event that said: "See Richard Turner (Iowa attorney general) turn on over Minnette Doderer demonstrating nude sit-in techniques in the lobby of the Fort Des Moines Hotel." The dinner invitation had a picture of a nude model wearing a Nazi helmet and a tattoo that said: "Sorry, Minette [sic] . . . You Little Sweetheart." Doderer's reaction reveals her relationship to feminism at the time: "I'm not the women's liberation type and I haven't been antagonistic to them, but I've listened enough. Now I know what these women's liberation types are talking about." [114]

In 1971 all of the women legislators received invitations to the dinner, even though the organization did not intend to admit them.[115] They asked Governor Robert Ray to boycott the event as a public statement against women's exclusion from it, but he planned to attend. They also asked Lieutenant Governor Roger Jepsen to boycott it but he responded: "When I go to the bathroom I don't invite any women to come in because that's especially a man's thing. Is that what women will want to do next?"[116] Lillian McElroy (Republican, Percival) called it a "matter of discrimination," saying: "If it's going to be for the Legislature, we all ought to be invited."[117] She wondered if the material would need to be cleaned up if women attended. Other women felt that they had more important things to do than object to their exclusion from the event. In 1975 the club extended a sincere invitation to Doderer, which she accepted. Seated at the head table, a newspaper article noted that her ad libs included some of the "better bits of comedy" in the program. She also used the opportunity to tell the club to "clean up some of the lousy ads involving women."[118] McElroy had identified the problem: if the entertainment was for legislators, then the organizers needed to include all of the members, not just the male ones.

The exclusion, derision, and suspicion that have met women when they entered the legislature have been noted in several studies, and while it has created barriers for some women by silencing them or leaving them out of the fundamental decision-making process, it is not the most important feature of women's experiences as lawmakers. Far more important are the ways women have adapted to the legislative culture. Those women who rendered themselves silent or accepted invisibility, because they believed those effective strategies, also limited their ability to contribute their ideas and experiences to the process of forming state policy. In addition, those women, satisfied that the leadership kept them informed of the decisions made by others, surrendered their power to influence. They did, however, avoid the heat of debate, the risk of humiliation, and the pressure of proving themselves as contestants in the struggles for power.

In order for a legislator to make a difference in state policy, that legislator must be informed, visible and vocal. If, as others have argued and will be argued later, women bring new ideas and perspectives to policy-making, then they must find ways to articulate and present them in compelling ways. Women like Betty Jean Clark, Minnette Doderer, Joan Lipsky, Jean Lloyd-Jones and others have identified and defined their power when they had an issue they wanted addressed, a cause they wanted remedied, that is, when they wanted something and needed power to obtain it. The authors of *Women in Power* have given the kind of power exercised by Iowa women legislators and the women in their study a name, WomanPower, emphasizing that it "includes a reason for being, a purpose, an agenda to be advanced."[119] The power Iowa women legislators have exercised does not include the dominance traditionally associated with the word, yet when women have worked from a position of strength they have succeeded. Passivity, wondering why one was not asked to run for a leadership position almost like hoping for a suitor, does not advance a political agenda. It takes boldness, confidence, and the understanding that defeat is as great a possibility as success. In the stories told above, women actively pursued their agendas and asserted themselves on the quests. The examples above have also shown the variety of ways that women have identified their power, using humor, withholding votes, threatening to go to the press, forming a caucus, and other strategies. At the same time, using their power has demanded that women have self-confidence, the willingness to take risks and the courage to endure ridicule.

CHAPTER 4

Women's Issues

As feminists in the 1960s and 1970s identified legal barriers to women's full participation in American life, they found that few male legislators shared their sense of urgency or commitment to remedying the problems. In response to men's ambivalence, women vowed to recruit and elect more women to lawmaking bodies. Yet, as described earlier, few women candidates campaigned as feminists or on a feminist agenda. In addition, some women have insisted that women's issues do not exist as a separate category, claiming that all issues are human issues. A few have staunchly opposed the principles articulated in feminist proposals. Other women who have been inclined toward supporting feminist issues have resisted becoming closely identified with them, concerned that their credibility on other issues would be diminished. Still others have shrugged off their reticence and persuaded their female and male colleagues to alter policies affecting women.[1]

Even those women lawmakers who generally support feminist issues have struggled with the question of how they should allocate their time in the legislature between the concerns of their districts and those of women. They wonder if they can adequately represent their constituents if they primarily devote their energies to passing bills for women. Others contend that men have ignored women's issues for decades and that female lawmakers can make their most substantive contributions to state policies by identifying, advocating, and passing legislation intending to improve women's status. Some women who had been ambivalent about women's issues began to have a different opinion of them after their constituents explained their experiences and the discriminatory biases with which the law has treated them.[2]

An Iowa legislator closely identified with women's issues, Minnette Doderer (Democrat, Iowa City), provides one of the best examples of a legislator whose experiences in the General Assembly transformed her from a person who referred to "those women libbers" into one of the state's most persistent advocates for feminist proposals. Doderer entered the legislature as a League of Women Voters advocate for reapportionment. Outspoken, unafraid, and quotable, she received attention from the press for her provocative ideas and public statements on issues ranging from state employee policies to tax policies. The press coverage she received made her name widely known in the state and prompted letters from women who saw a bold woman in power and wrote to her, woman to woman, about abusive husbands, unfair employment policies, insurance inequities, and estate problems, among others. The letters and the telephone calls, along with her own experiences, brought her an understanding of what "those women libbers" were trying to change, and she became one of them. Other women legislators have described comparable changes in perspective and have also become committed to using their legislative power and status to promote change for women.

Even though opposition to women's issues has often developed as proposals progressed through the legislature, it is important to remember that just as all women did not support these bills, not all men fought them. The critical roles women have played in their passage have been identifying problems, offering alternatives, and persistently advocating their passage. Without men's support in the forms of favorable committee and subcommittee assignments for the bills, in addition to their votes, the bills would have died.

The reader might challenge the topics included in this chapter because equal rights and privacy rights are not found here but in a later chapter. Those two topics are constitutional issues and are matters of the relationship between citizens and the fundamental philosophy of the nation. The topics considered here deal with gender, that is, the social roles assigned to women. They deal with women's visibility, honor, and safety, and the economic value of their work.

The tradition of women raising issues relevant to gender stretches back to the first woman in the Iowa General Assembly, Carolyn Pendray (Democrat, Jackson). During her first session in the legislature, Pendray and L. B. Forsling (Republican, Sioux City) sponsored and gained approval of legislation granting women new property rights in two ways. Before the Pendray-Forsling bill, male debtors could keep specific items (i.e., a library, clothes, two cows, two calves, fifty sheep, furniture, etc.) exempt from debt collection. Under the Pendray-Forsling bill, the same exemptions extended to the wife if she was the debtor and if she owned those items. The bill also allowed a married woman who was a debtor, even though not head of the household, to keep a sewing machine and poultry worth fifty dollars from debt collection. In the late 1920s, when an economic depression struck agriculture before other segments of the economy, these changes provided substantive relief for some families. For example, poultry and the eggs they produced often became an important part of a family's cash income. In later years, the legislature eliminated those gender-based provisions.[3]

The Pendray-Forsling bill did not begin a pattern of women legislators' advocating policies beneficial to women. During most of the 1930s and 1940s, Iowa and the rest of the nation focused attention on first the depression and then war. In the 1950s Gladys Nelson introduced a bill for equal pay for equal work, but the bill died a speedy death in committee. Nelson did, however, successfully shepherd a bill for colored oleomargarine through the legislature, arguing for it as a housewives' bill. (See Chapter 7.) With these exceptions, women who served in the General Assembly before the mid-1960s do not recollect considering gender connotations as they worked on state policies. In addition, they did not remember any issues that might have been proposed to address women's legal status. As in other state legislatures, it was the modern feminist movement that confronted lawmaking bodies with the need to identify and consider women's issues.

Of the many issues raised by the feminists, few people would label one group of women's proposals as radical. Believing that language carries subtle messages about gender identification and visibility, women wanted to end the use of male pronouns and nouns like fireman and policeman in the *Code of Iowa*. They wanted women's presence acknowledged in the code and discriminatory language as well as sexist implications and substance removed from it. The process began early in the 1970s and continued through the 1980s, comprising a number of variations on a theme. June Franklin's (Democrat, Des Moines) amendment to a bill revising voter registration and election laws in 1972 offers an early example. Her amendment changed the names on the sample ballots in the code to make half of them women's names, saying that in addition to updating its substance, she wanted to update perceptions as well.[4] She told the House that: "I'd like to change the thinking of this assembly and I'd like to remind you that 51 percent of the people of this state are female." She wanted women "recognized in the election laws of Iowa."[5] House members found the idea amusing and laughed at it. Richard Radl (Democrat, Lisbon) made fun of the amendment by saying: "This is a women's lib amendment. I am against women's lib advocates and their male supporters. They speak honeyed words of equality and emancipation when what they really have in mind is piracy and robbery."[6]

The debate deteriorated when Radl used the new women's restroom in the back of the House chamber as an example of "women's tyranny," explaining that the ratio of women to cubicles was less than that for men.[7] Joan Lipsky (Republican, Cedar Rapids) entered the debate and responded: "I want to assure the gallant gentlemen that I'll do everything in my power to change the ratio."[8] Franklin asked Radl to keep his comments on the topic, and the House Speaker agreed with her but asked Radl for a copy of the rest of his comments, showing his approval and amusement at the debate. Franklin's amendment did not propose a fundamental change in state policy, it only attempted to recognize that women candidates existed. Radl's accusations of robbery and piracy indicate the antipathetic culture in which women worked. The amendment passed, but only after the chamber had amused itself at Franklin's expense.[9]

Over the years, women legislators sponsored and passed numerous bills that intended to make women more visible in the *Code of Iowa* and to eliminate discriminatory state policies. The many reviews of the code for sexism included a 1982 bill to remove masculine pronouns and nouns. Several years earlier, the Legislative Service Bureau had altered the style for drafting legislation from using masculine nouns and pronouns to employing gender-neutral words. For example, firemen became firefighters, and nouns were substituted for he, him, and his. Sections of the code that had not been amended since the change continued to have masculine pronouns, which Doderer changed with a 1982 bill. To emphasize the extent of the old usage, Doderer's clerk highlighted the masculine pronouns in two of three volumes of the Code.[10]

Incremental changes in the Code resumed after a state panel completed a review of it in 1984. President Ronald Reagan, an ERA opponent, suggested that states review their laws, identify sexist provisions, and change them as an alternative to guaranteeing all citizens equal rights in the

Constitution. Following the president's recommendation, Republican Governor Terry Branstad appointed a committee of private citizens and state employees to identify implied and functional sexism and make recommendations to eliminate it. The committee found about one hundred areas in which the effect of the policy resulted in sex discrimination. For example, life insurance companies used sex in determining premiums, military veterans received preference in hiring for civil service jobs, and inheritance laws regarding intestate succession treated widows and widowers differently. In accepting the panel's report, Branstad expressed hope that the findings would help remove barriers to women's equality, but he resisted many of the substantive changes recommended in the report. Over time, however, the legislature enacted many of them.[11]

From Franklin's proposal to include some feminine names on sample ballots through the state panel's comprehensive evaluation of state policies and numerous other revisions, the goals changed from including women in a specific code section to identifying and removing sexist state policies. The locus of action moved from one woman's attempt to pass an amendment, to a governor's committee, adding new resources and attention to the state's policies on women. Through the process, the intent behind the changes remained the same: equitable treatment for women and men. The language changes, described by some as neutering the code, should not be dismissed as trivial even though the meaning of many laws remained the same. The earlier use of masculine pronouns and nouns excluded women, despite arguments that the language did not have that intent. The inclusive language symbolized a consciousness of women's existence and participation in the life and activities of the state.

The same belief in acknowledging women through words and images that had prompted Franklin's amendment resulted in a controversy over an Iowa Department of Agriculture brochure. Sue Mullins (Republican, Corwith) objected to the department's slogan "The Iowa Farmer . . . He's Quite a Man," which appeared in the brochure. Mullins farmed with her husband and she wanted women included in the piece, pointing out that neither the text nor the images included women. She cited the pictures of a dairy cow and some ewes as the only females of any species in the brochure. Using her own experience as an example of women's role in farming she described her research on conservation tillage, pointing out that she and her husband had changed their farm management practices to use it. Mullins insisted that farm wives contributed to farming decisions and deserved to have their work recognized by inclusion in the agriculture department's literature. Iowa

Secretary of Agriculture Robert Lounsberry said that he had not intended to offend anyone, but he had not thought about women's roles in agriculture. Lounsberry destroyed the few remaining copies, but he criticized Mullins, accusing her of having a chip on her shoulder. The reprinted version did not include the slogan, but Mullins did not believe that the text had been improved.[12]

Women legislators also wanted more women appointed to state and local commissions. They believed that these advisory and policymaking groups would benefit from the contributions women could make by adding other viewpoints to decision making. In 1973, Doderer asked Governor Robert D. Ray to appoint more women to state boards and commissions, criticizing his record of choosing only five women for 38 of the most recent major positions. At the time, women held about 200 of the 1,146 appointive positions in state government. Doderer believed that both parties had women with the necessary qualifications, despite the governor's claims that he could not identify them. She wanted the governor to consult a list of 400 women compiled by the Iowa Commission on the Status of Women, "even though his assistants say the list was somehow lost."[13]

In the late 1980s and early 1990s, Johnie Hammond (Democrat, Ames) decided the time had come to stop asking governors and mayors to appoint more women to state and local boards and commissions. Working with several other women in the General Assembly, Hammond consistently added an amendment to bills dealing with state boards and commissions. Known as the "usual amendment" among the women legislators, it required that half of the members be female. Hammond eventually passed a bill to mandate gender balance on all state boards and commissions. She later pursued the change on the local level. Dorothy Carpenter (Republican, West Des Moines) believed it would "empower women" as they participated on boards and commissions, and Mary Lundby (Republican, Marion) supported the bill as a fairness issue rather than one of gender. The local bill also required minority appointments in proportion to the percentage of their population in the community.[14]

In the 1970s, the spirit of acknowledgement and recognition led Mary O'Halloran (Democrat, Cedar Falls) to work to name a proposed new state office building for a woman but Richard Norpel (Democrat, Bellevue) wanted to name the building for Ansel Briggs, Iowa's first territorial governor. O'Halloran suggested Carrie Chapman Catt, the Iowa woman who had led the final stage of the crusade for woman suffrage and who was founder of the

League of Women Voters. O'Halloran acknowledged that many legislators had not heard of Catt saying: "The reason you don't know is obvious. The history books are written by men."[15] The House rejected her plea, and voted to name the building after Ansel Briggs. According to Doderer, O'Halloran lost because the Statehouse crowd began referring to the building as the Catt house. After the name became a joke, Doderer dropped Catt as a possibility, but she objected to naming the building for Briggs because she thought he "was nothing but a drunken stagecoach driver."[16]

Doderer agreed with O'Halloran that the building should be named for a woman and suggested Carolyn Campbell Pendray. She conceded that the controversy over naming the building could end up with it having no name, but explained: "That may be appropriate. Then it would be a female building because all women lose their names. That's the reason we wanted a building named after a woman so we could stop being anonymous."[17] Doderer temporarily won the battle when the Senate State Departments Appropriations Subcommittee substituted Pendray's name for Briggs' name on the building, but the issue remained unresolved at the end of the 1975 session.

Naming the building became an example of unrelated issues getting tied together. In 1976, the Senate Transportation Committee refused to release a bill prohibiting long trucks on Iowa highways. Doderer opposed long trucks but wanted the bill debated, so she joined others who circulated a resolution to pull the bill from committee. The resolution needed four more signatures for the President of the Senate do so. On the Senate floor, Norpel "boomed out at Doderer" that he had the four votes and that he would "sell" them if she would come up with four votes to name the building for Briggs. Doderer took his offer, preferring to keep the long trucks off Iowa highways to naming the building for Pendray, but Norpel lost his own challenge because he did not have the votes. After the Senate erupted in laughter, the majority and minority leaders called their members into caucus, temporarily ending the debate.[18]

Norpel and Doderer continued their battle over naming the new building in the 1977 session, and it continued to be part of completely unrelated debates. Known for his active vote trading, Norpel offered to trade his vote for a lake project Don Avenson (Democrat, Oelwein) wanted for Avenson's vote to name the building for Briggs. When Doderer heard about the offer, she rushed to the House to convince Avenson to support Pendray's name for the building. Doderer made Avenson the same deal Norpel had, but substituted Pendray's name for her support of the lake. Avenson refused both of them. A state contest for schoolchildren to name the building became an unhappy compromise for both senators, but it was unsuccessful. In the end, the building was named for Herbert Hoover. In the 1980s, the Iowa Commission on the Status of Women, the state Department of Education, and others cooperated to name a vocational rehabilitation building for Jessie M. Parker, a former state superintendent of public instruction.[19]

In addition to recognizing women's contributions to the state, legislators have wanted the value of women's work acknowledged in their pay checks. Women's wage rates and women's poverty have a sad history in this country. Since before the Civil War, women have organized, struck, demonstrated, demanded, and begged for living wages. Time has not ameliorated the problem, only given it a name: the feminization of poverty. Raising women's wage rates to a level comparable to those received by men has consistently ranked highest among the possible solutions for alleviating women's economic disadvantages.[20]

The earliest identified attention to women's pay issues appeared in 1953 when Gladys Nelson (Republican, Jasper) introduced a bill for equal pay for equal work, but the legislature did not take any action on it. A decade later Congress passed the Equal Pay Act, requiring employers to pay men and women performing the same job the same salary. Not all pay discrimination, however, appears in such obvious ways. Jobs dominated by women generally pay less than those dominated by men, a situation which the mandate of equal pay for equal work does not address.[21]

Examples of pay discrimination can be found in two events a decade apart. In the first instance, the House debated increasing the state traveling library director's salary by $4,000, to $15,000 in 1971. A woman had held the job for several years, but at the time of the proposed increase, a man held it. Delbert Trowbridge (Republican, Charles City) believed that the responsibilities of managing the staff justified the pay increase, explaining that "few women can handle 76 employees." He believed that because a man held the position, the pay needed to be at the higher level. Trowbridge had not suggested increasing the salaries of the state law and medical librarians; women held these positions which would remain at $11,000. June Franklin (Democrat, Des Moines) objected: "Suddenly we have a man in the position and we want to raise this one sky high without paying any attention to the salaries of the other two women librarians." Joan Lipsky (Republican, Cedar Rapids) added: "Give salaries according to ability and don't make distinctions because of sex or any other non-essential facts."[22] The House defeated Trowbridge's amendment and increased all three librarians' salaries to $11,500.

More than a decade later, a similar situation developed when the legislature increased the Chief Clerk of the House's salary from $30,000 to a ceiling of $40,000. Under the Republican majority in 1982, Elizabeth Isaacson, who had held the job for about fifteen months, had earned $28,080 a year. After Democrats obtained the majority following the 1982 general elections, Joe O'Hern was appointed and would receive the increased salary. Dorothy Carpenter (Republican, West Des Moines) accused House Democrats of sex discrimination, but Jean Lloyd-Jones (Democrat, Iowa City), a member of the majority leadership, defended the increase as part of upgrading the position. Privately, however, some women in the House Democratic caucus shared Carpenter's evaluation of the increase. They voted for it in a party line decision, bowing to party discipline.[23]

Minnette Doderer regularly criticized the state's employment and compensation policies. When the Senate debated a collective bargaining policy for state employees in 1973, she wanted to include all legislative employees (most of whom worked only during the session). Doderer said she wanted the Senate to stop treating them as servants, but she lost. The next year she criticized the eligibility rules for legislative employees' pay increases because they discriminated against that group when compared to other state workers. She also objected to the discrimination that resulted in women who taught at community colleges earning an average of $1,500 a year less than men.[24]

In 1981, Doderer began to research and develop a plan that addressed women's salaries from a different direction. She introduced a resolution to consider comparable worth as the method for determining state employees' salaries, an approach that had been around since World War II. Its resurrection began in the 1970s as unions, women's groups, and the EEOC looked for ways to explain the wage gap between men and women workers that persisted despite equal pay for equal work laws. Sex segregation of jobs was part of the problem. Jobs in which women were predominant, regardless of the education, management, or responsibilities required by the jobs, paid less than those jobs where men predominated. Feminists looked to comparable worth, which uses a point system to evaluate the skill, effort, working conditions, and responsibility required in a given position, as a method for evaluating jobs to change the systemic biases in pay.[25]

Doderer enlisted the support of a freshman Republican woman, Dorothy Carpenter from West Des Moines, along with several other women of both parties. The women's caucus, becoming more organized in 1981, provided opportunities for developing an initial base of support for the measure. In addition, several women served on the House State Government Committee, which handled the bill. Doderer and Carpenter provided leadership in their respective partisan caucuses and the women's caucus provided the network for arguing the points and for explaining the idea to the balance of the legislature. Together these women successfully gathered the votes for a resolution to form an interim study committee in 1982. Interim committees work in the months between sessions, conducting hearings and gathering information with the goal of making recommendations to the legislative body. Through the committee meetings, members learn more about the issue as specialists present information and as interest groups argue for their positions.

With a favorable interim study report, comparable worth supporters asked the next session of the legislature to fund an independent study of the state's pay structure. From the beginning supporters believed that the study would show that jobs dominated by women paid less than those dominated by men, and they knew that the state could not afford to make the increases in one action. In addition, Jean Lloyd-Jones (Democrat, Iowa City) explained: "It's politically not feasible to talk about cutting pay" for those positions identified as overcompensated. But she offered the possibility of withholding increases from positions that the study revealed as being overpaid.[26]

As chair of the committee examining the issue, Doderer and other women legislators met with Governor Terry Branstad to ask for his support. Later, Branstad decided to look at the issue, and appointed a task force to study "equity in state employee pay scales." Known as the Task Force on Comparable Worth and Equal Pay, the group recommended that $75,000 be made available to the Iowa Merit Employment Department to conduct a comparable worth study. Doderer did not believe that the governor and the legislature would compete over the issue, but she wanted an independent study, not one conducted by a state agency.[27]

The House approved paying for an independent study, which had an estimated cost of $150,000 and the bill went to the Senate, which held the bill for several weeks. Observers conjectured that the reasons for the delay resulted from an old political feud between Doderer and George Kinley (Democrat, Des Moines). The two had clashed over the distribution of power among Senate leaders in the 1970s which some speculated had left antagonistic feelings between them. (See Chapter 3.) Others theorized that the Senate had stopped the bill for more contemporary reasons, citing Doderer's attempts to kill Kinley's pari-mutuel betting bill that session. (See Chapter 8.)

With the pressure and vigilance of Charles Bruner (Democrat, Ames) and others, the Senate amended and approved the bill. After the bill received Senate approval, a colleague asked Doderer: "Was the messenger who brought the bill from the Senate riding a horse?" She replied: "Yes, but only because a dog was too small," referring to the bill for gambling on horse and dog races.[28]

The comparable worth study revealed that women in state government earned about 12 percent less than men in comparable jobs. In addition, an average difference of 30 percent in pay existed between men and women, about one-third of which could be attributed to gender. Jobs dominated by women were an average of 6.6 pay grades lower than those dominated by men. Some of the difference could be ascribed to differences in the skill, effort, and responsibility required to perform the jobs, but 2 to 2½ grades of the difference related to the fact that men dominated the jobs. Governor Branstad recommended reducing the pay of some employees to pay for the increases due in some of the positions held by women, but Doderer disagreed: "We have rejected that, not in a formal vote, but in discussion, because we think it's illegal and not fair. People who have been discriminated against do not get fairness and justice by having someone reduced to their level."[29]

The consultants projected that it would cost $30 million to bring jobs to recommended pay levels. When confronted with the cost of comparable worth adjustments, the governor suggested ways to delay implementing the findings of the study. A court decision in Washington state became ammunition for Doderer's argument that Iowa must begin action quickly: "We're too far down the road to put it off. If we put it off now we'll be sued and then we'll be subject to back pay for two to three years."[30]

Doderer pressed for $10 million to begin implementing the pay plan, but strong opposition came from a Johnson County colleague, Arthur Small (Democrat, Iowa City), who wanted the Iowa Merit Employment Division to be responsible for upgrading wages. Small claimed that his constituents did not accept Doderer's proposal and he questioned the legislature's involvement in an area of government that more directly came under the executive branch. Doderer retorted: "Arthur Small doesn't understand comparable worth. Arthur Small didn't study this issue for six months as we have. If Merit Employment was so anxious to improve pay grades, why didn't they do it before we mandated it? . . . It is only when women would get their pay increased that anyone objects."[31]

The legislature passed the $10 million appropriation in 1984 to begin implementing comparable worth and created a seven member oversight committee. But obstacles continued to develop after the bill's passage. In 1985 some workers wanted to appeal the assigned value of their jobs and sought a process for that. Comparable worth pay increases became entangled with union negotiations, leading to results that Doderer opposed. She and others tried to find ways to separate comparable worth pay increases from bargained wages, but no satisfactory solution had been found when the legislature adjourned. The legislature established an appeals process and appropriated $19 million to fund more increases, but the governor reduced that amount by $2 million. In addition, a lawsuit filed by the Iowa Nurses' Association in 1986 further complicated the problems. In general, the pay issues after 1985 rested in the courts and in the executive branch which acts as the labor negotiator. The legislature had established the policy and appropriated the money to pay for it, but found that other problems were beyond its scope.[32]

In addition to the policy change represented by comparable worth, Doderer's strategy and the legislative processes involved deserve attention. She incorporated the resources within the legislature to educate her colleagues on the topic and to enlarge the group of informed legislators. The interim study committee, other women legislators, and the House and Senate leadership learned the vocabulary, purposes, and philosophies of comparable worth as the concept progressed through the process. By 1984, when the time had arrived to implement the plan, the idea had been circulating in the legislature for over two years, and advocates in both chambers had worked on it in various capacities. In addition, the press had discussed it at length, familiarizing the public with the underlying concepts.

Another of the many issues women raised on behalf of other women involved the state's policies for prosecuting rape charges. Feminists in the 1970s explored many areas of women's lives, often assigning political significance to them. Susan Griffin and Susan Brownmiller in separate works persuasively argued that rape constituted a violent act of dominance and was unrelated to sexual desire. Early in the decade, women formed rape crisis centers, organized hotlines, and in other ways brought the public's attention to the crime. Over the years legislators have made changes in Iowa's rape laws which they intended to assist county attorneys in obtaining convictions and to encourage rape victims to report the crime.[33]

Several women credited the Iowa Women's Political Caucus with bringing the problem before the public and with pushing for changes in rape laws. Mary O'Halloran (Democrat, Cedar Falls), who was a former Roman Catholic nun, explained that: "It became increasingly clear that we needed to focus on rape reform. . . . It was so bad; the rape laws were terrible, just terrible. If we were going to liberate women, one of the most important things we needed to do was to liberate us from sexual terror, for God's sakes." O'Halloran continued: "Our laws were constructed to protect rapists in ways that no other criminals were protected by the law, and one of them being this matter of corroboration, that unlike other laws, one had to have a witness, literally, often in order for rape to be prosecuted."[34] In 1974 Iowa was one of five states that required the prosecution to produce a corroborating witness in order to obtain a conviction, the only crime which had that requirement in the state.[35] Many women believed that removing the necessity for a witness would encourage more women to report rapes and to press charges on the attackers. Doderer argued that men had written the state's rape laws and that, in cases of rape, "women are guilty until proven innocent."[36]

Tom Riley (Republican, Cedar Rapids) and Doderer worked in the Senate and O'Halloran in the House. They sought to remove the necessity for corroborating evidence.[37] O'Halloran told the House that the law requiring corroboration "not only is of questionable constitutionality, but indicates some inherent mistrust of the testimony of a woman in a rape trial." She argued that women often did not report rapes because they did not have corroborating testimony. O'Halloran believed that the time had arrived for "women to get a fair break in court."[38]

O'Halloran recollected years later: "It was awful debating it." She explained: "Male legislators felt the need to point out that the law was such as it was because, strangely enough, arguments were made that women would cry rape in order to get their way against a man that they didn't like. . . . And there were the usual amount of 'they're asking for it' arguments, that we had to protect men against the cry of rape, because there were, of course, women that by their dress, their manner, and all sorts of things, invited rape. And you could see what a primitive barbaric attitude toward the human race that expresses. It was very discouraging to work on this." O'Halloran also pointed out that: "Most male legislators with any sense of propriety at all found it difficult, if not impossible, to be pictured as being supportive of rapists," which helped pass the bill.[39]

As part of a massive rewrite of the state's criminal code in 1975, the campaign to change rape laws continued. Doderer convinced the Senate to prohibit judges from discriminating against a victim's testimony. She explained that judges often used a 300-year-old statement to discredit rape victims' accusations when they instructed juries that a charge of rape is "easy to make, difficult to prove, and more difficult to disprove." Doderer argued that the instructions, used only in rape cases, created a different standard for rape convictions than other crimes. Her campaign was successful.[40]

As the bill progressed two additional issues developed, marital rape and whether or not the victim had adequately resisted the attacker. Diane Brandt (Democrat, Cedar Falls) sponsored and passed an amendment that eliminated the requirement that a woman fight her attacker in order for the event to be considered rape. It also expanded the definition of force to include threats of violence or future violence, surprise, and inappropriate medical treatment or examination.[41] In the Senate, Doderer argued for Brandt's amendment, saying: "The only thing that more resistance would get her is more misery and she has plenty of that." Elizabeth Shaw (Republican, Davenport) agreed: "Sometimes it is better to talk an attacker out of it instead of actively resisting, because screaming and fighting could only intensify his maniacal intentions toward the victim."[42]

Joan Lipsky (Republican, Cedar Rapids) introduced an amendment changing the definition of sexual abuse. If force was used, if resistance was impossible, if one person was a minor, or if one person had a mental defect, the act would be sexual abuse. She included spouses in the definition. Lipsky told the House: "Women in general have been considered as chattel in ancient societies, first by their fathers and then by their husbands. Although that is not a modern idea, sexual abuse between husbands and wives follows that ancient concept."[43] The House passed the amendment.

When Lipsky's amendment reached the Senate, Gene Glenn (Democrat, Ottumwa) opposed it because he believed that it invited "the charge of rape in any incident of force, no matter how minimal."[44] Doderer asked the body to "give a wife the same protection as a woman who is not married," and won Senate approval. Before the Senate released the bill, however, it reconsidered the marital rape provision, and Doderer told the assembly: "I don't understand a law which allows a woman who is a prostitute to file a rape charge against a customer, where a woman can file a charge against a man she is living with without benefit of marriage, which will allow anyone to file a rape charge except a woman against her husband."[45] Eugene Hill (Democrat, Newton) argued against Doderer, saying: "Have you ever had a woman lie to you? They do you know. A lying, vindictive woman could send her husband to jail. It makes a mockery of our judicial system." Glenn, who had worked hard on the criminal code revision, so strongly opposed the

Senate's retention of the marital rape provision, that he voted against final passage of the bill, explaining: "I will not vote to make sexual intercourse between husband and wife a criminal act."[46] The bill passed with the Senate with the marital rape provision, but the two chambers continued to disagree over other parts of it.

When the bill went to conference committee, that group changed the marital rape provision to allow the charge of sexual abuse only if there were serious injury or if a weapon had been used.[47] Glenn raised his voice against the physical force provision in the bill because: "Physical force is a frequent act of sexual intercourse in a husband and wife relationship. This amendment said nothing about a requirement that it be against the will. . . . It troubles me because in my experience, both personal and otherwise, the very act of intercourse involves this application of physical force."[48] In the final version, spouses could charge their marriage partners with sexual abuse if threats of violence were made or physical injury was inflicted.[49]

Lipsky said that the legislature required different standards for defining rape between married people than those for people who were not marriage partners because: "I don't think they liked to think that husbands raped wives, even though they deep down inside them know that they do. I think it was more that emotional problem they had accepting that than the assertion of the rights of the husband that kept them from endorsing it."[50]

A decade later, the House allowed third degree sexual abuse charges against a spouse, meaning that the victim did not have to sustain injuries or be threatened with a weapon in order for a rape to have been committed. The reported debate took place among men, with Michael Peterson (Democrat, Carroll) managing the bill. While no one accused women of being liars, as had occurred in 1976, some legislators expressed disbelief that rape could occur in marriage. The House approved the bill, but it died in the Senate.[51]

Three years later, James Riordan (Democrat, Waukee) successfully and easily gained Senate acceptance for a bill making sex against the will of one's spouse illegal (no threat of force involved) and marital rape a felony (threat or use of force involved). In the House, again with little debate, Ralph Rosenberg (Democrat, Ames) managed the bill and gained that chamber's approval. Behind the scenes, women like Dorothy Carpenter had worked to convince their caucuses to consider carefully the extent of the problem and had discussed it privately with many of their colleagues.[52] Thirteen years after extended debate and almost twenty years after the first introduction of the proposal, the legislature passed a bill to make marital rape a crime. By the time Iowa included marital rape in the criminal code, thirty-four other states had acted. Doderer, who had participated in the marital rape debates all those years could not explain the legislature's ultimate decision. She conjectured: "Nobody wants to get up and argue for some male's right to rape his wife. For ten years, somebody always got up and argued the point. You know these things change finally."[53]

The controversies surrounding various aspects of rape laws again reveal the culture in which women legislators worked. Their colleagues regularly argued against changing rape laws on the basis that women cannot be trusted to tell the truth. The expression of fundamentally malevolent views toward women appear in other debates. For example, Berle Priebe (Democrat, Algona) told the Senate that 12-year-old girls fearing a rape needed to learn to "run faster."[54]

Those women and men who worked to change Iowa's rape laws demonstrated a different perception of women than those that had prevailed in the past. They believed women have the same range of honesty and integrity as men. They argued that rape constituted an act of violence unrelated to sexual desire. Dismissing the excuse that the problem was a misunderstanding between two people, they argued that a significant difference existed between a victim and a consenting partner. They believed that a woman who submitted to the attack rather than risking her life fighting it could still charge that a crime had been committed against her and have a prosecutable complaint. Regarding her role as an amendment sponsor, Joan Lipsky remembered that: "I probably wouldn't have had the guts to do it as a newcomer. I had earned my spurs as it were, and I was a member of leadership."[55] She believed that her decade of experience in the House helped avoid some of the most demeaning aspects of the debate.

An issue far less emotional than rape involved health care delivery to low-income Iowans. People without private insurance or financial resources to pay for their health care and who do not qualify for federal programs have the option of applying for "state papers" with the State Indigent Patient Program. The legislature created the program in 1915 for two purposes: to provide health care for low-income citizens and to provide patients for teaching medical students at the University of Iowa Hospitals and Clinics (UIHC) in Iowa City. The state appropriates funds for the program, which are allocated on the basis of specified priorities and a quota system to counties. Persons meeting their county's standards apply for state papers and receive medical care at UIHC. A large percentage of the patients receiving treatment under the program are obstetrical patients and their newborns.[56]

The statewide program offered services only in Iowa City, located in the eastern part of the state. UIHC provided transportation to patients, but for many pregnant women waiting in Iowa City for three weeks or more to deliver their babies, the separation from friends, family, and other sources of support left them feeling isolated and depressed. In the early 1980s, a group of women legislators began proposing a variety of plans to take the medical care paid by the indigent patient fund to the patients, instead of taking the patients to the care. Ways to decentralize the services included developing a medically needy program, setting up satellite clinics, and establishing training facilities at local and county hospitals. Administrators at UIHC rejected those ideas because they would diminish the patient base at the hospitals and reduce the teaching opportunities.[57]

Several women had participated in developing the alternatives, along with men such as Charles Bruner (Democrat, Ames). Sue Mullins (Republican, Corwith), whose district was in northwest Iowa, far from Iowa City, argued for changing the program because of the distance her constituents had to travel to receive the services. The bill she managed proposed making all services locally available by allowing county relief directors to charge the state for services and UIHC receiving reimbursements only for the services it provided. Mullins repeatedly stated that it only made sense to provide services locally, but UIHC officials claimed it would destroy their training programs.[58]

An important addition to the cause came with Jo Ann Zimmerman's (Democrat, Waukee) election to the House in 1982. A nurse, a health educator, and an activist in health-related issues, Zimmerman joined the fight on the side of decentralization. As a medical professional, Zimmerman countered the objections to decentralization raised by UIHC and argued for the economic and medical benefits of providing local services. When decentralizing the entire indigent patient program became a dead issue, Zimmerman and others worked to salvage part of the idea. Focusing on pregnant women, their obstetrical needs, and their newborns, they devised a plan to offer those services locally, with some exceptions. Women lawmakers crafted a plan in 1986 that would better serve low-income women and that attracted enough votes for passage.[59]

The quality of medical care provided at UIHC was not ever the issue in the debate. Testimony offered at a public hearing praised the care but also expressed the difficulties of being separated from loved ones during important and emotional events. Zimmerman, Mullins, and other legislators responded to the "emotional pleas" to find alternatives that would allow women to obtain the family support denied them by distance. They put those concerns above the needs of the teaching hospital, believing that women should not suffer in order for medical students to have patients.[60]

By placing women's needs at a higher priority than medical training, women legislators rejected the status quo and demonstrated their beliefs in women's importance. In a culture that almost deifies doctors and often holds women in low esteem, the choices these legislators made provide further illustration that women often take different priorities to the State House than their male colleagues. The values these legislators propounded placed individual women's needs above institutional ones.

Obstetrical care for women and the other issues discussed here came during a time in which several factors came together. A strong feminist movement throughout the country helped women identify discriminatory practices and propelled them into action. Through their lobbying, they pressured legislators into recognizing the indignities that women were subjected to by state laws. About the same time, women in the Iowa legislature had begun to increase their visibility and to use their power. In addition, a number of women had served several terms, giving them the political skills necessary to manipulate these bills through the process. And, as Joan Lipsky pointed out, she had "earned her spurs," had found the courage to introduce emotion laden issues, and had the added status of belonging to leadership. Other leaders in these debates could point to comparable evidence of their legislative maturity and the power it gave them to negotiate these issues.

Another factor contributing to the success of the measures can be found in the numbers of women serving simultaneously. Most of the legislation discussed here passed after the mid-1970s, when fourteen to sixteen women served in each session. Many of those years, the House and Senate caucuses of both parties had women among their members. This distribution allowed women to argue their points in all four caucuses and gave them opportunities to counter opposition in that semi-private environment, as opposed to the public debate. The reasons women gave their caucuses to support a bill may have included the righteousness of the proposal, but one woman told her caucus that political reasons also existed: the party should not want to be identified as opposing women's issues if it wanted success at the polls in the next election. Messages like hers would probably not be well-received during floor debate, but could be stated straightforwardly during a closed caucus meeting.

The many roles women performed in passing feminist legislation point to the crucial nature of their presence if women's issues are to receive the attention and approval of the General Assembly. After male legislators understood the problems and the proposed solutions, they regularly supported making the necessary changes. While confrontations, objections, and rancorous debate surrounded the process in many instances, female and male legislators affirmed the importance of developing public policies that recognized the state's responsibility to attempt to balance the needs of all citizens.

Democrat Carolyn Pendray of Jackson County presiding over the Iowa Senate in 1933. Photo courtesy of the *Des Moines Register.*

Democrat Ada Garner of Butler County at the Statehouse in 1933. Photo courtesy of the *Des Moines Register.*

Republican Kathlyn Wick of Taylor County in 1947. Photo courtesy of Kathlyn Wick.

Republican Edna Lawrence of Wapello County at her desk in the Iowa House in 1949. Photo courtesy of the *Des Moines Register.*

Republican Gladys Nelson of Jasper County on the right conferring with American Soybean Association lobbyist Norval Hodges of Illinois regarding the oleomargarine bills in 1953. Photo courtesy of the State Historical Society of Iowa-Des Moines.

Democrat Katherine Falvey Zastrow at her desk in the Iowa House in 1959. Photo courtesy of the *Des Moines Register.*

Democrat June Franklin of Des Moines reading mail at her desk in the Iowa House in 1967. Photo courtesy of the *Des Moines Register.*

Republican Joan Lipsky of Linn County on the steps of the Statehouse in 1971. Photo courtesy of the *Des Moines Register.*

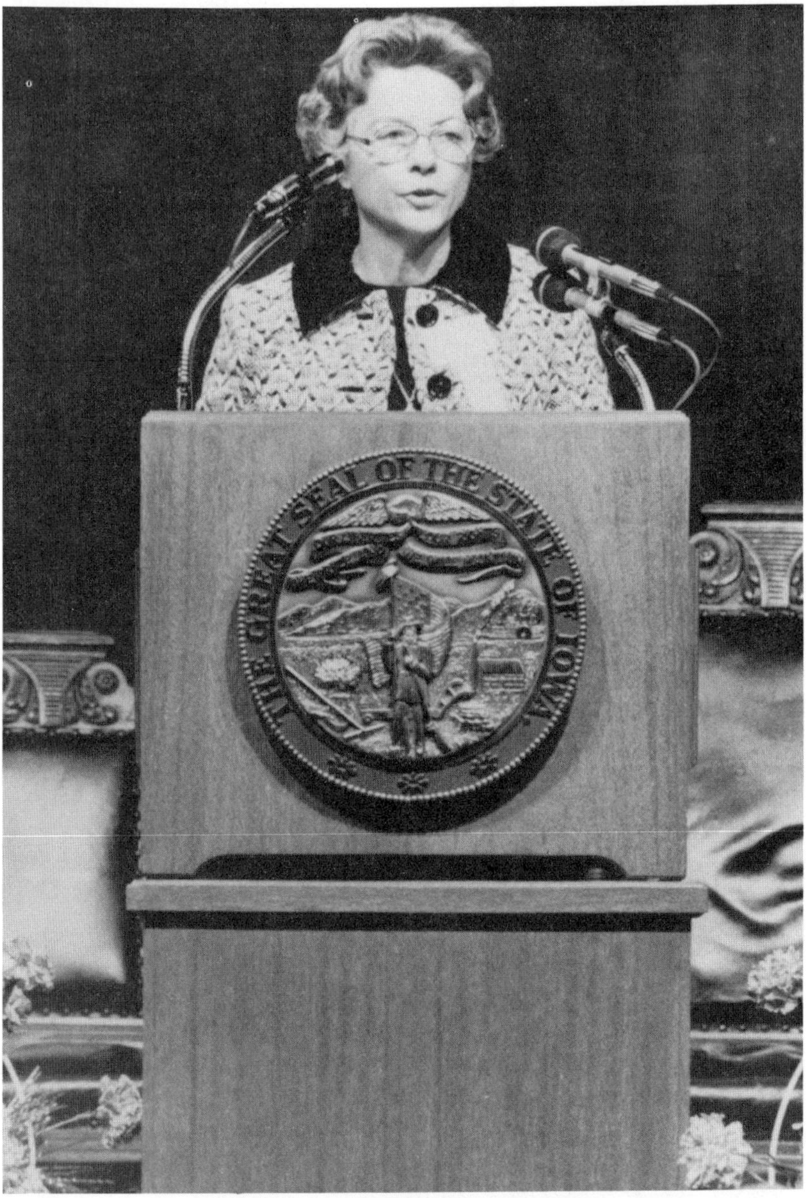

Democrat Minnette Doderer of Iowa City on the January day in 1975 she became president pro tempore of the Iowa Senate, shown here presiding over the governor's inauguration at Veterans Memorial Auditorium in Des Moines. Photo by Carl Voss, courtesy of the *Des Moines Register.*

Democrat Mary O'Halloran of Cedar Falls on the floor of the Iowa House in 1978. Photo by Warren Taylor, courtesy of the *Des Moines Register.*

Republican Betty Jean Clark of Rockwell wearing her gambling hat during her fight against a lottery bill in 1984. Photo courtesy of the *Des Moines Register.*

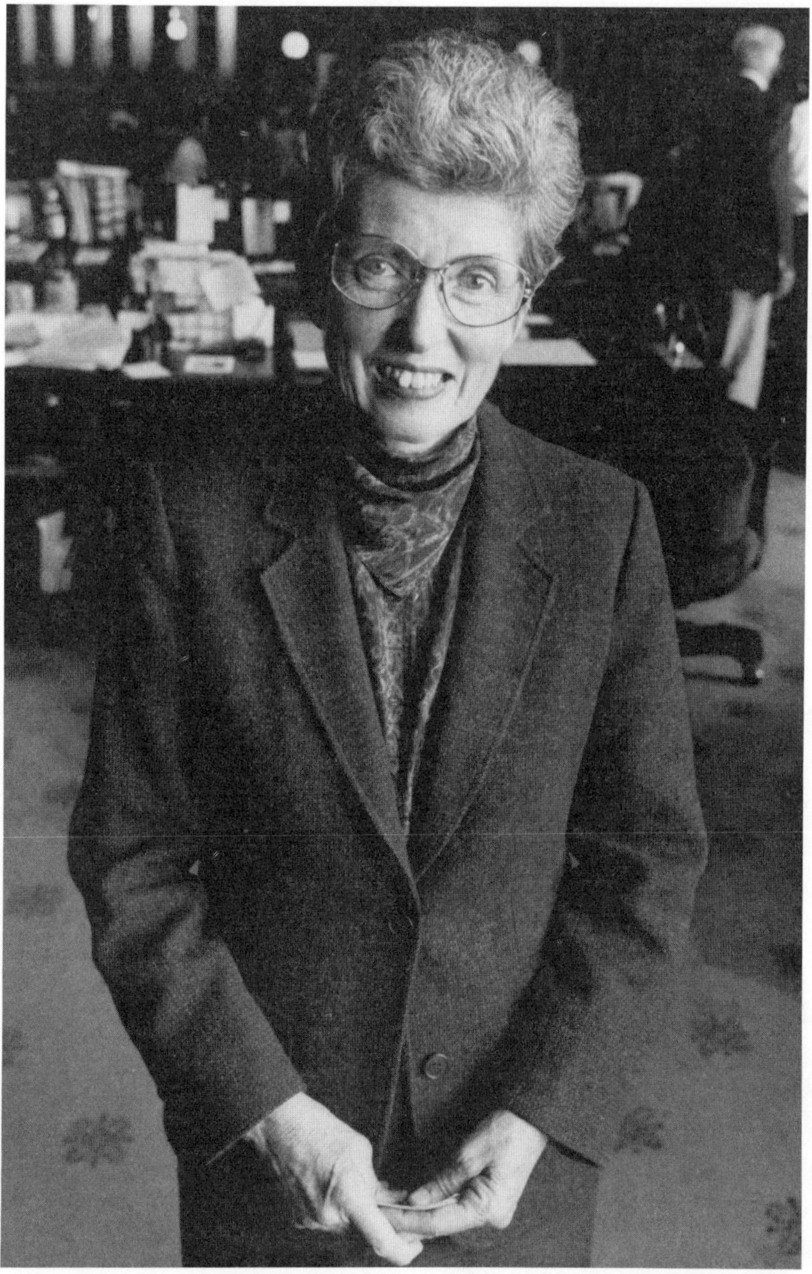

Republican Dorothy Carpenter of West Des Moines in the back of the Iowa House in 1993. Photo by Bob Nandell, courtesy of the *Des Moines Register.*

CHAPTER 5

Children

Of all the roles women hold, the closest to universal must be that of mother. Bearing, feeding, nurturing, protecting, and teaching children has occupied women for centuries. Since the nineteenth century, women have also become children's advocates outside the home and have taken their concerns for children into the public sphere, leading crusades to establish kindergartens, abolish child labor, improve infant and child health, and build playgrounds. The many examples of women working to protect children and to improve their lives include Lillian Wald and Jane Addams who ran settlement houses that provided child care and sponsored youth programs. They also crusaded for the formation of the Federal Children's Bureau, which another woman first headed after its creation in 1912. These women and others throughout the country raised their voices in the Progressive Movement to reform the nation's policies for children. As might be anticipated, women entering state legislatures have taken their experiences as mothers, girls' club leaders, and teachers with them and added their concerns for children to policy debates.

A 1988 study by the Center for the American Woman and Politics at Rutgers University found that women more likely list women, children, and families as priority interests than men and that while men sponsor legislation affecting families and children, women more often introduce and obtain passage of their proposals than men. The authors suggest that the reasons may be that women have more credibility in these areas and they may be more persistent in their advocacy of them. In addition, a higher proportion of women in the legislature appears to increase the probability that legislation affecting families and children will pass. Another aspect of children's issues has been suggested by the authors of *Megatrends for Women* who assert that children's issues are no longer "women's issues" but have become political issues, and that women's advocacy for and emphasis on them are the reasons for success in their passage. All of these researchers agree that women have clearly made a significant difference in the attention given to policies affecting families and children in recent years. As would probably be found in other states, Iowa women have been active in developing state policy in these areas for decades.[1]

Women in the Iowa General Assembly have sought ways to protect children from disease, abuse, state policies, and other threats to their well-being. In addition, despite hopes for another outcome, some children become the state's responsibility because of unavailable or inadequate parental care, and other children require attention from the state because of their unlawful acts. The state also defines the point at which children are considered capable of making adult decisions. These issues are complicated. Identifying the situations in which the state should intervene and in what ways has often become the most trying aspect of the debates. As legislators have sought to craft policies for children's safety, protection, and care, they have encountered opposition from parents and lawmakers who resisted the state's intrusion into family life and disagreed with establishing children's needs as a state priority.

A number of related factors place children's issues in a class by themselves. First of all, children can not vote for their state legislators or anyone else in public office. If they disapprove of their legislators' actions, they have no way to remove them from office and replace them with people more inclined to represent their concerns. In addition, governments have resisted becoming involved in family life until recent decades. Under English common law, children were considered to be chattel and belonged to their fathers. While governments no longer strictly subscribe to that philosophy, they have continued to regard children as the responsibility of their parents unless other circumstances, such as abuse, call for involvement. More directly related to legislatures is the fact that children seldom have paid lobbyists working on their behalf to provide lawmakers with research or to bargain their issues in a back room. These conditions often leave children and their needs relatively invisible. Women's presence in the legislature has increased the visibility of these issues and altered the perspective from which they are viewed.

The tradition of the state's female lawmakers working to protect children began with an issue from the Progressive Era. The first two women in the Iowa legislature, Carolyn Pendray (Democrat, Jackson) and Ada Garner (Democrat, Butler), worked to gain the state's ratification of the Child Labor Amendment to the United States Constitution.[2] Approved by Congress in 1924, the amendment would have permitted the federal government to "limit, regulate, and prohibit the labor of persons under eighteen years of age." In the late 1920s, supporters, including the Women's Joint Congressional Committee and the Women's Trade Union League, appeared unable to avoid its defeat by business interests and the American Farm Bureau Federation. Legislators around the nation, however, attempted to resurrect the amendment in the early 1930s.[3]

Pendray began her effort to gain Iowa ratification of the Child Labor Amendment in the Senate during the 1933 Regular Session of the legislature, but it failed. Early in the legislature's 1933-34 special session, however, Ada Garner prepared to lead the House fight for its ratification. After the House committee on constitutional amendments recommended indefinite postponement, Garner, the farmer's wife, worked to override the decision by lobbying her colleagues. With House leaders divided on the resolution and with most House members, especially rural ones, opposed, Garner's chances for success appeared minimal.[4]

With the House stalled on the resolution, Pendray obtained its approval in the Senate, and chances for ratification further improved when Governor Clyde Herring asked for its passage. The House committee voted again and changed its decision from indefinite postponement to no recommendation. With Garner continuing to lead the ratification effort, the House finally approved it. The *Iowa Recorder* declared Garner's success "an event of national importance." Winning ratification in an agricultural state gave supporters hope that the amendment would be accepted in enough other agricultural states for ratification. Instead, New Deal policies rendered moot the need for the amendment.[5]

After Garner's and Pendray's success with the Child Labor Amendment, women legislators worked on education policies but they tended to focus on administrative issues rather than children's more direct needs. In the 1960s and 1970s, however, a number of issues affecting children's welfare received new or renewed legislative attention from two women in particular. Joan Lipsky (Republican, Cedar Rapids), a psychologist and mother, and Minnette Doderer (Democrat, Iowa City), a political activist and mother, repeatedly led the legislature by creating an awareness of issues concerning children and by working to devise solutions to problems. After 1968, Doderer served in the Senate and Lipsky in the House, giving the issues advocates in both chambers. In addition, the women's willingness to cooperate and cross party lines provided opportunities for two caucuses to hear the reasons for the desired legislation. Lipsky and Doderer each had her own areas of specific interest as well as those they developed together. In some situations one woman had greater visibility than the other, but the level of activity in the areas of children and families in the 1960s and 1970s may well be attributed to their combined insistence on the importance of the issues.

Reasonable people of goodwill legitimately question the impact and relative merits of many of the policies discussed here. Two of them, however, have had direct and speedy benefits for children: immunizations against childhood diseases and child safety restraints in automobiles. In the 1960s Doderer attempted to require immunizations against measles for children, but the bill did not progress. She regularly introduced the bill over the years, but it received little attention. Then in 1976, the House passed a bill requiring mandatory immunizations for German measles, mumps, diphtheria, whooping cough, tetanus, and polio before entering public school, but the bill died in the Senate. Charles Miller (Democrat, Burlington) had killed it, even though he professed to have little interest in it. At the time, only Iowa, Idaho, and Wyoming did not require these immunizations for school children.[6]

In 1977, a measles epidemic hit Iowa and public health officials believed the only way to stop it was through mandatory immunizations. At the time, about 70 percent of Iowa's schoolchildren received the immunizations, but supporters believed the balance needed the protection for themselves as well as for others. Jo Ann Orr (Democrat, Grinnell) and Doderer again introduced the immunization bill in the Senate and once again Miller attempted to kill it by assigning it to a burial subcommittee. The controversy centered on the allowable exemptions. Doderer and Orr had agreed to allow them for religious and medical reasons, but Miller wanted a conscience clause that would permit anyone to forego the immunizations for any reason. Doderer insisted that the conscience clause would gut the bill, rendering it useless.[7]

In the House, Gregory Cusack (Democrat, Davenport) had introduced the companion bill to that of Doderer and Orr. During the debate, Joan Lipsky explained that measles is "debilitating and results in lifelong handicaps. It's destructive of hearing, causes brain damage and the loss of sight. And there's no reason for any child today to have measles."[8] She added that saying the immunizations were the parents' responsibility was not adequate because they were not fulfilling it. The conscience clause, which had stopped action in the Senate was not even introduced in the House and the bill passed. When the bill went to the Senate, the body considered and rejected the conscience clause amendment, but added others, requiring House approval of the changes.

Back in the House, Gregory Cusack, the bill's sponsor, had undergone a change of heart and decided that the conscience clause had merit and attempted to add it. Julia Gentleman (Republican, Des Moines), a self-described civil libertarian, argued against the conscience clause, saying that a person's rights should only be limited in order to protect the rights of others. She added: "Those are clear cut times, and this is one of those times."[9] The House rejected the conscience clause, approved the Senate amendments, passed the bill and sent it to the governor, who signed it.

After the bill had been in effect for a year, the state health department announced that the number of measles cases dropped from 4,333 in 1977 to 76 in 1978, the first year the law was in effect. As a sidelight, Doderer, who worked on policies that affected nearly every aspect of government and held several leadership positions in the legislature, later recollected that she was most proud of her role in passing the bill. She believed it made a significant difference in children's welfare.[10]

In 1983 Jean Lloyd-Jones (Democrat, Iowa City) began another fight to protect children, those riding in motor vehicles. The measure she won in 1986 required children under 2 years old to ride in approved child safety seats and those 2 to 4 years old to either be in a safety seat or buckled with the seat belt. The measure included a monetary penalty for those who did not comply. To support her arguments for state requirements to buckle up babies, Lloyd-Jones explained that in 1981, 772 children had been killed or injured in auto accidents in Iowa. One opponent to the bill, Horace Daggett (Republican, Lenox) complained: "This would not allow me to take my grandchildren to the drugstore for a Coke."[11] Other opponents accused supporters of invading privacy and beginning a police state.

The proposal faced greater obstacles in the Senate than it had in the House. A vocal and powerful opponent, Joe Coleman (Democrat, Clare) chaired the Senate Transportation Committee, assigned himself chair of the subcommittee for the bill, and buried it. He believed: "We can't protect everyone from everything. There is no way that I am going to tell parents how to take care of their children."[12] Berl Priebe (Democrat, Algona) also on the subcommittee thought: "Voting against this is like voting against motherhood," but acknowledged his was only one of three subcommittee votes.[13] Lloyd-Jones continued to strategize ways to pass the bill and succeeded the next session.[14]

These policies for child immunizations and for safety restraints required parents to take specific action to protect their children. Legislators did not question the value of the protections by arguing that immunizations were ineffective or that child restraints did not help save children's lives. Opponents did not want the state involved with such elementary levels of family life. The same opposing opinions can be found in the debates on child day care licensing.

Sue B. Mullins (Republican, Corwith) spent much of her legislative career advocating policies to protect children in day care by requiring more categories of day care providers to register with the state, obtain licenses, and permit state inspections of their facilities. Putting children's care into perspective, she wrote in a newspaper opinion article: "In this state, to protect consumers we license bait sellers, car dealers, egg handlers, grain dealers, restaurants, health-care facilities, pesticide applicators, foster families and a host of other providers. We do not, as yet, mandatorily regulate the surrogate parents whom we call family-day-care providers."[15]

Karen Mann (Republican, Scranton) disagreed with Mullins and wanted to remove licensing and registration requirements for private centers, which do not receive public funds. Mann questioned the need for state involvement in these centers: "Shall the state confiscate the authority of the parents in determining what is best for the care of our children? Are we ready to say that parents are no longer responsible for their children? That the Department of Social Services shall be the authority in determining a standard of care?" She argued that removing the licensing requirement for private centers "puts the responsibility on the shoulders of the parent or guardian involved."[16] Mullins did not intend to replace parents but wanted to assist them by helping them identify places that would provide safe care for their children. Mullins left the General Assembly without her vision of child care legislation completed.

The premise of the day care and other legislation described above was that the state had a role in making policies that would prevent children from being harmed. The state also intervenes when adults abuse children. By the mid-1960s, laws making child abuse a crime already existed, but many abused children were not identified and helped.

In 1965 Doderer introduced a bill in the House making physicians and nurses mandatory reporters of child abuse. The Senate version, which passed, was essentially the same as Doderer's, which required mandatory reporting of child abuse to the county department of social services and for that department to report to the county attorney. The goal of the policy was to protect children from abuse by prosecuting the offenders.[17]

By 1974, Doderer had come to believe that child abuse was far more prevalent in the state than reports indicated and that new approaches to identifying and ending child abuse were needed. The university hospital at Iowa City had conducted studies on child abuse and researchers had discussed the inadequacies of the existing laws with Doderer. Working with the researchers and Josephine Gittler, a law professor at the University of Iowa, Doderer drafted and passed legislation to make significant changes in the policy.[18]

The most important aspect of the legislation rested in the change of emphasis the bill proposed. Instead of identifying abusive parents and reporting them with the intent of prosecuting them, helping parents learn alternatives to abuse became the objective and within that the hope of ending the cycle of abuse. Doderer explained: "Today's battered child becomes the battering parent of tomorrow." She believed: "They [parents] don't want to harm the child. They're emotionally upset and the child is the most handy victim of their temper."[19] Under the legislation, county departments of social services were required to provide services, such as counselling, to the child and the abuser.

Doderer also believed that doctors did not report all of the abuse they encountered. She included a $100 fine for failure to report, saying: "Doctors always report gunshot wounds; why can't we condition these people to report child abuse cases?"[20] The legislation added a wide variety of other professionals, such as teachers and social workers, to the group of mandatory reporters. In addition, it established a central registry and a 24-hour answering service to receive reports.

The only person recorded as opposing the legislation during debate and voting against it in either chamber was Eugene Hill (Newton, Democrat), who did not believe that any bill could reduce the problems of child abuse. Hill may have been correct. The legislation has not ended child abuse, but it has improved the likelihood that an abused child will be helped.[21]

In another area of child protection, the state becomes involved when parents are unable or unwilling to take responsibility for them. Orphanages, foster care, and adoption have been the resources used by the state, but Joan Lipsky found that state policies resulted in discrimination among certain categories of children. After Lipsky won her 1966 race for the Iowa House, she toured several of the state's institutions, among them the Annie Wittenmeyer Home in Davenport. She recollected:

> I was absolutely shocked beyond belief by my visit to the Iowa Annie Wittenmeyer Home, because the children who were there didn't belong in an institution. It was, in fact, an old-fashioned orphanage. There was not a difficult child in the place. There was not a child who wasn't eligible for placement in a perfectly nice family home. . . . It was like stepping back 50 years. . . . There were some very good people running a very good school there—that was the only thing I saw that was really good.[22]

Talking to the superintendent, Lipsky learned that many of them were veterans' children and that the state paid for their care at the home, but would not if they went into foster care in their home counties. Counties often chose to place the children at Annie Wittenmeyer to save money, leaving the children's care to the state and its funds. Lipsky believed that the policy worked to the children's disadvantage by denying them the potential benefits of foster care.[23]

Lipsky remembers: "I decided that the first thing I would do would be to get a law passed saying that the state would pick up the tab for veterans' children wherever they might be, and that there was no reason to discriminate against the veteran's child."[24] After getting the bill passed in the House, a friend and legislative observer pointed out that the Senate still had to approve it. She heeded his advice, went to the chairman of the Senate committee assigned to the bill and discussed the proposal with him. He agreed that the bill was worthy of passage, but Lipsky felt that he did not have enough influence to get the job done alone. Lipsky describes her next step: "I went to a couple of the Senators who were interested in veterans' programs, and I said, 'Just because you're unfortunate enough to be a veteran's child, why should you have to go to a crummy institution instead of to a nice foster home? I think it's terrible.'"[25] With their support the Senate approved the bill, but the story is not over.

Lipsky's friendly observer reminded her that the governor still had to sign the bill and that: "'You never know who's out in the woodwork working against you, maybe the head of that school down there that you're going to deprive of kids, or somebody he knows.'"[26] Republican Lipsky had only met privately with Democrat Governor Harold Hughes once before on an unrelated matter. It had been with the state senator from her district, and while their conversation had been pleasant, Lipsky felt that yet another unrelated matter may have left the governor less than willing to sign a bill she had sponsored.

Taking the initiative, she called the governor's aide, saying: "I am so excited because I have gotten a bill passed, and it has gone through the House and it has gone through the Senate in my very first session. And I would like to request that the governor let me be present and let me take a picture when he signs my bill." The aide said that she would be invited to the bill signing. On the appointed day, Lipsky says: "I put on my best outfit, and I went into the governor's office and asked someone to take a picture, and he signed my bill. I still have the picture. But it was not the end of the trouble for the bill. The bill had really not run into trouble yet; I had done it so fast and so alone and without much fanfare or press attention, that it got in before the department or the bureaucracy even knew it was there."[27]

When Lipsky returned to Des Moines a year and a half later for the biennial legislative session, she discovered that child welfare administrators had not begun implementing the program. Instead, they had convinced the state comptroller, the state treasurer, and the state attorney general to hold the bill in abeyance because no way existed to certify foster care and they had other objections to the bill. Lipsky called a meeting of the concerned parties to sort out the problems. She began the meeting by asking the child welfare staffers if the program would help children. After they answered affirmatively, she turned to the others gathered and asked for their help in resolving the interdepartmental problems, which they did.[28]

As Lipsky pointed out, she truly had relatively few problems passing the bill. It was her good fortune to have a friend who advised and coached her through the legislative process. It is to her credit that she listened and responded to it and had the creativity to make the bill appealing to men who might not have otherwise been as interested in it. In many ways, the bill highlights the differences women's presence in the legislature makes in policies for children. Learning about the state institutions and discussing their operations and policies involved a large time commitment on Lipsky's part. In addition, her identification of the situation as a problem points to her awareness of children's needs and her willingness to find a solution. None of the research on this bill suggests that men opposed it, fought it, or in any way obstructed its progress. But as Lipsky explained: "Everyone talks a good game, but when push comes to shove, if it's the truckers against the kids [in getting a bill on the debate calendar], you know which bill is going to get on the calendar."[29] By making the problem a priority, by strategizing ways to gain its acceptance, and by following the bill through the process, it became enacted as a state policy.

A related area, adoption, has a number of competing interests. When parents voluntarily terminate their rights or when the courts order the action, the state regulates and authorizes adoptions. In addition to protecting the child's interests in an adoption, the state recognizes that the birth parents and the adoptive parents have privacy concerns that they want safeguarded. Some birth parents want their identities carefully concealed, especially those mothers who may fear that their child, whose very existence may have been kept a secret, may suddenly appear and disrupt her life. Some adoptive parents want to keep their identity confidential to avoid the possibility of a birth parent reclaiming the child they have nurtured and raised. Some adopted children want to find their roots or need their family's medical history for health reasons. These competing interests have involved the legislature in numerous policy debates. In addition to the many debates on adoption, only a few of which are discussed here, the issue stands out for another reason. In every other policy area relating to children, women legislators, particularly Doderer and Lipsky, have more likely defended children's rights and protections over those of the adults in their lives. In some aspects of the adoption debates, women placed a high priority on protecting the birth mother's privacy.

Until a U.S. Supreme Court decision in the 1970s, only mothers had to terminate their parental rights before a child could be adopted. The decision required that fathers must also terminate their rights. Joan Lipsky sponsored a proposal to include that provision in state law. Her bill had other provisions, including the requirements that both parents receive counselling prior to terminating their parental rights and that an investigation of the adoptive parents be conducted before the adoption.[30] Lipsky also attempted to limit adoption placements to the Department of Social Services and licensed social agencies and eliminate doctors and lawyers as private adoption avenues, arguing that doctors and lawyers did not have "the facilities, the professional qualifications or the time to adequately investigate prospective adoptive families." Emma Jean Kiser (Republican, Davenport) successfully argued against that point: "If you close up private adoption procedures, the abortion rate is going to climb."[31] In addition, the House decided that if the father had not been identified a notice of the pending adoption had to be published. When the bill reached the Senate, Minnette Doderer amended it to eliminate the publication notice of the pending adoption if the father had not been identified. Though the bill was intended to protect paternal rights before a court terminated them, Doderer believed that it would humiliate the mother and could prevent her from placing the child with an adoptive family.[32]

The birth mother's privacy became an issue again in the 1980s. Adults whose adoption records the state had sealed wanted to simplify the process for identifying and finding their birth parents. Janet Carl (Democrat, Grinnell) floor managed a bill to open the records of some adoptees, saying that: "It is the birthright of each citizen in the state to know the identity of his or her parents. Adoption is a special arrangement between children and two sets of parents."[33] Doderer and Sue Mullins (Republican, Corwith) argued against the open records, again defending the birth mother's privacy. Doderer believed that opening the records would break the contract of confidentiality made at the time of the adoption. Mullins told the chamber: "We are saying that in instances that are most private, most personal, a woman has no right to privacy."[34] Beverly Hannon (Democrat, Anamosa) echoed the sentiment: "A woman who gave up a child to adoption may never have told anyone. I can't think of a reason why we should allow such disruption."[35] Although the bill died in the Senate Human Resources Committee in 1986, the concept continued to be an issue in the Iowa legislature.[36]

The intensity with which some women legislators defended the birth mother's privacy may well be related to the time in which they grew up. Janet Carl, who wanted adoption records more readily available, was twenty-five years younger than Doderer and twelve years younger than Mullins, who both opposed it. The shame attached to an out-of-wedlock pregnancy has diminished over the decades and these women's opinions may be expressions of the eras in which they spent their youth. The women opposed to opening adoption records wanted to protect the mothers who had made difficult decisions about their and their children's futures. Without hesitation, these lawmakers sought to protect the mother's interest: she had taken care of her child by placing it in an adoption agency's care and legislators sought to protect her from family and public scorn. Women who grew up in an era when an unmarried daughter's pregnancy brought shame to the entire family could understand the potential trauma for others in their generation if the baby, whose existence had been a well-guarded secret and who a woman may have reluctantly surrendered, reappeared later in her life as an adult. These concerns may explain the reasons opponents to making adoption records more easily available placed greater importance on the birth mother's interests than on those of the adopted child.

Several women who believed that the state had a responsibility to protect children also believed that it extended to those who had broken laws. Providing help to them rather than punishment appears as a theme espoused by women in the mid-1960s. At the time, the courts could send children deemed delinquent or incorrigible to one of the state's correctional institutions. Children who ran away from home or skipped school or whose parents had difficulty with them could be sent to the schools. Several women legislators opposed the state's policies for these children and believed the state could better address the problems by helping youth through counselling than by punishing them. In 1965 Gertrude Cohen (Democrat, Waterloo) opposed a proposal for regional detention facilities for children because she believed that children in trouble with the law needed to be protected from themselves and that the facilities would not help them. Instead, she asked for "state-supported group foster homes or shelter homes which would house perhaps up to eight youngsters. These should be available at a moment's notice for a youngster on detention awaiting his juvenile court hearing."[37]

Early in her legislative career, Joan Lipsky also advocated protecting children who had broken laws. In 1967 Lipsky worked with several other legislators to give judges the option of closing court proceedings involving juveniles to the press. She felt that youngsters in trouble already had enough problems and that publicizing their activities did not help them. She also fought attempts to have children treated as adults in certain situations and wanted juvenile courts to have exclusive jurisdiction over delinquent, neglected and dependent children.[38]

These early attempts at changing the state's policies toward juveniles began to develop more fully in the 1970s. Through work on various study committees over several years, Lipsky and Minnette Doderer developed a large package of juvenile justice reforms with the help of University of Iowa law professor Josephine Gittler. The proposals included a fundamental change in one aspect of juvenile law. If an act were not a crime when committed by an adult, they believed that it should not be a crime if a child committed the same act, meaning that running away from home and skipping school would no longer be criminal offenses for children. It became the most controversial component of the proposed new juvenile laws. Lipsky asserted that most status offenders were runaways and that imprisoning a child who escaped incest or other abuse was neither sensible nor fair because adults in those situations could leave without criminal penalty. She believed that children belonged with their families but that some families needed help. Doderer and Lipsky also believed it unconscionable to force the children to return to the people who had mistreated them.[39]

Another aspect of the proposal included placing all juvenile laws into one chapter of the *Code of Iowa* to guide lawyers, judges, social workers, and others dealing with children in making their decisions. Lipsky believed that by codifying the decisions, children's rights could more easily be protected because authorities would have greater awareness of them. Drafters also wanted children treated in the least restrictive manner and given as much responsibility for themselves as possible.[40]

While the underlying philosophy of the proposal had been in development for close to a decade, transforming it into a specific bill involved numerous consultations with dozens of experts and advisers. For example, in 1976 Doderer chaired and Lipsky was a member of a study committee that investigated the state's juvenile justice laws. Josephine Gittler worked with probation officers, juvenile justice judges, and other professionals before she drafted the proposal which Lipsky introduced in the House and Doderer submitted to the Senate. Despite the preparatory work done for it, the bill had many opponents: law enforcement officers, judges, state administrators, and juvenile authorities, some of whom had been consulted in its crafting.[41]

During debate on the bill, some legislators recounted their own experiences as children and as parents. Betty Jean Clark (Republican, Rockwell) said that she "skipped school a lot" but had "reasonably good judgment," so did not get involved with the courts. Clark also spoke from a mother's experience, describing her own children as having difficult times growing up, but she had not wanted them involved in the juvenile justice system.[42] In the final version sent to the governor, runaways and truants did not come under the jurisdiction of the courts.

The juvenile justice bill passed by the legislature in 1978 accomplished many of the goals planned for it by Lipsky and Doderer, but as Doderer explains: "We were going to work on getting more services in the various communities after we cleaned up the law. We never got that far because we kept fighting off the ones that wanted to return to putting kids in jail. We still do [have the fights]."[43]

Another issue has involved defining when a child is no longer a juvenile and can begin exercising adult rights and privileges. Creating policies for young people of varying maturity at a given age has plagued legislators. One of the rites of passage from childhood to adult status for some young people includes buying that first beer on the birthday that it becomes legal. The legislature has had a difficult time deciding at what age citizens can buy that drink. In less than twenty years, Iowa reduced the legal drinking age from 21 to 19, lowered it to 18, raised it to 19, and then raised it back to 21. After the country ratified an amendment to the United States Constitution allowing 18-year-olds to vote in 1971, the Iowa legislature began debating which other adult rights should be extended to them. Chief among these was the purchase of alcohol. During the Vietnam War years, some lawmakers argued that citizens old enough to fight and die in battle were also old enough to purchase and consume beer and liquor.[44]

The odyssey began in 1972, when the legislature lowered the legal drinking age from 21 to 19. Some senators fought to lower it further to 18. Charlene Conklin (Republican, Waterloo), mother of five teenage and preteen children, argued for the lower age because she believed: "We'll have fewer high school students buying drugs. . . . It is too easy to buy controlled substances today. We can teach the effects of alcohol but not of controlled substances because we don't know their effects yet."[45] Minnette Doderer generally had an opinion on most topics, but here she was uncertain. She co-sponsored an amendment reflecting her indecision and her sense of humor, recommending age 43 for legal alcoholic beverage consumption. After jokingly suggesting that age 43 could be a compromise between those arguing between 18 and 19 for the legal age, she withdrew her amendment and supported 18. In 1972 the legal drinking age became 19.[46]

A year later, the legislature again debated the issue and lowered the age to 18. Then in 1976, raising the age back to 19 passed in the House but slowed down when it reached the Senate. The problem of 18-year-old high school students purchasing alcohol and sharing it with their younger friends had prompted the change. In the Senate the bill went to a burial subcommittee, of which Doderer was a member. She and others pointed out that some 19-year-olds attended high school, and she did not believe that raising the age would solve the problem. She explained: "People, especially school people, are looking for a simple answer to a difficult problem. . . . Schools are charged with teaching the hazards of smoking and drinking and they haven't succeeded. So they have come to us for a solution."[47]

Senators Elizabeth Miller (Republican, Marshalltown) and William Plymat (Republican, Urbandale) believed that raising the drinking age to 19 would limit, if not solve, the problem. The bill was deeply buried, but Miller sponsored and Plymat co-sponsored a procedural move to pull it out of its grave. They obtained the necessary 26 signatures of their Senate colleagues on a petition to require debate. The Democratic leadership then asked two of their partisans to withdraw their names from it, which they did. Miller insisted she had met the Senate's rules, but an ethics issue arose over removing the two signatures. According to a newspaper article, Miller did a "slow burn" over the Senate leadership's tactics.[48]

After the 1976 session ended without action, Miller again introduced the change in 1977. She continued to argue that high school students provided younger classmates with alcohol. She also cited problems with students attending class while intoxicated. Governor Robert Ray contributed his support for raising the age, and school administrators continued to plead for it. Responding to public and political pressure, the legislature raised the legal drinking age to 19 in 1978. The increase to 21 came when the federal government tied some of its financial assistance to the states to a higher age. Fearful of the financial loss, lawmakers finally agreed.[49]

The age at which children can make the decision to marry and their parents' roles in the decision pose similar questions on the point at which children can make adult decisions. The 1972 bill that allowed 19-year-olds to buy alcohol also granted other adult rights at 18, including marriage without parental approval. At age 16 girls, and at age 17 boys could marry with their parents' consent, but Doderer wanted to add a judge's approval as another requirement, and she wanted to remove pregnancy as a reason that a judge could allow adolescent marriages. She successfully argued that: "Society's solution to the problem of a girl who is pregnant is marriage, but this often turns out to be no solution at all." She believed that parents forced their young pregnant daughters to marry because they wanted "to avoid a scandal."[50]

Her proposal stated that a judge could authorize the marriage "only if he finds the underage party or parties capable of assuming the responsibilities of marriage and that the marriage will serve the best interest of the underage party or parties." It further stated: "Pregnancy alone does not establish that the proposed marriage is in the best interest of the underage party or parties." James Briles (Republican, Corning) disagreed, arguing that pregnancy was "a pretty good reason to get married," because "the baby needs a name."[51] Briles did not convince the chamber and Doderer's proposal passed. Doderer's goal was not to punish the pregnant child, but to protect her from an ill-fated marriage and her parents' fears of scandal.[52]

Doderer's desire to protect and not to punish pregnant girls provides one more example of the perspective that women regularly supported in state policies for children and their parents. Particularly regarding adults who abused children and juveniles who broke laws, women offered alternatives to the prevailing policies by emphasizing programs to help and to educate rather than to punish. They wanted solutions that might require more time and services but that also anticipated more satisfactory long-term results. To them, keeping families intact even though an abusive adult was involved was the goal and incarcerating the adult would not achieve that end without endangering the child when the adult returned home. Providing adults with parenting skills and with counselling increased the probabilities that the family could remain together and the child would be safe within it. In much the same way, the intent behind the juvenile justice laws was to remove children from the court system as much as possible and instead offer services that would help them learn the skills they needed to avoid further criminal activity. Women did not introduce the legislature to the problems of child abuse or juvenile justice; their role was to alter the premises of the policies and the state's responses to them. Without powerful lobbyists to plead children's causes, to explain the dilemmas, and to negotiate proposals, children's issues do not receive the same attention as economic development or agriculture. Lawmakers who made protecting children a legislative priority devoted one of their primary assets, time, to a group with no political power. These lawmakers could not expect votes or political action committee contributions to their next campaign for office from this constituency. Yet, they committed their political resources to representing the needs of children in ways that directly affected the children's welfare and safety.

CHAPTER 6

Rights: Expansion and Definition

The men who drafted the United States Constitution established high standards for the new government. According to the Preamble, they sought "to form a more perfect union, establish justice, insure domestic tranquility, provide for the common defense, promote the general welfare, and secure the blessings of Liberty" for themselves and their posterity. While they began the Preamble with the words "We, the people," in reality, these noble and honorable concepts became the preserve of free, white, male citizens. In the more than two hundred years since its acceptance, stateswomen and statesmen have attempted to remove the qualifying adjectives and to guarantee these glorious ideals for all citizens.

These patriots have endeavored to persuade the nation that a broad vision of the tenets incorporated within the U.S. Constitution benefits everyone. Even though women have not had the luxury of enjoying all of the protections provided under the Constitution, their labors to have themselves and others included under its umbrella may well be the clearest testimony to their belief in the concepts found in that document. One could argue that the methods women have used, educating, demonstrating, arguing, and often pleading with those holding power to include or exclude, rather than inciting insurrection and revolution, bear witness to their faith that the justice resident within this system of government will ultimately prevail.

Throughout the nineteenth-century abolitionist and suffrage movements and the twentieth-century civil rights and modern feminist movements, women's voices have been among those explaining the hazards of denying these rights to some citizens and describing the blessings that would accompany their expansion. These dynamic leaders have held mirrors before this nation and called on citizens to see the unflattering reflections. Sojourner Truth, Lucretia Mott, Elizabeth Cady Stanton, Carrie Chapman Catt, Rosa Parks, Gloria Steinem, Bella Abzug, Shirley Chisholm, and hundreds of other women have challenged Americans to grant the rights initially given to free, white males to those without freedom, not white, and not male. Through their actions and words, these women have helped change a nation. Other women have helped change a state.

Working for the causes of justice, and civil, equal, and privacy rights, Iowa women legislators have encouraged their colleagues to reject the death penalty, taught them the realities of racial discrimination, pleaded to be included in the state and federal constitutions, and strived to obtain and protect women's access to abortions. These emotion laden issues demanded all of the tenacity, procedural expertise, and experience the women could bring to the debates. Women have humbled themselves as they have recounted the indignities they and others experienced in efforts to describe the circumstances which compelled them to persevere in their quests. Despite decades of dedication to these ideals, the issues remain unresolved and the controversies continue.

The decision to raise and pursue a difficult topic may evolve out of a person's innate sense of justice. It does not require that one has been an experienced crusader, or even a particularly vocal member of the legislature. Such was the case with Katherine Zastrow (Democrat, Monroe), who entered the legislature in 1959, after running for her deceased husband's seat. During her three terms in office, her party was in the minority, but she emerged in 1963 as the leader in a cause so unlikely to succeed that initially it attracted far less attention than such a controversial issue would normally provoke. Zastrow wanted to end the death penalty in Iowa.

Zastrow insists that: "I'm not a sob sister by a long shot. I could argue some of the hard facts of life about things." At the same time, she believed that the death penalty "was no deterrent to killing people."[1] A white, comfortably middle-class woman, Zastrow also argued that the courts and juries inconsistently delivered the sentence, sarcastically calling capital punishment the "luxury of the poor."[2] She believed that economics sometimes determined who would live and who would die because wealthier people could pay lawyers' and other fees to appeal decisions which the poor could not. She raised the issue of race and the disproportionate number of African-Americans sentenced to death.[3]

At least one of the four women in the House at the time, Lenabelle Bock (Republican, Hancock), supported the death penalty. She acknowledged the idealism of those who opposed it, but believed that "you should have some practicality along with it." While Bock thought a different method of execution might be preferable to hanging, she maintained that protecting society needed to be a priority and asked: "How can we know whether a criminal is rehabilitated so that, beyond question, he will not kill again?"[4]

Other House members, both Democrats and Republicans, supported Zastrow's proposal in 1963 to end the death penalty, as did Governor Harold Hughes who had included it in his inaugural address. House leaders allowed the bill to proceed because they felt that enough members were interested in it to warrant using the chamber's to debate it. Zastrow knew the bill had little chance for passage, an opinion others shared, making the leadership's decision to debate the bill unusual, because legislative leaders avoid using the body's time to debate a bill that they expect to fail.[5]

Undeterred by the bill's assumed fate, Zastrow researched professional opinions on capital punishment and prepared her arguments. In casual conversations before the debate, Zastrow came to believe that: "Men seem not have the sense of values that I had. . . . They contrasted what it cost to keep a person [in prison], and my argument against that was that there's always a whole series of appeals if a person is given the death penalty . . . and those have to be paid for."[6] Yet, during the House debate, Charles Grassley (Republican, New Hampton) joined Zastrow, saying that "the injustice of our system is that some murderers are hanged and some are not."[7] Others called for the end of this "hangover from the dark ages," and argued: "It's time to stop sacrificing human lives on the altars of our own retributions."[8] Zastrow added: "The value of the individual is a fundamental tenet of our free society," and "each execution by the state is an implicit denial of this principle."[9] She characterized the death penalty as "a symbol of terror and of irreverence for life."[10]

When debate ended, the bill passed. According to political writer Frank Nye: "The Iowa House surprised itself . . . by voting to abolish the death penalty for all crimes except kidnapping."[11] The element of surprise entered when legislators changed their votes after listening to the debate. Only rarely does floor debate offer adequately compelling arguments to change votes.

After the House approved ending the death penalty except in the case of kidnapping, Zastrow tried to get the Senate to debate and pass the bill. There she confronted the opposition of Cliff Nolan (Republican, Johnson), who had been a partner in a farm with Zastrow's husband, Lawrence Falvey, and who chaired the committee assigned to handle the bill. When Nolan's opposition became clear, Zastrow arranged a public hearing to demonstrate the depth of antipathy to the punishment. Wardens from three federal penitentiaries and others spoke against the death penalty, but the effort failed. Nolan refused to let the bill out of committee, where it died.[12] After Zastrow retired from the legislature, Democratic majorities in the House and Senate abolished the death penalty in the state in 1965. Philosophical about not being present when the bill finally passed, she said: "I don't mind, particularly, who gets credit for things, if what you're interested in is accomplished."[13]

Zastrow's belief that the death penalty needed to be abolished in the state prompted her introduction and advocacy of the policy change, but it does not explain how a woman in the minority party could take center stage for such an important bill. Other women legislators before and after Zastrow have explained that one of their best legislative strategies for passing a controversial bill involved finding a male legislator to introduce it. The woman legislator would sign on the bill as a co-sponsor, but give the man first billing. They believed it gave the issue greater credibility and enhanced its chances for success. With all of the men, both Democrats and Republicans, who signed and spoke on the bill, Zastrow could have asked one of them for assistance. Maybe she did. One possibility may be that the subject was so controversial that none of the men wanted to take the risks involved with being the lead sponsor. As with Gladys Nelson and the colored oleomargarine debate (see Chapter 7), a majority of Zastrow's male colleagues ultimately supported the issue. In neither case, though, did men take the political risks involved. As a woman and a minority member, Zastrow may have had less to risk than her colleagues who were competing for committee chairs (she chaired Mines and Mining only in 1959), leadership positions, or other perks of office.

Women have also intensified the legislature's attention to civil rights. Many Iowans have grown up without ever meeting a person of color primarily because the minority population in the state is so small. People from rural areas may have had little or no contact with African-Americans or other minorities. For many people, the matters of racial discrimination and the onerous burdens it imposes often seem remote and foreign. Yet, discrimination in employment, housing, public accommodations, and restaurants have been a part of life for African-Americans in Iowa. At the same time, people of goodwill have risen to the challenge and attempted to construct legal barriers to discrimination.[14]

One woman in particular, June Franklin (Democrat, Des Moines), used her office as a bully pulpit to dare Iowans to face the racism in the state and to rectify its errors. The story of civil rights legislation, however, began before Franklin entered the legislature. In 1965, as Dr. Martin Luther King, Jr., marched from Selma to Montgomery, Alabama, Willie Glanton (Democrat, Polk) and her husband Judge Luther Glanton fasted in sympathy, and the Iowa General Assembly debated a civil rights bill. Supported by Governor Harold Hughes, the bill created a commission to investigate racial and religious discrimination in employment and public accommodations. The state already had the Governor's Commission on Human Rights, but it had no funding and no enforcement power. The proposed Civil Rights Commission would have both.[15]

One of the bill's sponsors, Gertrude Cohen (Democrat, Waterloo) explained: "The accepted approach now is an attempt to procure voluntary compliance through education, training, and arbitration."[16] If those attempts failed, the commission could hold formal hearings and court orders could result. Despite her sponsorship of the bill, Cohen believed it inadequate: "[I]t is my contention that this bill is too conciliatory in the area of housing, since it only provides for investigation of discriminatory practices in this area. It seems to me that a person's race, religion or national background must not be allowed to pre-determine the advantages or disadvantages he will receive in the social order."[17]

The legislature created the Civil Rights Commission that year and in the next session amended it. June Franklin and other legislators addressed the weakness identified by Cohen in 1965. An African-American, Franklin had experienced racial discrimination in housing and employment when she had moved to Des Moines in the 1950s. Unable to find adequate housing, she and her family had resigned themselves to renting an apartment in a converted house with five apartments and one bathroom. At the time, Des Moines had a fair housing law, but it lacked enforcement provisions, leaving African-Americans' housing options limited to the racial ghettos.[18]

The forecast for success with the bill was not good. Franklin remembers asking Governor Harold Hughes if he would sign it should it pass. After he read the bill, Hughes told her: "You'll never get this son of a bitch through the legislature," but if it got to his desk, he told her: "Hell, yeah, I'll sign it."[19]

Republican Tom Riley and Democrat John Ely, both from Cedar Rapids, started the controversial fair housing bill in the Senate. Despite opposition from the Iowa Realtors Association and other groups, the Senate passed the bill but added the requirement that a $500 bond had to accompany complaints filed with the Iowa Civil Rights Commission, asserting that this was necessary to avoid nuisance actions. From the Senate, the bill went to the House Industrial and Human Relations Committee which unanimously passed it out of committee, an action described as a tribute to Franklin and Cecil Reed (Republican, Cedar Rapids), another African-American. Both Reed and Franklin opposed the bond requirement, but a lobbyist had convinced Reed that he had the votes to defeat the bill should the bond requirement be removed.[20] While managing the bill during debate, Reed expressed his distaste for the bond, but urged passage of the bill. Franklin believed that the better strategy would have been to have legislators on record voting against a strong bill rather than voting for a weak bill. Reed later wrote: "It wasn't easy going up against her [Franklin], she was an effective legislator and highly respected."[21] In 1967, the bill passed with the bond provision and Franklin vowed to change the provision.[22]

In 1969, Franklin described the bond requirement as a "stumbling block," accepted "under the guise that it would stop harassment" from citizens who objected to the practices of realtors and apartment house owners. She argued that "there are no bonding companies which will write that kind of bond, so it means $500 cash."[23] She succeeded in removing the requirement that year.

A civil rights activist, Franklin extended her influence beyond the House chamber and into the community. In 1967 she challenged the Des Moines Association of Professional Firefighters (A.F.L.-C.I.O.) to assist African-American applicants seeking jobs with the Des Moines Fire Department. Even though the union had no direct role hiring firefighters, Franklin wanted it to find a way to help minority job candidates.[24] The next year she addressed the Des Moines City Council, pointing to several racial problems in the city and demanding action. She wanted the Des Moines City Council to sue the city's school board for the functional segregation of many black students. She also called on the city to end discriminatory hiring practices, citing the 97 African-American city employees out of the city's 1600 employees. She told the council that if changing hiring practices required "cleaning out the employment service, then clean it out. If it means a new city manager, then get a new city manager." She also told the city council that it needed to implement a penalty to enforce the city's fair housing code: "You should ask the white community to say to the white bigots who perpetrate racism and alarm the people, 'Either change your ways or get out of town.'"[25]

Franklin also addressed racism in public and higher education. She wrote to the Iowa Board of Regents, explaining that she would oppose its funding requests because of the racism on the Iowa State University campus. She explained: "I felt that so long as black students are treated as second-class citizens on the campus and in the city of Ames, and black female students are the subject of demoralizing epithets hurled by students as well as by residents of Ames, and housing and job discrimination are the fashion both on and off the campus, then I cannot vote for any appropriation to support racism." She referred to a group of African-American student athletes who had withdrawn from Iowa State University to protest the Iowa State Athletic Council's decision to delay hiring an African-American assistant football coach, adding: "The black athletes felt that a black coach on the football staff would alleviate the necessity of being subjected to the word 'nigger,' which is a prominent word in the vocabulary of the entire athletic staff."[26]

In another area of education, a Waterloo high school had been a center of racial unrest. A citizens' committee, a grand jury, and the state department of public instruction had investigated conditions at the school, but the school board had not acted on the recommendations. Franklin wanted the legislature to withhold state funds from the district until it responded to the racial problems, and she asked her legislative colleagues to visit Waterloo and "walk the black reservation" to see the problems for themselves.[27] Charles Grassley, House Education Committee Chair, did not think that the legislature had a role to play in a "purely local situation." Franklin felt that Grassley did not understand and that, if he would visit Waterloo, he might see it differently. She felt that rural legislators did not understand the problems of the cities because small communities did not have the same racial and poverty problems. At the same time, she praised the lawmakers for their willingness to listen and work with her, even though they believed their districts did not face the problems of racism.[28]

In addition to her calls for action from the white community, Franklin admonished the African-American community at a memorial tribute to Martin Luther King, Jr. Speaking to marchers assembled on the steps of the Iowa Statehouse, with rage in her voice, she said:

> It is time for the few black citizens of Iowa who sit on policy-making boards and commissions, or who hold jobs where they can help their black brothers to stop compromising, stop scratching, stop shuffling, stop grinning, stop accepting half a loaf, stop being handkerchief heads and Uncle Toms . . . to stand up and step forward and be counted. Let's pray together, march together, work together. Let us all be black together. Dr. King never accepted half a loaf. He was never an Uncle Tom. He walked in peace and fought for the dignity and equality of people. It is time for the black ministers of this city and state to stand up and step forward and show leadership—start leading our people into the promised land.[29]

Refusing to use euphemisms, and discarding undue tact or diplomacy, Franklin described the racism she saw and confronted policymakers and community leaders with it. Franklin's pleas, cries, and demands for justice called on all citizens to use their power to end racial discrimination in the state. One of only two African-American women who have served in the Iowa General Assembly, Franklin clearly and persuasively spoke of the racial issues to a predominantly white male audience in the legislature. As an antagonist who repeatedly raised racial issues, and as a woman and an African-American, Franklin could have relegated herself to the fringes of legislative politics, a voice in the wilderness, a nuisance without credibility. But that was not the case. Franklin won election to minority whip, evidence of the respect her partisans held for her and of her inclusion in the decision-making process at important levels.

The problems of racial discrimination continue to receive sporadic attention from the legislature as specific issues appear. For example, in 1984, after an African-American man was refused admission to a bowling banquet at the Moose Lodge in Cedar Rapids, Minnette Doderer (Democrat, Iowa City) and Phil Brammer (Democrat, Cedar Rapids) worked to outlaw private clubs' discriminating on the basis of race, age, religion, or sex. If the club had liquor licenses or sales tax permits, under their proposal the person could file a complaint with the Iowa Civil Rights Commission.[30] Doderer explained: "What we are saying is if the government gives you a license, then you should open up to the public."[31] The new policy did not limit private clubs' discriminatory practices regarding membership, but it provided that when those clubs allowed non-members to use it and charged a fee, they could no longer discriminate.[32]

With the emergence of the modern feminist movement in the 1960s, another demand for equality has been made and energetically opposed. Many women came to believe that one answer to gaining women's social, economic, and political equality rested in the Equal Rights Amendment. After lingering in Congress for almost fifty years, the Equal Rights Amendment (ERA) gained congressional approval on March 22, 1972, and went to the states for ratification.[33]

In the last days of the 1972 legislative session, Minnette Doderer, Charlene Conklin (Republican, Waterloo), and Joan Lipsky coordinated efforts to ratify the ERA passed by Congress only one day earlier. In order for the legislature to consider the resolution to ratify, the women had to obtain approval to suspend the rules in each chamber, a difficult task when legislators have their sights set on ending the session and going home.

The drama began on Thursday, March 23, in the Senate Constitutional Amendments Committee where an early obstacle appeared: professional lobbyists had organized to defeat it. The lobbyists' success in convincing committee members to oppose ratification led supporters to abandon it for the session, rather than have Iowa become the first state to reject the amendment. The next morning, however, the professional lobbyists had retreated from the issue as the story of their involvement circulated through the legislature. Doderer described the opponents as being "scared off," implying that the lobbying had been inappropriate.[34] Also according to Doderer, Lieutenant Governor Roger Jepsen "did a backroom thing and got enough votes" to get the bill through the committee.[35]

With the professional lobbyists silenced, women who supported the ERA and who had special relationships with legislators began lobbying. Several legislators' wives had gone to the Statehouse to witness the last day of the session and became advocates for passing the ERA by lobbying their husbands. Rudy Van Drie's (Republican, Ames) wife asked Joan Lipsky to convince Van Drie to support the amendment, which he did on final passage, although he had voted against it earlier. Another group of women, generally silent and relatively invisible, spoke out. Legislative secretaries lobbied and bargained with their bosses for passage.[36]

During debate, Doderer told the Senate: "I know you want to protect us from equal pay, from equal educational opportunities, from every equality you have and we want."[37] She urged them to take the historic opportunity to be among the first states to ratify the amendment. Senate opponents to ratification, however, wanted time to study and consider the amendment. Eugene Hill (Democrat, Newton) told the chamber: "I don't know if I'm for or against this resolution. I haven't discussed it with my wife."[38] Another senator asked Doderer if the Equal Rights Amendment would allow Hill to be a Playboy bunny. Doderer responded that Hill would have the "same rights that a woman his age has."[39] Whether or not women could be drafted also became an issue, but James Schaben (Democrat, Dunlap) told the assembly: "If you draft both and they're going to live in the same bunks and building, you won't need the draft anymore—a rush of volunteers will come forward."[40] The resolution passed the senate with only Hill voting against it.

In the House, Richard Radl (Democrat, Lisbon) argued against ratification on the basis that the world's problems had been caused by "female Amazons" even though he characterized most women as kind and "very lovable." Radl explained: "The present furor over the status of women is part of the fractured insanity which is now surging through the civilized world. When the dust settles, females will still be chips out of Eve who led, not followed Adam down the primrose trail."[41]

Charles Grassley (Republican, New Hartford) asked the legislature to delay debate to allow time for study and research. He said it would be all right if Iowa were the thirty-eighth state to ratify the amendment, instead of the fourth.[42] He told the House: "This has been before the congress for 50 years and it has been before the Iowa legislature only 24 hours." Lipsky replied that "Equal rights means equal rights for all citizens. It is a concept we all believe in. It is nothing new."[43] Despite his request for delay, Grassley voted for ratification, explaining: "If I was getting out of politics, I'd have voted against it."[44]

Hallie Sargisson (Democrat, Salix) first voted against the resolution but then changed her vote to yes. The only woman who voted against the resolution, Elizabeth Miller (Republican, Marshalltown) issued a statement: "Mrs. Sargisson went and changed her vote because she was afraid she might lose the women's vote. I'm not afraid at all of that. I don't think the average woman really wants this thing."[45] Miller expressed concerns that other opponents had identified: drafting women and sharing toilets.

Among several factors that contributed to Iowa's speedy ratification of the amendment was the leadership provided by Doderer and Lipsky. The two women had served several terms in the legislature and both had highly developed political skills. In addition, the pressure to adjourn combined with the opportunity to be among the first states to ratify created excitement and an intensity to act. The women who supported ratification had worked together in other efforts and had a network already in place to respond to ratification, while opponents had not organized or developed their counter arguments. Doderer also believed that her male colleagues did not want to be "swept away by history and they wanted to be on the winning side."[46]

By 1975 the situation had changed. ERA opponents had developed their arguments, organized their allies, and fashioned their strategies. Eugene Hill reopened the debate when he announced that he planned to file a resolution to rescind ratification of the ERA. Reading from material prepared by anti-ERA leaders, he described his reasons for rescission, which included vague and imprecise language, preservation of the family, women's desire to choose their own lifestyles, and the haste with which Iowa had ratified. Elizabeth Shaw (Republican, Davenport) responded by pointing to the ERA's importance with a personal example of discrimination. Some time earlier, she had applied for and been denied a credit card in her own name. It was only after her status of state senator was revealed did she receive the card. Jo Ann Orr (Democrat, Grinnell) told the chamber that while no one disputed equal pay for equal work, women had been "patient too long for their own good." She expressed disappointment that "the women of Jasper County" had not talked to their "deeply prejudiced senator [Eugene Hill] about ERA."[47] Senate President Pro Tempore Doderer said she would assign the resolution to a committee other than Hill's and bury it.

With the rescission battle going on, Philip Hill (Republican, Des Moines) introduced a resolution for a state ERA. Explained Hill: "It occurred to me that in the event the federal ERA is not adopted, we should have something ready to go in Iowa. I would prefer to have the federal one passed. This would be simpler. We would only have to amend one Constitution instead of 50. But it appears it might not make it."[48] He also introduced it to serve notice that the legislature did not intend to rescind its ratification of the federal ERA. Ultimately, he was correct and the federal ERA failed to obtain ratification from the required thirty-eight states.

Philip Hill's efforts to serve notice did not deter his colleague Eugene Hill. In March 1977, rescission supporters filled the Senate gallery to offer Eugene Hill support as he filed the rescission resolution. To announce their presence ERA opponents delivered loaves of bread to every senator's desk, including a note: "Vote for the Homemaker. Rescind the ERA." Eugene Hill called the day the legislature had ratified the federal amendment "a black day," adding that women had reason to be concerned about the amendment because it would change their lives. Elizabeth Miller (Republican, Marshalltown) drew applause from the gallery when she said she voted against the ERA and had been re-elected twice since. Doderer "responded emotionally" to the resolution, refuting allegations that the ERA would force men and women to share restrooms and that career women had abandoned their families.[49]

After weeks of discussion, the Senate agreed to hold a public hearing on rescission but then delayed it until the next January.[50] In response to the delay, pro- and anti-ERA groups planned rallies, one on each side of the Statehouse. Speaking for Stop ERA, Donna LePorte said:

> We have consistently asked for the right to be heard on this important proposed amendment to the United States Constitution, and our requests have been consistently denied. We hope that the Judiciary Committee of the Senate will start behaving in a responsible manner and grant us what should certainly be the right of all Americans, a chance to speak our opinion on a proposed amendment which would affect all our lives.[51]

Illinois lawyer Phyllis Schlafly told the anti-ERA forces that women "are the most privileged class of people who ever lived on the face of the earth."[52] She maintained that laws already gave women equal pay and equal educational opportunity but the ERA would allow men to abandon their wives, make women subject to the draft, and eliminate single sex schools and colleges.

On the pro-ERA side, Rosa Cunningham, who had been a suffragette, told supporters to question candidates about their stands on equal rights for women: "Do not take any weasel words about it, either. Get a flat yes or no. Tell those who say no, that means a no vote. That is your weapon." When Doderer spoke, supporters serenaded her with "Happy Birthday to You," and sent her bouquets of yellow roses. Doderer told the group: "I am not fighting for my right to be a woman. That happened to me the day I was born. I am fighting for my right to be included in the Constitution of my country."[53] Also speaking at the rally, Joan Lipsky said: "There can be no security, no value in perpetuating a system of discrimination against one entire sex and that ultimately is the real and only issue of ERA."[54]

The next year, with an Iowa ERA stalled in the Senate, Terry Dyrland (Democrat, Elkader) introduced another version of it in the House. Dyrland used language based on the federal ERA, and the House quickly took it up. During the debate Terry Branstad (Republican, Lake Mills) succeeded in adding an amendment to the resolution that stated that the ERA did not alter the state's laws prohibiting homosexuality and same-sex marriages. Branstad's amendment was only one of twenty-two amendments filed on the resolution in attempts to kill it. The bill stalled.[55]

A couple of weeks later, John Brunow (Democrat, Centerville) introduced a new version of the amendment, one which simply added the words "and women" to Article One, Section One of the Iowa Constitution.

Brunow's version read: "All men and women are, by nature, free and equal, and have certain inalienable rights—among which are those of enjoying and defending life and liberty, acquiring, possessing and protecting property, and pursuing and obtaining safety and happiness." It also added: "Neither the state nor any of its political subdivisions shall, on the basis of gender, deny or restrict the equality of rights under the law."

During the hours of debate on those words, emotions ran high. Two legislators, both men, required a third to keep them apart after one went storming to the other's desk. According to one newspaper report, Norman Jesse (Democrat, Des Moines) used oratory so compelling that it "halt[ed] the milling about that characterizes legislative debate." He accused opponents of "appealing to all that is worst in society" and of posturing in an election year.[56] The House passed the ERA 70-25. Its supporters were elated. Mary O'Halloran believed that the level of support would push the Senate into considering the resolution and pointed to another factor in the passage of the ERA: "I can't forget that it was a majority of men who passed the ERA tonight."[57] At the time 88 men and 12 women served in the House. In the spirit of recognizing men's contributions to the ERA's passage, Doderer, remembering the loaves of commercially baked bread distributed by anti-ERA women the year before, presented Terry Dyrland with a 28-inch loaf of bread she had baked, and credited Dyrland's labors with helping gain the House's approval of the state ERA.[58]

The Senate still had to act on the amendment, and it finally held a hearing on the ERA, but it was not the one promised the year before. The Judiciary Committee held a hearing on passing the state ERA, not one on rescinding the state's ratification of the federal ERA. The more than 200 people who spoke at the hearing included a Davenport minister who testified that "God does not support the ERA." Another person dismissed the ERA as a symbol.[59]

On March 7, 1978, the ERA subcommittee of the Senate Judiciary Committee added an amendment to the House version of the resolution: "It is declared to be the intent of the Legislature that a classification on the basis of gender shall not be held to deny or restrict equality of rights if it can be established that such a classification was necessary to accomplish a compelling state interest."[60] The Judiciary Committee later removed the intent section.

Having voted against ratifying the federal ERA and having led the effort to rescind its ratification, Eugene Hill prepared to fight the state ERA. Hill explained his opposition: "Those women [ERA opponents] fear the American way of life will be changed and disrupted. They feel that they can no longer remain in the home to care and nurture their families but must leave home to support their families if the ERA is adopted."[61] He submitted several amendments with the hope of defeating the resolution, but Lieutenant Governor Art Neu ruled three of them out of order and the Senate defeated the fourth. The Senate approved the intent language proposed by the subcommittee and rejected by the Judiciary Committee.

The passage of the intent language provoked anger among men and women senators. James Redmond (Democrat, Cedar Rapids) and Doderer attacked their party's leaders who supported the intent language. Calling their votes appalling, Redmond heatedly criticized the leadership for supporting an amendment that confused the issue. Doderer cited her fourteen years in the legislature and said that the legislature had not included intent language on any constitutional amendments in that time. The Senate passed the Iowa ERA with the intent language intact. A few days later, the House approved the intent language and the resolution.[62]

With legislative approval obtained in 1978, the amendment still faced two major hurdles before it could be included in the state's constitution. In Iowa, two general assemblies must approve amendments, allowing an election between the two occasions on which it is passed. Then it is placed on the ballot for voter approval during the next general election. In sharp contrast to the battles in 1978, the resolution passed the House and Senate easily in 1979. The next year, however, voters defeated the constitutional amendment at the ballot box. Phyllis Schlafly and her supporters had inundated the state with television advertisements depicting gay rights parades and suggesting direct ties between abortion rights and equal rights. Observers believed that the homophobia, in particular, provoked by the ads led to the amendment's defeat.

The legislative success of the state ERA may have resulted in large part from the persuasive and political abilities of its supporters in the chambers. Another factor surely involved the many citizens outside of the legislature who demonstrated their support by lobbying legislators and participating in the Statehouse rally. Moreover, when the legislature approved the state amendment, it did not become law because it still required voter approval. This last step provided legislators with an escape when confronted with anti-ERA voters. Lawmakers could explain that while they did not necessarily support women's equality, they believed that a popular vote best served the state's interests.

When Iowa ratified the federal ERA, the decision took place during a time of visible and widespread support for the concepts it represented. While opponents existed, they did not have the publicity that supporters had attracted and developed. In response to congressional passage of it and some states' speedy ratification, opponents identified and recruited their allies in order to stop it. Phyllis Schlafly effectively articulated arguments opposing constitutional guarantees of legal equality for women and equally effectively organized women against it. She appealed to women's fears of abandonment, military service, and sharing toilet facilities with men, as well as Americans' homophobia. By 1977 Schlafly had brought her skills and arguments to Iowa, first to unsuccessfully demand rescission of the federal amendment and later to successfully oppose the state amendment.

In 1990, Doderer again attempted to include women in the Iowa Constitution. The resolution successfully made its way through the legislature the required two times. Opponents led by Phyllis Schlafly used essentially the same arguments they had used to fight the federal amendment and the 1980 state amendment. Proponents did not articulate their cause adequately, nor did they effectively rebut Schlafly's arguments. In 1992, voters again refused to extend to women the protections guaranteed to men.

One of the issues that has entered debates on women's equality is abortion. For many Americans the word provokes visceral responses. Those who identify themselves as pro-life believe abortion is murder. For those who identify themselves as pro-choice, abortion restrictions provoke images of women suffering in back alleys from illegal and unsafe procedures that can result in physical damage to the mother and sometimes death. On both sides of the abortion debate, citizens previously uninvolved in politics have become outspoken advocates of one position or the other.

Abortion became a highly visible issue in Iowa politics in 1967, when John Ely (Democrat, Cedar Rapids) introduced a bill to change Iowa's abortion laws. At that time, Iowa law allowed abortions only to save the life of the mother. Ely's bill would have allowed abortions when the pregnancy posed grave mental or physical risks to the mother, the fetus had severe mental or physical defects, or when pregnancy resulted from rape, incest, or other felonious intercourse. The Iowa Society of Obstetricians and Gynecologists, the Iowa Civil Liberties Union, and Iowa Methodist Hospital in Des Moines supported Ely's bill.[63]

Doctors and hospitals wanted the change because they had to refuse the procedure to women who faced health risks by continuing their pregnancies. Because the pregnant women probably would not die, the law required them to carry the fetus to term, regardless of other health implications. One physician explained that his support for the bill resulted from seeing the difficulties some women faced with problem pregnancies. Another physician said that doctors openly consulted each other about performing abortions which did not meet the state standard of life of the mother, but then performed the procedure because they felt it justified. Lawyers familiar with rape and incest cases pointed out that the offender might go to prison, but would eventually be released, while the victim would bear the effects of the crime for the rest of her life. Doctors, hospitals, and lawyers struggled with the health and ethical issues involved with these pregnancies, sending women who sought their help back and forth to each other. But a pregnant woman had few options in the state, she could continue the pregnancy or obtain an illegal abortion. If she was wealthy enough, she could seek an abortion outside the state or country.[64]

Some conservative Iowa politicians in the 1960s and 1970s also wanted to change the abortion laws to make the procedure legal and more available. They saw abortions as a way to limit government spending for children who would need welfare programs. That conservative position changed when the right-to-life movement became a powerful force within conservative coalitions.[65]

When Governor Robert D. Ray advocated changing Iowa's abortion law to "protect a mother's health, prevent the birth of a defective child or end a pregnancy caused by rape or incest" in his 1969 inaugural address, pressure for changing the law increased.[66] The Iowa Medical Society and the Iowa Council of Churches (composed of twelve Protestant denominations) endorsed his proposal. The conditions had been accepted by other states, but some legislators expressed opposition to the health provision because of its breadth.[67]

The women in the legislature expressed varying levels of support for Ray's proposal. Minnette Doderer (Democrat, Iowa City) expressed the greatest support and articulated the rationale that she would use for almost three decades: as a medical procedure, the decision to continue or to terminate the pregnancy belonged with the woman and her physician. She compared it to an appendectomy, saying she did not need the General Assembly's permission for that operation. Other legislators approached the topic more cautiously. Elizabeth Shaw (Republican, Davenport) felt that reasons probably existed for abortions, but she did not want the decision made casually. Joan Lipsky (Republican, Cedar Rapids) believed that rape or a deformed fetus justified abortions, but questioned other reasons.

Charlene Conklin (Republican, Waterloo) did not believe that an unwanted pregnancy justified an abortion. Elizabeth Miller (Republican, Marshalltown) wanted the laws eased because of the number of illegal abortions performed in the state. June Franklin (Democrat, Des Moines) supported changes for rape, incest, and a deformed fetus. The variety of opinions expressed by women legislators reflected the range that also existed among their male colleagues and the public.[68]

Doderer took up the pro-choice standard in the Senate, beginning her career as one of the legislature's leaders to change the state's law. She came to the issue almost by accident; a committee chair assigned her to the bill's subcommittee. She said she did not know how she felt about abortion but knew that the state should not make the decision for a woman. Despite some religious denominations' approval of the changes, Doderer identified the major opponents as religious groups, primarily the Roman Catholic Church. She argued that they espoused the position that the woman had sinned and must suffer for it by bearing the child.[69]

The mother of two, Doderer had found childbearing a joy that should not be forced on women as punishment. Citizens responded to Doderer's position by sending her letters in which some writers called her a murderer and others encouraged her to continue her crusade. Her daughter Kay, who served as her legislative secretary, destroyed the most malevolent of the letters before her mother saw them. Charlene Conklin, who also supported fewer restrictions, received so many threatening letters and phone calls that her family became alarmed for her safety and they discussed the problem with law enforcement officials. Doderer and Conklin were not alone in receiving mail; other senators reported receiving more correspondence on abortion than on any other subject.[70]

Before the Senate debated the abortion bill, the chamber convened as a committee of the whole to allow proponents and opponents the opportunity to present their positions on it. In emotional presentations those on both sides of the issue laid out their views. An opponent equated abortion with execution and stated that allowing abortions would not solve poverty, social, or psychological problems.[71] One of the bill's supporters, however, offended legislators with his attack on the Roman Catholic Church. His description of that denomination's position as "archaic, barbarian ecclesiastical law imposed by a tyrannical hierarchy" did not win votes.[72] Instead, he was blamed for the bill's defeat.[73]

During debate, Joseph Coleman (Democrat, Clare) told the Senate that "under this bill we will put to death millions of children who will never have a chance."[74] Many opponents focused their arguments on the mental health provision, claiming that it would allow women to obtain abortions for any reason. Doderer countered that assuming all women would get abortions did them an injustice, and she asked lawmakers to imagine themselves in the woman's position.

After the bill's defeat in the Senate, Doderer pledged that abortion rights supporters would return to the legislature until women's demands for help had been answered. She also changed her position on the bill, no longer supporting the conditions in the Ray proposal. Instead she advocated total repeal of any limits on women's access to legal abortions. She continued to argue that abortion posed a medical problem not a political problem.[75]

Charlene Conklin introduced a bill that, like Doderer's position, would end state involvement in deciding limits on abortion. Conklin's only restriction would be that a licensed physician perform the procedure.[76] The mother of five children and the wife of a physician, she had also come to believe that abortion should be treated like any other medical need, that the woman and her physician should make the decision, and that it was not a decision for the legislature to make. She wanted the changes to protect women seeking abortions from injury and death, and she hoped that the bill would end the practices of what she called "quack abortionists."[77] She pointed out that anyone, whether a physician or not, could perform abortions with the law then in effect. The only restriction was that the abortion be performed to save the life of the mother. She did not expect the legislature to debate the bill because the anticipated lengthy and emotional debate did not fit in the leadership's plans for an early adjournment. In addition, the House leadership did not think that the bill would pass and did not want to spend the time debating a doomed bill. Conklin acknowledged those problems but noted that there was always another session.

The Senate Social Services Committee did hold a public hearing on Conklin's bill that year. One woman told the committee: "Do not fertilize Iowa with precious babies' bodies instead of good old manure."[78] Supporters and opponents of Conklin's bill raised many of the issues raised in other forums: the tragedy of unwanted children and the sanctity of human life. With the help of Senate Social Services Committee Chairman Ernest Kosek (Republican, Cedar Rapids), Conklin's bill cleared the committee and was placed on the Senate debate calendar, but it progressed no further.[79]

Abortion rights advocates began using two new arguments. They pointed to a group of clergymen that identified legal sources for abortions out of the state and country. This referral service became a counterpoint to the moral issues raised by and the opposition of the Roman Catholic Church. Supporters also relied on a number of court decisions to augment their reasons for change. Courts had found unconstitutional abortion laws that allowed the procedure only to save the life of the mother. Wisconsin, Texas, and the District of Columbia all had laws similar to Iowa's, and all had been rejected by the courts, thereby leaving the states with no restrictions. Charlene Conklin argued that the similarity between the laws in those jurisdictions and Iowa's laws could lead to a court challenge with the probability that Iowa's law would also be declared unconstitutional, and Iowa would be left with no limits on abortion.[80]

The House Judiciary Committee approved an abortion bill in 1971 that had several provisions. It allowed abortions only in the first twenty weeks of the pregnancy, except to save the life of the mother, required that abortions performed in the twelfth through twentieth weeks had to be done in hospitals, required sixty days of residency, and prohibited advertising abortion services. When the House debated the changes, June Franklin (Democrat, Des Moines) accomplished what few have done, she changed votes with her comments and defeated the bill. In her pleas against changing the abortion laws, Franklin raised racial, social, and economic issues. With passionate words, she declared that human life had never been a top priority in America but that property had. She pointed to the treatment of Native Americans and the enslavement and lynching of African-Americans as evidence. She criticized the expenditures for sending men to the moon while hungry people lived in the country. She characterized as phony the arguments that changing the abortion law benefited African-Americans and poor women, and she insisted that those groups were threatened by overzealous social workers who might force them to have abortions. With her powerful appeal, she convinced others to vote against the bill, and it was defeated. (See Appendix B.)[81]

Joan Lipsky and Hallie Sargisson (Democrat, Salix) voted against the bill. Sonja Egenes (Republican, Story City), Lillian McElroy (Republican, Percival), Elizabeth Miller (Republican, Marshalltown), and Elizabeth Shaw (Republican, Davenport) supported it. In a parliamentary move known as a double barrel, an opponent filed a successful motion to reconsider and to lay the bill on the table. The motion had the effect of killing the bill for the session, unless two-thirds of the House voted to bring it up for debate.[82]

In January 1973 the United States Supreme Court decided in *Roe v. Wade* that a right to privacy existed and that the right included women making their own choices between continuing and ending a pregnancy. The decision did not end the debate in Iowa or in the nation; instead it signaled the beginning of new battles. *Roe v. Wade* rendered Iowa's statute unconstitutional, and the legislature turned its attention to writing a constitutional law on abortion.

Minnette Doderer, John Murray (Democrat, Ames), and George Milligan (Republican, Des Moines) worked for three weeks to develop a new state policy on early termination of pregnancies, allowing abortions during the first twenty-four weeks of pregnancy. To everyone's surprise, Doderer voted against the bill, saying: "This is just a bad bill. I think we ought to just let the Supreme Court ruling be in effect in the next year, see how it works and then put our own restrictions on abortion next session. We have the law on our side, so why get into a big squabble?"[83] She insisted that leaving Iowa open for abortions was not her motive. The bill died, leaving Iowa with no restrictions on abortions.

Finding themselves unable to convince the legislature to limit the conditions under which a woman could obtain the procedure, opponents tried other approaches. In 1975 the Senate passed a feticide amendment to a criminal code revision, which made it a crime to intentionally kill a fetus of twenty weeks or more that is aborted alive or to allow it to die if it shows signs of life. Doderer called it a return to "the dark ages" for women.[84] When the House took up the bill the next year, Julia Gentleman (Republican, Des Moines) attempted to remove the provision, arguing that the killing of any living person constituted murder, which the code covered. Willis Junker (Republican, Sioux City) argued successfully to keep the provision in the code. He told the House: "If we take it out, we provide for some snap decision on the part of a woman who reaches her third trimester and decides she does not want that child."[85] Third trimester abortions remained illegal in Iowa.

In 1974 Iowans for Life had proposed and George Kinley (Democrat, Des Moines) had filed a bill to allow hospitals and medical personnel to refuse to perform abortions. Doderer protested that the bill would effectively end women's access to abortions in Iowa.[86] The next year senators passed a conscience clause bill to protect a nurse or doctor who refused to perform or assist in abortions; Doderer protested: "We have ordained a woman's body can be labeled a public utility and the legislature is in the process of regulating that utility." She asked: "Where else can a person refuse to perform his job and get away with it? Why should the situation be different in a hospital than any other kind of employment?"[87]

The House continued to work on the conscience clause bill in 1976. The Iowa Women's Political Caucus (IWPC) wanted to amend it by including a provision for saving the life of the mother and to create a liability if a hospital or its employees refused to help with the procedure. Julia Gentleman (Republican, Des Moines) offered the amendment in committee, but it lost. When the IWPC and Doderer huddled to develop strategy, the group decided it could not lobby on its own amendment because the IWPC steering committee had not taken a position on it. Doderer demanded: "You mean we have a difference within the Women's Political Caucus on saving a woman's life? Because, if we do have a difference on that, how in the heck can we ask male legislators to put their jobs on the line to back us?"[88] When the House debated the exception to the conscience clause, Gentleman argued that "the lives of thousands of mothers are at stake," but the amendment lost and the bill passed that year.[89]

After a series of U.S. Supreme Court decisions that allowed states to refuse public funding for abortions, some Iowa legislators wanted to do the same. Governor Robert Ray, however, wanted the state to continue paying for poor women's abortions.[90] When the Senate debated the issue, Doderer asked: "The question is, do the 12-year-olds want children? To suggest that they should know better than to get pregnant is to ignore the problem. Of course they should."[91] Elizabeth Miller (Republican, Marshalltown) asked: "Shouldn't poor women have the same right as women of means? I can't understand this—you talk here all the time of helping the poor. Especially you Democrats, you're known for that [and] you don't want to help them."[92] The effort to maintain full Medicaid abortion funding lost. The legislature decided to limit Medicaid funded abortions to those occurring under the rape, incest, and the life of the mother umbrella.[93]

The successful campaigns for the feticide provision, the conscience clause, and the restriction of Medicaid funding for poor women limited access to abortions. Women who could pay for the procedure and could afford to travel continued to have the right to decide their own futures. Without making the procedure illegal, the legislature had effectively narrowed the classes of women who could exercise the right to choice established in *Roe v. Wade*. The pro-life movement had not achieved its goal of eliminating the procedure as a legal medical option because the Supreme Court decision had placed that out of reach. But the pro-lifers had restricted accessibility and demonstrated their power and influence.

In 1979 pro-life supporters wanted the Iowa legislature to send a request to Congress for a pro-life amendment to the U.S. Constitution. In light of the successes their candidates had enjoyed during the 1978 primary and general elections, they had reason to believe that their priorities would receive favorable attention from the legislature. Instead, Speaker of the House Floyd Millen assigned the resolution to the Human Resources Committee, chaired by Betty Jean Clark (Republican, Rockwell), a pro-choice leader in the House. She used her prerogative as committee chair to assign the bill to a burial committee of three pro-choice legislators. The speaker had another option, the resolution could have gone to the Judiciary Committee, chaired by Nancy Shimanek Boyd (Republican, Monticello) who likely would have assigned the resolution to a more favorable subcommittee. Observers believed Millen's decision indicated that he did not want abortion debated.[94]

During the next session, pro-life advocates began to work on another opportunity to restrict abortion funding in the state. In 1981, the legislature took up the issue of state funding for abortions at the University of Iowa Hospitals and Clinics (UIHC), debating whether or not the state indigent patient fund should continue to pay for abortions performed at the Early Termination of Pregnancy (ETP) Clinic.[95]

The Senate decided to limit abortion funding at UIHC to saving the life of the mother and to prohibit the use of state funds to support the ETP clinic as part of a multi-faceted appropriations bill. In a series of dramatic events, the final outcome took shape as the House debated the bill. The chamber had begun work on the appropriations bill and then adjourned for lunch. While the House generally resumed work reasonably close to the appointed time, it usually began a few minutes late. On this day, however, the Speaker gaveled the House back into its afternoon session promptly, even though not all of the members had returned. Doderer had prepared an amendment to strike the Senate restrictions and it came up as the first business of the afternoon. With only a few minutes of debate, the House passed it 46-42. Enough of the amendment's supporters had returned to vote for it, while too few opponents had returned to engage the House in a more comprehensive debate and defeat it.[96]

The House went on to consider other amendments to the bill, but returned to abortion when Douglas Smalley (Republican, Des Moines) brought up his amendment to allow state funds to be used only in cases where the woman's life was endangered, the fetus was deformed, or the pregnancy resulted from rape or incest. Smalley believed he offered a compromise, but others felt that the House had already decided on the issue. Some like Doderer pleaded with House colleagues to resist the amendment and not send poor women "back to butchers." She begged: "Don't, don't make this mistake today."[97] Jean Lloyd-Jones argued that poor women would abort themselves and risk their chances for future pregnancies.[98] After the

House limited abortions at the ETP Clinic to rape, incest, life of the mother, or a deformed or retarded fetus, Doderer accused her opponents of being against women, adding "they do not like women generally."[99] A few days later, Doderer attempted to get Medicaid funding for abortions expanded to include a list of diseases such as diabetes, cancer, sickle cell anemia, renal disease, and others, but the House rejected it.[100]

In the years since, abortion opponents have made other proposals to create obstacles for women seeking to end their pregnancies. Among them are parental notification and statistical reporting. Parental notification requires women under 18 years of age to obtain a signed statement from their parents or guardians acknowledging that they know their daughter or dependent intends to obtain an abortion. After more than a decade without an abortion debate in the General Assembly, the House debated parental notification in 1994. Dan Boddicker (Republican, Tipton), who managed the bill, said it was "not a pro-life or a pro-choice bill. This bill merely states that if an abortion is performed on a minor, the parents have a right to know."[101] Rick Dickinson (Democrat, Sabula) said that bill was more than "parental notification. I see it as parental obligation." In an emotional plea, Doderer countered: "In this bill there is no love for this little girl. None. It is a vindictive, punitive, anti-female bill. . . . Why don't you control your sons? Why don't you put that in a bill?"[102] The bill included a judicial bypass provision which would allow a girl to appeal to the courts to decide if she was mature enough to make the decision, as well as other exceptions. Dorothy Carpenter (Republican, West Des Moines) expressed her reservations about the bypass provision: "What I believe will happen is the girls least able to care for a child will be least able to find their way through this difficult waiver process . . . and will keep their babies."[103] The bill passed 63 to 35 after nine hours of debate. When the bill went to the Senate, it was assigned to a committee chaired by Elaine Szymoniak (Democrat, Des Moines), who buried it for the rest of the session.

The other measure right-to-life supporters want, statistical reporting, requires physicians and facilities performing abortions to collect data and submit it to the state. Doderer has accused proponents of statistical reporting of wanting to "stamp the woman with a scarlet letter. A woman has 'sinned' and we want a report on it."[104] The Iowa General Assembly has repeatedly buried it in committee.

Some legislators have speculated that parental notification and statistical reporting have adequate appeal to win approval. During House Speaker Don Avenson's (Democrat, Oelwein) eight years (1983-1990) in that position, he consistently buried the bills in unfriendly committees. Bob Arnould (Democrat, Davenport), who followed Avenson in the Speaker's chair (1991-1992), provided the same service for his pro-choice colleagues. These two men used their position to prevent debate on these issues. It was only after Republicans gained the majority in the House that a bill on parental notification was debated.

Keeping statistical reporting and parental notification out of the *Code of Iowa* have been the only identified victories of the pro-choice movement in the state. Efforts to change the state's abortion policy before *Roe v. Wade* in 1973 failed despite determined and organized struggles to allow women greater access to the medical procedure. Even Governor Robert Ray, a moderate Republican who had great and long-lasting appeal to voters, could not influence enough legislators to change the policy or to maintain full Medicaid funding. The zeal and the fervor demonstrated by the pro-life movement has not been matched by those who believe in choice.

Since *Roe v. Wade*, pro-life advocates have won several significant battles in Iowa. The conscience clause, the feticide provision, and limits on Medicaid and indigent funding for abortions have limited women's access to abortions. Attempts to expand the reasons for allowing poor women to obtain abortions paid by these tax-supported programs have failed. The U.S. Supreme Court, however, has also accepted parental notification and statistical reporting as constitutional limits on abortion. While Avenson and Arnould used their power to halt the progress of those proposals, legislators have other tools which could be used to circumvent the committee process. Two possibilities could explain the legislature's resistance to the changes. Most legislators dislike debating the issue of abortion in any form. On this emotional issue, anger quickly rises to the top in heated exchanges that accompany abortion debates. In addition, moderate legislators who are not crusaders on either side of the issue may be satisfied with the status quo. The limits already established may have contented this center group as being fair and representing public wishes, and they see no reason to create additional requirements.

The twenty-five year abortion debate, however, has left neither side pleased with the results. Those in the right-to-life movement continue to want increased restrictions until the procedure becomes illegal. Those in the pro-choice arena continue to defend the status quo, despite significant losses in the past.

Fundamental to the issues discussed here has been the education women provided their colleagues. Using committee hearings, rallies, private conversation, and public debate for their classrooms, the women who believed in the premises of civil, equal, and privacy rights taught their colleagues the indignities of living without them. June Franklin's belief in the integrity of her colleagues was so great that she felt that if they would only visit the scenes of segregation, they would reject the policies that had permitted it and find new remedies. This has not always been a gentle education. In bold, clear, aggressive words, women like Franklin and Minnette Doderer thundered their objections to the continued exclusion of any citizens from the full benefits of being an American. Unrelentingly, they exhorted their colleagues to answer their pleas for equality.

The rights that these and other women advocated to further the cause of justice remain part of the public debate on the philosophies contained in the Bill of Rights. By raising issues such as the death penalty, civil rights, women's equality, and privacy rights, lawmakers challenged their colleagues to reconsider whether or not the status quo best served the needs of our society. They believed their proposals would contribute to remedying inequities in the state and to improving all citizens' chances for fairer treatment under the law. The debates these women provoked in the legislature extended far beyond the Statehouse and involved citizens in defining and formulating the pros and cons. Seeking justice for criminal offenders, minorities, and women, lawmakers identified injustices and sought remedies. Their successes and failures point to the complexity of the problems they sought to alleviate as well as to their inherently controversial nature.

CHAPTER 7

Agricultural and Environmental Issues

Iowa is an agricultural state. Fields of corn and soybeans cover its rolling hills and gentle slopes. Driving the state's highways, an odor that farmers call the smell of money regularly accompanies the hog and cattle feedlots near barns and farmsteads. Often the silhouette of a grain elevator on the horizon is the most visible clue that a town is nearby. Iowa residents who stay in the cities are reminded of the agricultural base of the state through noon crop reports on the radio and weather reports that include subsoil moisture content and soil temperatures, information important to farmers planting crops or concerned about the progress of their growing crops. In the late winter, Iowans hear the relative merits of various brands of herbicides and fertilizers for crops through television advertisements, and they watch Boar-Power (for hog semen) advertising along with the ten o'clock news. Summertime in Iowa means dozens of county fairs across the state that conclude with the state fair late in August. Even though most Iowans no longer live on farms, agriculture, and the land that supports it, remain part of the state's cultural and social life as well as important components of the state's economy.

Until the 1960s, more legislators worked in agriculture and farming than any other occupation, and many legislators, then and now, who list other occupations grew up on farms or have owned farmland. In addition to the many lawmakers familiar with agriculture, a powerful lobbying interest in the state has been the Farm Bureau. With this abundance of sympathy, support, and power for agriculture, the issues related to it regularly command the legislature's intense interest and action. Despite many policies favorable to agriculture, remedies for some economic problems elude lawmakers. Iowa farm products are traded on international markets, which set the prices. The money policies that determine interest rates are made on the federal level, as are production, soil conservation, and dozens of other policies, all of which are beyond the scope and influence of the Iowa General Assembly. For those issues that are within the state's purviews, such as roads for delivering crops to grain elevators and attempts to save family farms, many leaders have emerged, only a few of whom have been women. In ways that appear to mirror men's support for the issues discussed earlier, these women have generally filled supportive roles in passing agriculture and environmental legislation. There are, however, exceptions to this generalization, a few of which receive attention here.

One woman led the debate to remove a tax on oleomargarine and to legalize the sale of oleomargarine with yellow food coloring mixed in it. Another woman wanted to clean up the environment by creating incentives to reduce litter. A third woman believed that the disintegration of the state's railway system needed to be stopped. All of them urban legislators, they found themselves in the centers of controversies that sometimes resembled summer thunderstorms rolling across the state. While these policies did not constitute deliberate assaults on agriculture or business, the groups affected by them responded as if they were.

The state's dairy farmers felt besieged in the early 1950s as increasing oleomargarine sales began to threaten the market previously dominated by butter. It also appeared that the marketing barriers against increasing oleomargarine sales that they had created were about to fall. The story began in the 1890s when the legislature began regulating the manufacture, sale, and packaging of butter substitutes, including a prohibition against selling oleomargarine with yellow food coloring mixed in it. Then, in 1931, the Farm Bureau lobbied for and won a five-cent-per-pound tax on oleomargarine.[1]

The prohibition against selling yellow margarine received most of the attention from housewives. Small packets of coloring accompanied the margarine, and consumers kneaded the two together to get the more familiar and appealing color of butter. The task took about ten minutes. In 1953 Iowa was one of only five states in the nation that still banned the sale of colored oleomargarine. Gladys Nelson (Republican, Jasper) wanted to remove the tax and to legalize the marketing of colored oleomargarine.[2]

When Nelson entered the Iowa House of Representatives in 1951, she began her term knowing many of the legislature's personalities and procedures from her years of lobbying for the League of Women Voters. After spending her first term observing and learning, she later recalled that: "I joked that if I ever sponsored a bill, it would be so complicated and intricate that no one would know what it was. It was always the simple things like naming a state bird that drew the loudest debates."[3] The loudest debate in her second term developed over oleomargarine: everyone understood a nickel tax and white-vs.-colored margarine. It was variously described as the hottest subject, the biggest issue, and the most emotional issue of the 1953 session. The legions of lobbyists that the dairy and soybean associations recruited from within the state and imported from other states bore testimony to the high stakes they believed they could win or lose.[4]

Dairy farmers recognized the potential for lost sales and lobbied against the change. The 1951 *Iowa Year Book of Agriculture* described the dairy cow as "one of the cornerstones of the Iowa agricultural economy."[5] Industry sales totaled over $200 million in 1950, with butter contributing $120 million of that amount. The *Year Book* also noted that butter no longer had the secure market it once had and that competition from other fats and oils could adversely affect it. While the industry had begun advertising to increase butter sales, the *Year Book* pointed to reduced butter consumption and to the larger profit margin retailers realized from fats other than butter as threats to the economic future of butter producers.[6]

Another agricultural group, the American Soybean Association, supported the elimination of the tax and the color ban. The association argued that margarine users received no special benefits from the tax. They compared it to the gasoline tax that was used for road construction and maintenance. And unlike cigarettes and beer, margarine was not a luxury. Calling it a matter of justice, the association asked for the change, adding that its members produced the major ingredient in margarine and wanted to supply the market.[7]

In addition to the dairy and soybean associations' economic interests and housewives' desire for the convenience, grocers on the state's borders lost millions of dollars a year in sales when shoppers crossed state lines to buy colored oleo and bought other groceries while there. They wanted the changes in order to protect their retail sales. Another factor involved the state treasury: when consumers spent their money in other states, Iowa lost the sales tax revenue.[8]

Before the session began legislators knew that colored oleo would be an important issue. It reportedly played a role in the Republican caucus's choice for House Speaker. The newly elected Speaker created a special Dairy and Foods Committee to handle the various oleo bills in preparation for the upcoming controversy. He appointed Nelson to the committee.[9]

As part of its deliberations, the House Dairy and Foods Committee held a public hearing on the issue early in the session. Told that they needed to show support for maintaining the status quo, an estimated 1,000 dairy farmers attended the hearing, out of an estimated 1,500 observers. Attempts to convince the committee of the superiority of butter and the health risks of margarine included the testimony of a Des Moines housewife who told the panel that an experiment in Milwaukee, Wisconsin, had shown that the use of oleo retarded the development of secondary sex characteristics in children. A colored oleo supporter argued that the housewife had not read the entire report because it also said that children raised on oleo developed as well as those who used butter. Another oleo supporter argued that: "Neither butter nor oleo has any 'God-given right' to the color of yellow, and the law won't permit the patenting or copyrighting of a color."[10] Of course, the real arguments behind legalizing colored oleo had little to do with children's secondary sex characteristics or with divine rights.

Nelson managed the bill on the House floor. She argued for it as a housewife and as a representative of housewives, stating that she favored neither the dairy nor the soybean industries. In remarks during debate, Nelson responded to many of the issues raised during the hearing. She argued with the dairy industry's assertion that removing the color ban would result in unfair competition, saying that margarine packages included artificial coloring in the list of ingredients while butter packages did not (during some seasons, creameries added food coloring to make the color of butter more consistent year around). Nelson discussed the costs of sales lost to adjoining states, which were estimated at about $50 million. She also pointed to the moral issue involved with the widespread bootlegging. Throughout her speeches, however, she emphasized the housewife's desire to buy colored margarine without paying a tax on it. Nelson's strategy of characterizing herself as a housewife and the bill as a housewives' issue attempted to make it a consumer issue instead of a fight between the dairy farmers and the soybean growers. She probably used the approach more easily than her male colleagues who likely would have been drawn more deeply into the contest between the agricultural interests.[11]

Nelson's choice of tactics notwithstanding, newspaper accounts report that the Farm Bureau and the dairy associations devised strategies to subvert the goals of margarine supporters. At one point, the bill required colored margarine to be sold in a triangular shape to alert consumers that they were not buying butter. According to Nelson, equipment had not been designed or manufactured that could package margarine in a triangular shape.[12] She admonished the Farm Bureau for the amendment, saying: "I know the Farm Bureau has put tremendous pressure on you to do this. I know that votes have been traded away from this great consumer issue to help special interests." Continuing her strong statements: "The Farm Bureau has, for me and the great mass of Iowans, sold its prestige as a great state organization down the river for a mess of rancid butter."[13] Nelson believed that her colleagues had voted for the triangle shape knowing that equipment did not exist to package it, in order to be able to tell their constituents they had voted for colored oleo. She appealed to her colleagues' partisan interests, saying: "Among the losers will be my party, and your party—the Republican party. You have tagged it as hopelessly reactionary and the tool of selfish interests. You have lost it votes." Nelson's aggressive attack on the Farm Bureau and her characterization of her partisans as reactionary show her to be a woman who did not fear the political repercussions of her words. The chairman of a Newton union sent a telegram calling her position gallant, and lauded her courage and "untiring leadership."[14]

When the session ended, Nelson had won the repeal of the tax and the legal sale of colored oleomargarine in any shape. She had successfully championed a housewives' issue despite the opposition of the state's powerful Farm Bureau lobby. As the champion of a housewives' cause, Nelson, the only woman in the legislature that year, appears to have been the logical choice to floor manage the bill in the House. Perhaps other factors entered the leadership's decision to choose Nelson to manage the bill. The leadership could only expect strife, bitterness, and anger from debate on the oleo bills, and perhaps fail to pass anything. The person who managed the bills would be a target for that anger, which Nelson was. The bill's manager confronted fifty farmer House colleagues, the Farm Bureau, and the dairy industry. The political consequences of opposing these groups could be devastating whether the issue won or lost. The floor manager could win but then risk losing a leadership position or a committee chair the next session or suffer other forms of political exclusion. Nelson's colleagues may have felt that no glory existed in handling the oleo bills and that they did not want to take the political risks involved in handling the bill.[15]

Gladys Nelson's leadership in the butter battle contrasts with Mary O'Halloran's (Democrat, Cedar Falls) attempts to pass environmentally conscious policies. One difference is that when Gladys Nelson entered the fray on oleomargarine legislation, widespread public interest and support for the measure had been developing for some time. Environmental issues in the early 1970s, when O'Halloran became interested in them, were still somewhat new to the general public. Some Americans had participated in Earth Day and others had long been involved in Arbor Day, but for many citizens environmental issues were not something in which they were directly involved.

Another difference is related to the women themselves. Nelson does not appear to have sought leadership positions or other forms of institutional power, even though her party held the majority, Although she received accolades for her work in the legislature at the time of her retirement, she does not appear to have received an uncommon amount of publicity or other kinds of attention during her terms in office. And, as mentioned earlier, Nelson even camouflaged her campaign for office by using pictures from a family trip as a campaign tool. Despite her high level of visibility during the oleomargarine fracas, it was not characteristic of her political career.

Mary O'Halloran entered the legislature as a strong feminist, a committed liberal, and a politician with ambition. She found a culture that was unwilling to accept an energetic and strong feminist who was in pursuit of power and higher office. The macho culture of the legislature did not easily tolerate this brash young politician who for her part did not tolerate the sexist comments and actions she heard and saw among her colleagues.

One other aspect of the legislative environment enters the equation. As described earlier, men in the legislature sometimes sexualized the women with whom they worked. Comments made about O'Halloran suggest that some legislators could not accept a young, attractive, single woman as an equal colleague and instead focused on those attributes rather than her ability to participate in policy development. O'Halloran said it this way:

> I often wore slacks and jackets and blouses. That was my almost daily dress. I didn't wear dresses very often. Yet I had long hair and wore lots of makeup. So I think that I was a pretty androgynous person, and I don't think they could relate to that at all. They just didn't know what to do with me. I didn't fit into any molds—former nun, yet androgynous; ambitious, yet attractive from their perspective; single and yet a feminist who affiliated

> herself with the older married women in the groups. . . . So that was puzzling and threatening.[16]

She also described an incident in which a male colleague told her that his wife did not like it when she talked to him. She said: "That was very painful and difficult. You just don't think about things like that, you know. I didn't anyway. I mean, really, did somebody's wife actually think that I was after him because I had to do business with this guy. . . . It was often intensely personal and manipulated in order to keep me from threatening or seeking power or becoming powerful. So that was difficult."[17]

Despite the difficulties, O'Halloran found her voice and used it. Early in her political career, she began accepting speaking engagements to discuss rape legislation, environmental issues, and the Equal Rights Amendments all around the state. Her speeches, which reportedly were consistently well-received, served to heighten her visibility outside of her legislative district, which is unusual for state legislators who do not hold leadership positions. As she explained: "I was becoming a persona, maybe, a person to be dealt with, less inside the legislature than outside, as is always the case of people who are not part of the club."[18] In addition, her change in vocations from Roman Catholic nun to politician received generous attention in newspapers. She quickly became one of the rising stars in Iowa politics. The combination of her ability, energy, youth, visibility, desire for power, and willingness to work would be tremendous assets for a politician seeking higher office, if the politician were male. In the 1970s, men in the legislature appeared to resent them in a woman.

As a freshmen legislator in 1973, O'Halloran considered focusing on social issues, but she decided: "It just seemed natural that I would let Joan Lipsky and Minnette Doderer do social services. They were so skillful and so knowledgeable, that there wasn't really a place for me, and there wasn't a big need for me to go off and try to . . . spend four or five years becoming an expert in the incredible maze of social service legislation that had to be just digested and studied."[19] She also noted that she did not have legal training and so felt that the Judiciary and Law Enforcement Committee would not be an appropriate place to focus her attention.

O'Halloran decided to express her interest in social issues from another direction. A self-described environmental feminist, she said: "I saw saving the earth as saving women, saving life, saving hope, saving the planet, making life livable."[20] An urban woman, O'Halloran's family heritage included homesteaders and from that she developed a deep and passionate love for the land. She explained: "The land is alive; the land is a source of wealth; the land is what we have here. Texas has oil, Pennsylvania has coal, New York has harbors, we have this unbelievable black soil."[21] She believed that protecting the land needed to be a priority in the state's policy development, whether that meant making concessions to the land in highway design or other land use policies.[22]

During her terms in office, O'Halloran offered several proposals to protect the environment. She advocated banning fluorocarbons as aerosol propellants, greater use of solar and wind energy, implementing a state energy conservation plan, regulating low-level radioactive material and other hazardous waste disposal, and assisting homeowners with insulation expenses. From 1975 until President Jimmy Carter appointed her to a position with the federal Department of Energy in 1978, O'Halloran worked to preserve Iowa's farm land for agricultural uses because it was being converted to other uses at the rate of 30,000 acres a year. O'Halloran met opposition from farmers who believed they would lose control over their land and from cities that did not want their growth limited. The House passed land-use planning programs twice, but Senate opposition stopped both bills.[23]

Through those years, O'Halloran had also worked on another environmental issue which would be more successful: reducing litter on the state's streets and highways. She knew that outlawing cans and bottles alone would not end street and highway debris, but she believed it would make a significant improvement.

Several things came together that helped O'Halloran launch the crusade for what became a bottle deposit bill. In 1973, she had included the Natural Resources Committee among her requests for committee assignments and received it. In preparation for her committee work, she researched Oregon's bottle deposit program and began to regard that approach as a place to begin. After the session had begun, Tom Harkin (later a U.S. Senator) visited the Iowa Statehouse and discussed environmental legislation with O'Halloran. Harkin held a particular interest in beverage container legislation because he had recently completed a study on the topic while a law school student. Harkin's research, combined with that prepared by O'Halloran's clerk Sharon Robinson, provided O'Halloran with the background she needed to begin developing a bill. O'Halloran explained the benefits that would accrue from the proposal: "The possibility of saying no to the throw-away, no deposit, no return, no responsibility point of view . . . just fit in with my personal philosophy and my feminist thoughts about taking responsibility for our lives and turning this thing around."[24]

O'Halloran's original bill would have banned non-returnable bottles and cans, but the committee chair buried it. Despite her attempts to use procedural rules to get the bill out of committee, it stayed there.[25] The next year O'Halloran worked to get the bill out of committee, but House Natural Resources Committee Chair Dennis Freeman (Republican, Storm Lake) continued to oppose it because it dealt only with cans and bottles and not other forms of litter. Freeman also opposed the bill because it placed a storage and handling burden on grocers who would have to redeem the returnable bottles and cans. O'Halloran responded to his complaints: "Of course, it will cause some grocers storage problems, but we have to make some decisions about the storing of masses of litter on our highways, farmyards, and front lawns. This is in the public interest." She cited the Department of Environmental Quality's support for her legislation, and said: "This bill would allow Iowans to set up their own recycling centers and would provide lots of jobs." Refunds on returned containers would range from two to five cents. She pointed out that it cost the state twenty cents to pick up each piece of litter and "it is the responsibility of lawmakers to stop this and address themselves directly to the energy question."[26]

The politics within the legislature began to play important roles in the fate of the bottle legislation after the 1974 general elections. That year Democrats won the majority in the House and the tasks of organizing the body fell to them. Dale Cochran (Democrat, Vincent) and Norman Jesse (Democrat, Des Moines) competed for the position of House Speaker. O'Halloran cast the deciding vote for Cochran because she believed in his commitment to environmental issues. She soon had reason to question her decision, and she later encountered obstacles because of it. She recollects: "[H]is return of that favor was not to give me the committee that I wanted [to chair] but to give me the Energy Committee, which was nothing. It didn't exist."[27] As the session progressed, however, the Energy Committee became part of Iowa's response to the energy crisis of the mid-1970s.

O'Halloran explained her developing commitment to the bottle deposit bill: "Nothing much happened, and then boom, it just took off as an issue. And I got passionate about the subject. You do; the bottle bill is one of those things that became this symbolic issue in the House for the six years that I was there."[28] As chair of the Energy Committee, O'Halloran pushed her proposal a bit further when a bill outlawing pop-top cans and requiring deposits on all beer and soft drink containers went to the House floor. The committee did not expect the House to debate the bill but moved it to alert bottle and can manufacturers and retailers that the legislature intended to take action to limit litter.[29] O'Halloran knew that passing the bill would require patience: "There was no chance at all to pass this in the beginning. Labor opposed it. It was nonpartisan, that's for sure. Every major corporation in the country that had anything to do with packaging and bottling beer or liquor or soft drinks—you put that together, and you've got a good portion of the American retail power in this country focusing on the Iowa bill because they were bound and determined [to stop it]."[30]

When the 1977 session of the legislature opened, several of the components of the beverage container drama had become apparent. Individuals and groups had chosen sides and had begun lobbying the legislature and the public to join the fray. Opponents to deposits included the Iowa Federation of Labor, AFL-CIO, Retail Grocers Association, bottlers, brewers, Aluminum Company of America, and the Iowa Manufacturers Association. The Iowa Wholesale Beer Distributors also opposed the bill, saying it would not significantly reduce roadside litter. They proposed a tax on industries producing litter and using the revenues for roadside clean-up, recycling, and education to encourage recycling.[31]

Gene Kennedy, a former legislator turned lobbyist, opposed deposits but supported an anti-litter tax because he believed that the bottle and can bill discriminated against the industries that produced them and that other material contributed to the litter problem. He also believed that the bill would put people out of work. Kennedy said: "The people who hold our position are just as concerned about cleaning up our environment as anybody else. Our position is not a dodge."[32] O'Halloran disagreed: "The purpose of our bill is energy and resource conservation and an effort to turn around the throw-away ethic. Taxing everybody to go out and pick up somebody's discarded newspaper is a pretty half-hearted attempt."[33] Kennedy opposed the bill with determination. He was the driving force behind a $100,000 advertising campaign against it.[34]

In contrast to the powerful lobby opposed to the deposits, the American Association of University Women, the League of Women Voters, the Sierra Club, the Izaak Walton League, and the Iowa Public Interest Research Group supported them. Proponents received important support when Republican Governor Robert Ray asked for a study on beverage containers. The study reported that Iowans would have fewer choices in beverage container types, save money on beverage costs, have minimal savings in solid waste disposal, see some change in jobs, and enjoy substantial energy savings. The job shifts would come from a loss of jobs in metal fabrication and glass manufacturing and from a gain of jobs in container sorting and processing. The study also cited Oregon as a state that had been using bottle returns for some time and whose beverage prices had risen at the same rate as the states surrounding it, which countered the fear of higher prices resulting from recycling.[35]

In addition to the arguments that proponents and opponents to deposits prepared, another factor entered the picture: O'Halloran's vote for Cochran for House Speaker. Norman Jesse (Democrat, Polk), a leading liberal Democrat in the House, had also run for Speaker and had expected O'Halloran's support. Because O'Halloran had voted for Cochran, Jesse and his allies pledged to vote against any bill O'Halloran wanted. O'Halloran's relationships with some of her other colleagues had also become difficult by 1977. A newspaper reporter noted that "in an uncharacteristic display [House members] have taken swipes at her during debates on the House floor, and snipe at her behind her back." The reporter further explained: ". . . the situation can be attributed to good old-fashioned resentment—87 male House members aren't crazy about a young woman occupying such a prominent spot in the legislative process."[36]

Self-confident and bold, O'Halloran used her power as committee chair and took credit for the committee's work. Some members resisted her use of power and demonstrated their contempt for her. When the Energy Committee met to debate the bottle deposit bill, a member of the committee, John Pelton (Republican, Clinton) offered an alternative bill. As the time allotted for the meeting ran out, O'Halloran ended discussion on Pelton's proposal and called for a vote on her bill. In a clear affront to the chair, another committee member moved to adjourn before a vote. The motion passed. The majority party had broken the rules of courtesy when it voted to adjourn against the chair's wishes.[37] A local television station reported the story and cast it in personal terms as an attack on her. O'Halloran considered the news report a "raging example of sexism in politics. I wasn't the question; the issue was the question."[38]

O'Halloran explained her actions: "It appeared to some people that I was trying to force the bill. Well, any time you have something controversial, you have to push it. But some, particularly Rep. John Pelton, felt they did not have a chance to explore other options."[39] A week later, Pelton offered his alternative, but committee members rejected it as too cumbersome and too expensive. The committee supported the deposit bill.

Public interest in the bill was high, O'Halloran received fifty phone calls a day from people who wanted to know when the bill would be debated so that they could visit the Statehouse to watch the debate. Norman Rodgers (Democrat, Adel) said that he could not remember an issue lobbied as aggressively since the colored oleomargarine bill in 1953.[40] Another legislator said that public pressure was overwhelming lobbyists and noted that the public was ahead of the leaders on the issue.

O'Halloran had an important ally on the bill. Governor Ray had listed the bottle bill as a priority piece of legislation in his 1977 State of the State Address. O'Halloran had not known the governor's intentions, but when she heard him declare his support for the bill during the speech, according to one observer, "she jumped up and led the applause." Another commented that: "Once he [Ray] proposed it, that bill was going to pass even if he dropped dead." After making a commitment to the bill, Ray followed it up by working with industry leaders and legislators. He called lawmakers into his office to discuss it with them and to persuade them to support it, convincing several legislators to change their position on the bill.[41]

The House passed a tax on litter which would be paid by producers (i.e., newspaper manufacturers) and a ten-cent deposit on bottles and cans. When the bill passed the House, O'Halloran said: "Without public support, this bill would be in committee somewhere being kicked around by special interests."[42] The Senate passed a different version of the bill and it went to a conference committee. The final version included a ban on snap tops on cans, a five-cent deposit on liquor bottles, soft drink and beer containers, and provisions for redeeming the containers.[43]

In order to allow the businesses and industries involved with the recycling plan time to organize for the changes, the law did not go into effect until July 1, 1979. The state prepared for the new law by sponsoring a statewide event. On a warm, sunny, spring day in May 1979, about 45,000 Iowans helped with the Great Iowa Cleanup, filling a quarter of a million trash bags with tons of trash from the state's roadsides and parks. It was speculated that the project was the "biggest event of its kind anywhere ever."[44]

Another energy conservation issue also had agricultural aspects to it. In the late 1970s, the Milwaukee Road and the Rock Island railroads had undergone bankruptcy and the forecast was that the lines would be sold piecemeal because no bidder wanted the entire lines. The Rock Island was particularly important because it carried grain from the Midwest to other parts of the country for processing or export. Because transportation costs influence the price farmers receive for their produce, they have an economic interest in maintaining rail service. In addition, shipping the grain by train instead of hauling it in trucks consumes less fuel, which gave the issue appeal to those interested in energy conservation.

Jean Lloyd-Jones (Democrat, Iowa City) is among those concerned about energy conservation, and she is among those who love trains and travelling on them. She believed that it was important to keep the Rock Island rail line in tact, but as a freshman in 1979 and a member of the minority party, she was not part of the group that would decide the legislature's priorities that session. Nonetheless, as she drove home to Iowa City from Des Moines on the weekends, she would discuss the matter with Arthur Small, who was the senator for her district and a frequent passenger on the trips home. Lloyd-Jones would think of ideas for saving the line and Small would counter that it was a federal problem and the state could not do anything. Eventually, she started talking about her still amorphous ideas with other legislators and learned that Lowell Norland (Democrat, Kensett) and Clifford Branstad (Republican, Thompson) shared her interest.[45]

The irony of this story is that being a member of the minority party worked to Lloyd-Jones's advantage. Members of the minority do not have committees to chair or any of the other duties that are the privilege of the majority members, which leaves minority members with ample time to do other things. Sometimes they use the time to write endless amendments to controversial bills. Other times, minority members research proposals they hope to pass when they achieve majority status. Lloyd-Jones wanted to form a task force on railroads. She talked to Don Avenson (Democrat, Oelwein), the minority leader, about the task force and he agreed to it and told her to find other interested legislators. Lloyd-Jones remembers: "I started asking people, and it was amazing the interest that people had on this. They all wanted to be on the task force. I talked to Hutch [C.W. Bill Hutchins, Senate assistant minority leader] over in the Senate and he said absolutely he wanted to be on it."[46] Hutchins and Lloyd-Jones chaired the task force and held hearings around the state. From the hearings, they developed a number of bills.

The centerpiece of the proposals was the creation of the Iowa Railway Finance Authority (IRFA) which could "offer financial assistance for the acquisition, rehabilitation, construction, refinancing, extension, replacement, maintenance, repair or leasing of any rail facility."[47] The bill did not allow the state to operate train service; that would be done by a lessee. To pay for all of this the state would sell bonds that would be repaid through a new revenue source designed for that purpose.

In March 1980 concern for the fate of the Rock Island line dramatically increased. A federal judge ordered the liquidation of Rock Island's assets, which included the east-west main line connecting Chicago to the Davenport area, Des Moines, and Omaha, a vital link to markets and to north-south routes. The possibility that the track would be abandoned if the state did not act became increasingly greater. Governor Robert Ray did not believe that the state should be running a railroad, yet endorsed the IRFA proposal because, he said: "We're down to the point where it is the state or nobody else at all."[48] In addition, Republican leadership in both chambers had become committed to the IRFA, even as Lloyd-Jones continued to be identified as a primary leader for the bill.

Opposition to the plan quickly entered the picture. The chairman of the Iowa Transportation Commission, Robert Rigler, called the plan to sell bonds "monstrous" and said: "In my 25 years in state government, never have I seen a lousier bill."[49] Rigler opposed both the new bureaucracy that he believed would be created and the method for financing the plan. A spokesman for the Chicago and Northwestern Railway called it a "misconceived notion" that the state could succeed where private enterprise had failed.[50]

The fear that Iowans could be without rail service in some parts of the state overwhelmed the opposition. In the last days of the session, both chambers approved the Iowa Railway Finance Authority and authorization to sell $100 million in revenue bonds. Revenues anticipated from the lines would repay the bonds. The biggest concern was that no one would buy them because federal tax laws would make the bonds too expensive.[51]

A new obstacle became apparent in early 1981. The law was in place for the state to begin purchasing rail lines, but as Lloyd-Jones explained: "There is nothing we can do until the (Rock Island Lines) trustee liquidates the property, and there is no way we can force him to do it." She continued: "We need to have a greater interest in railroads. We need to come to a greater realization of how vital they are to our economy."[52] While waiting for the trustee to act, Lloyd-Jones appealed to the federal bankruptcy court to keep the Rock Island line intact so that it would remain usable.[53]

The other problem that emerged involved the intention to sell bonds to fund the purchases. The federal government refused to allow them tax-exempt status and the plan was abandoned. Another attempt to finance the purchases was passed during a special session in 1981. That plan imposed a locomotive fuel tax and a car mileage tax, but state and federal court challenges to the taxes were successful and they were removed.

Over the next three years, the IFRA collected $2.5 million in delinquent railroad property taxes and the legislature authorized a $15 million interest-free loan to the IFRA. The Rock Island trustee began accepting bids for the line and the IFRA helped finance acquisition for parts of it. By rotating the loan payments into new loans, at the end of 1993 the IFRA had loaned over $23 million to groups of grain elevators, shippers' groups, and a tourist group to purchase and rehabilitate over 700 miles of track.[54] Lloyd-Jones recollected that the railroad corporations had fought the IFRA proposal and then said with evident satisfaction that: "The minute we got it passed they all wanted to use it. Yes, it's real strange."[55]

The acceptance of the plan may have been strange, but Lloyd-Jones's approach to developing and passing it was based on solid research. She had begun with the persistent sense that the state could participate in maintaining rail service and from that worked first with her partisans to obtain ideas from the public through the hearings. She expanded her resources by working with majority party members in further refining the plan and at the same time developing their support and commitment to it. The research she had gathered and encouraged others to prepare became the source of ideas for proposals as well as the basis of her arguments supporting them.

In much the same way, O'Halloran's research offered her models of container recycling plans that had worked and those that had been less successful. Working from these models and material provided to her by others interested in the problem of litter, she modified her proposals over six years, until a plan passed. Public support also became crucial to the bottle bill's passage, overwhelming industry objections, a factor that significantly contributed to Nelson's passage of the oleomargarine bills.

None of these women appear to have done any work in these areas prior to their legislative service. Women have regularly explained that as officeholders they became exposed to policy areas that they had not before encountered and that through their committee work especially, but also through constituent lobbying, they learned the issues surrounding them. They have also explained that this exposure was one of the personal benefits of serving in the legislature.

Lloyd-Jones's work to preserve rail transportation, O'Halloran's to clean up the state, and Nelson's for colored oleomargarine suggest the wide range of interests women took to their legislative duties. As candidates, women have repeatedly told voters that theirs would not be parochial interests limited to those traditionally identified with women. They pledged that they would take a broad interest in legislative matters, and these issues provide examples of some of the ways they fulfilled it.

CHAPTER 8

Revenue Issues

One of the perennial topics in the legislature is tax policy. Attempts to lower one group's tax burden and to replace it with another tax that presumably is less politically painful or to find some new revenue source regularly appear on the legislative agenda. Lobbyists work to protect the interests they represent, lawmakers try to protect their districts (i.e., border counties resist sales tax increases because of potential sales lost to neighboring states), and the leadership huddles in back rooms to negotiate tax packages which often no one fully understands. Throughout the process of making deals and compromises, lawmakers insist that their primary interest is finding a fair plan to pay for state government and its programs.

In the 1980s, as the state underwent a number of related economic difficulties, revenues dropped and finding new sources of revenue emerged as a priority. Economic development also became a consideration in developing tax policies as the state wrestled with ways to identify new revenue sources. Proposals, such as legalized gambling, that had previously been rejected as inappropriate for Iowa began to be more attractive for the jobs and revenue anticipated from them.[1]

Whether the goal has been to attract jobs or to fill the state's coffers, the broad outlines of revenue policy appear to have been defined primarily by men in the legislature. Even when women have held assistant leadership positions or chaired the relevant committees, they do not seem to have been among the few who defined the agenda. While it is difficult to know precisely who was in the back rooms or at a poker party when the ideas were developed, neither the interviews used in this project nor newspaper reports suggest that women were involved as primary leaders. Without doubt, most men in the legislature were not among the inner circle that developed these plans, but the point here is that it does not appear that there were any women included. It could be that when women describe themselves as being excluded from the club, they are referring to the informal gatherings during which the early plans are crafted.

At the same time, women have not removed themselves from participating in developing the policies. They have followed the same strategies that have served them in other policy areas. After identifying a problem, they have proposed a solution and then lobbied their colleagues for its acceptance, often working outside of the formal power structure of the legislature. Research suggests that women have not successfully proposed sweeping new tax policies; instead, their role has been to modify existing ones, adding their conceptions of fairness and morality to them. This approach has not reduced the range of their proposals or the intensity with which they were supported and opposed.

Iowa's women legislators have challenged the trucking industry, had their ideas appropriated by the opposing party, have instituted a minimum income tax for high-income Iowans, and have fought the introduction of legalized gambling. For both women and men legislators, the search for equitable and innovative revenue sources raised moral and ethical questions regarding who should pay taxes, the rate at which they should be levied, and what the impact would be on the community. The power of the ideas women have presented has sometimes surprised their colleagues; sometimes women's inability to stop legislation has disappointed them in poignant and emotional ways.

Some of the proposals emerged after the introduction of a bill brought attention to an issue. When the trucking industry wanted the legislature to allow 65-foot-long trucks, an increase from the 60-foot limit, Joan Lipsky (Republican, Cedar Rapids) argued that the longer trucks "would do more damage to our highways, so we needed them to pay a little more to compensate for the damage they were proposing to do." To pay for road construction and maintenance, Iowa charges a tax on motor vehicle fuels and another for vehicle licenses. Lipsky maintained that "the casual user, like myself, pays a much higher percentage fee for the privilege [of using roads] than does the commercial hauler—the trucks."[2] In 1969 Lipsky proposed increasing both fees, based upon a highway commission recommendation. Truck license fees had not been increased since 1949 and did not pay their fair share to the road-use tax fund. Her formula for increasing truck license fees would add $13 million to secondary and municipal road funds. She also proposed increasing the $10 annual license fee for hauling overloads to $100, which would raise about $400,000. Lipsky used a bill making changes in the road use tax fund to carry her proposal.[3]

Responses to her amendments came quickly. Republican Governor Robert Ray expressed his support for increasing the license fees, and the Republican House leadership pledged that it would be debated.[4] Private citizens sent letters and phoned Lipsky expressing their frustrations with the trucking industry. She said that: "All those people that had been splashed or offended by those truckers on the highway supported me. . . . [It] was clear that people were really tired of being treated like the road belonged to the trucks and not to them. Whether they knew they were paying for more of it [roads] or not, they were wanting more courtesy."[5] Lipsky believes that many of the private citizens who called her did not fully understand her proposals. Through press reports, however, they identified her as a legislator fighting the trucking industry and they wanted to join her. Their windshields had been covered with mud by passing trucks, they felt truck drivers had treated them rudely on the road, and they told Lipsky their complaints, believing they were supporting her cause. Even though they may not have grasped the issues of truck fees, they recognized a common adversary and provided Lipsky with citizen support.[6]

Some freshmen legislators expressed their perplexity that the truckers had avoided increases in their fees because other taxes and fees had increased since 1949. One legislator explained that farmers used trucks to transport their produce to market and that many lawmakers' occupation was farming. Another reason was the power of the truck industry lobby.[7]

In addition to its own lobbyists, the trucking industry enlisted shippers, oil jobbers, and other related groups to fight Lipsky's proposal. At a public hearing on the proposed increase, opponents contended that it would result in many truckers leaving the state, and they forecast a 10-15 percent increase in the cost of living.[8] According to Frank Nye, the proposal to increase truck license fees had "shaken the industry right down to its dual wheels."[9] The *Des Moines Tribune* compared Lipsky to Harriet Beecher Stowe, calling her the "little lady who started the big war."[10]

The intensity of the controversy becomes apparent from political columnist Frank Nye's portrayal of debate on an unrelated bill, in which he described "pro-truck legislators" as "moving in on her." He wrote:

> They showed that when she handled a supposedly non-controversial bill on the floor last Friday. The pro-truck boys, scenting an opportunity to give her a bad time, fired a barrage of questions that forced a 40-minute debate. But she fooled 'em. Not only did she keep her own cool but her adept handling of the questions caused some of the gents doing the questioning to almost lose theirs.[11]

After haggling between the two chambers, the legislature made changes in the road-use tax fund, scrapped the longer trucks that Lipsky and others had opposed, and increased the fees Lipsky had advocated.[12]

The soundness of the plan and its public appeal convinced Ray and the party leadership to help push it through the legislature. Although a member of the majority party, Lipsky did not have a leadership position or a relevant committee chair from which to maneuver her proposal through the legislature. Instead, she relied on its fairness, citizen support, and lobbying her colleagues.

Another proposal for increasing fairness in tax policy held the House captive as the majority party leaders attempted to find ways to recover from the land mine that exploded when Minnette Doderer (Democrat, Iowa City) unexpectedly passed an amendment to a tax bill. In 1982 the state needed new revenues to balance the budget. As part of a bill to update state income tax policies to reflect changes in federal income tax laws, legislative leaders also planned to include other changes that would increase state revenues. With Republican majorities in the House and Senate and a Republican governor, that party's legislative leaders had the power and the responsibility to devise a plan for recommending the changes. After lengthy negotiations between House and Senate leaders, they reached an agreement to raise $39 million over eighteen months.

In these large tax packages, legislators attempt to find solutions that raise the desired amount of money and that consider their projected impact on various parts of the economy. The result is a collection of ideas carefully knitted together. Holding the pieces intact becomes a goal because any alterations in the package can unravel the entire proposal. The leadership's tasks include constructing proposals that their caucuses will support and then keeping the members disciplined, that is so they vote "right." Party discipline is important as individual members make a series of compromises to reach the agreements and because it becomes a matter of trust among the members that they will honor their commitments to cast their votes as promised. If a person agrees to vote for a part of the proposal which they do not support on the basis that another member has made a like pledge, any changes can upset the balance of the total package. If the caucus did not discuss or agree to a proposal, members vote as they want or they might wait to make a decision until the leadership's choices appear on the voting board and follow them. Presumably, the House Republican caucus had agreed to support the leadership's tax plan, although some members expressed doubts about at least one provision that added a tax on Individual Retirement Accounts. All of these factors came into play when the House considered Doderer's tax-the-rich amendment to the Republicans' tax package.

Doderer had quietly formed a bipartisan coalition to pass an amendment to close the loopholes that allowed some wealthy Iowans to avoid paying any state income tax. The minimum tax she proposed, modeled after a federal law, would produce $5 million and that would be enough to continue to give Iowans a tax break on their retirement savings, plans like Individual Retirement Accounts. Taxing the retirement savings had been an undesirable feature in the Republican leadership's plan, especially because the federal government did not tax those funds. Doderer's proposal had the combined appeals of attempting to tax those with incomes over $50,000 who avoided state income taxes through deductions and of preserving the retirement plan tax benefits.[13]

When the House members voted on Doderer's amendment, one Republican and one Democrat were absent, but Republicans still had a 54-44 margin to defeat any Democrat's amendment. Doderer's work within her party and with the majority to gain support for her proposal became apparent when four Republicans joined the 44 Democrats to pass the amendment, making the vote 48-48, which would defeat it. Republican leaders did not realize that one of their members, Richard Welden (Republican, Iowa Falls), had left the chamber, but Republican Sonja Egenes of Story City, did. She said: "I knew my vote was the one. When I stood up I looked down and I didn't see Dick Welden. I just thought it was time to force the issue."[14] She also explained that the caucus had not discussed the amendment, leaving Republicans confused about whether they had to follow leadership or could vote as they wished. Her vote passed the amendment, 49-48.[15]

House Majority Leader Larry Pope (Republican, Des Moines), whose plan had taken an unforeseen detour when Doderer's amendment passed, told the press that: "Frankly, I'm not overly upset by what happened. We'll fix it."[16] His comments contrast with his actions. After the vote, he stood by Doderer's desk, saying that she had ruined the tax plan. Republicans immediately went into caucus to discuss the change in plans. Jim Clements (Republican, Davenport), who had voted for the amendment, left the caucus angry "because of the personal attacks on people in caucus that are not only groundless, but highly inflammatory and uncalled for, not even within the realm of decency."[17] While the Republican leadership worked to discipline their ranks, Doderer commented: "I knew it was going to give them trouble, because Republicans do not ordinarily believe in people not paying taxes."[18]

When Pope could not convince the five Republicans who had voted with Doderer to change their positions, he said that the leadership had seen that substantial support for the amendment existed, but that Doderer's amendment was "ill-drafted, poorly worded," and needed technical revisions. Doderer insisted that her amendment had no flaws, and added: "They [Republican leaders] only have to change it so face can be saved and so Republicans who didn't vote for the amendment the first time will be able to vote for it again. I welcome the support."[19] Instead of the regular committee meetings that day and the next, Republican leaders huddled in back rooms and met with their caucus. A week later the House Republican leadership and the caucus agreed to implement a minimum state income tax for wealthy Iowans. The Republican version of Doderer's amendment was substantially the same as the original.[20]

As a veteran legislator, Doderer knew the political mechanics of lawmaking and knew where to seek support for her proposal. Obviously, she did not know that Welden would be out of the chamber, nor could she be certain that any of the Republicans would break party discipline to support her amendment. Her tenure in office, however, had taught her that some ideas could be so compelling that surprises occurred. Knowing that her amendment logically had little chance for passage, she did not let that dissuade her as she lobbied majority and minority members to support it. As a minority member she also knew that she could press for passing a concept that majority members, because of party discipline, could not.

When Democrats controlled both chambers of the legislature in 1983, Doderer chaired the powerful House Ways and Means Committee. From that position, she advocated another policy to tax the rich by limiting the amount of federal income taxes that Iowans could deduct from their state income taxes. She explained: "The federal deductibility mandates the truly blessed will pay a small amount to the state treasury for their blessings."[21] Her proposal passed the House but did not survive the rest of the legislative process. Iowans continue to deduct their federal income taxes from their state income taxes. More important than the proposal's failure is the philosophy behind it: Doderer believed that wealthy Iowans should pay their fair share to support the state, the same philosophy that had prompted the minimum tax which had passed the year before.

Focusing on the other end of the economic spectrum, Jo Ann Orr (Democrat, Grinnell) based her 1972 Senate campaign on repealing the sales tax on food and prescriptions as a way to help low-income people. She proposed a tax on luxuries to replace the lost revenue and to shift the tax burden to wealthier people. In the minority in 1973, Orr introduced the repeal but it went nowhere. In a one-woman crusade, Orr talked to interested groups in and out of the legislature about her idea and worked to develop support for it among the public.[22]

The next year, Republican Governor Robert Ray surprised his legislative partisans and Orr by including the repeal of sales taxes on food and prescriptions in his legislative agenda, after rejecting the idea only six days earlier. Leaders of both parties and in both chambers agreed with Ray that it would help solve a budget problem: a surplus in the state treasury. Observers saw Ray's decision as an artful political move, and Orr expressed her delight at the improved outlook for the idea. House member Delwyn Stromer commented that opposing such a popular idea "would be like voting against motherhood and the flag." With a coalition of conservative Republicans and liberal Democrats, the repeal passed that session.[23]

In an earlier search for ways to help low-income Iowans, Orr had proposed in 1970 to legalize pari-mutuel betting as a revenue source. At the time Iowa appropriated enough money to fund welfare programs at the rate of 81 percent of subsistence needs, but Orr wanted to increase it to 100 percent, calling it "unchristian and unconscionable" to force people to live on less.[24] She encouraged community action groups to support legalized gambling because her program designated the revenues for social services funding. She invited human services and community action representatives to meetings at the Statehouse to lobby legislators, but little happened until 1971.[25]

Orr was not in the legislature that year, but other pari-mutuel supporters had obtained its approval from the House Conservation-Recreation Committee. The bill included a significant change; it did not earmark the revenues for welfare programs. Elizabeth Miller (Republican, Marshalltown), who did not share Orr's enthusiasm for gambling, believed that: "We [the legislature] have some big problems to solve before we adjourn and I don't believe we should be horsing around with this." She added that "I might amend it on the floor to put in dog races and cock fights," showing her disapproval of the committee's passage of the bill.[26] However, it was only a false start and it would be years before any final action was taken.

In 1975 George Kinley (Democrat, Des Moines) convinced the Senate Ways and Means Committee to approve a pari-mutuel betting bill. Supporters pointed to the $3.1 million in revenue Nebraska received from pari-mutuel betting as a benefit Iowa might take advantage of if it was available. Having returned to the Senate, Orr saw further benefits: "I think it would help industry by providing trade for restaurants and motels. I'm for it as long as it is going to be cleanly operated and as long as the stakes are not too high—I hear that's when the trouble starts." Minnette Doderer said: "I'm undecided. I don't think it should be passed in haste, there's not time to pass it this session and it is not on the Democratic priority list."[27] Interest in passing pari-mutuel betting continued to surface regularly, with bills occasionally being debated but not approved for several more years.[28]

The concept of legalized pari-mutuel betting had lurked around the Statehouse for more than a decade by 1983, when it began to look as though passage was possible. That year, the bill originated in the House State Government Committee. When the committee voted on its recommendation, with several members passing rather than voting, the vote tied at 11 to 11. Then, Jean Lloyd-Jones (Democrat, Iowa City) fulfilled a pledge to gambling crusader Jack Woods (Democrat, Des Moines) to vote for passage if that was necessary to get the bill out of committee. It passed on a 12-11 vote. Close votes, difficult choices, and pressure from other legislators would continue to be a part of the bill's progress.[29]

After passing the House State Government Committee, the bill went to the House Ways and Means Committee, chaired by Minnette Doderer. She was now a determined opponent of pari-mutuel betting and voted against it, thereby defeating it (15-16) in her committee. Although apparently killed in committee, the bill's death knell had not yet rung as long as some legislators continued to fight for it. Some legislators accused Doderer of holding onto the bill as revenge for political indignities suffered in the 1970s at the hands of George Kinley (Democrat, Des Moines), one of pari-mutuel's strongest and most enduring supporters.[30]

The Senate meanwhile was holding a bill that Doderer and other women legislators wanted that called for a study of the state's salary policies to determine whether or not women received less pay than did men for jobs of comparable worth. The comparable worth bill had passed the House and the Senate, but James Gallagher (Democrat, Jesup), who supported gambling, filed a motion to reconsider on the comparable worth study, keeping it in the Senate. He vowed: "I'm going to hold onto it [comparable worth] until I get some horses running."[31]

At a Tuesday night poker game regularly held at a lobbyist's home, a legislator offered to release the comparable worth bill if Doderer would change her vote on pari-mutuel betting. Acknowledging that she could be jeopardizing the future of the study, Doderer refused to change her vote. The next day she and the bargaining legislator dismissed the deal as a joke, with Doderer adding: "It won't look good in the headlines if they trade horses and dogs for women."[32] Three days later the Senate let the bill out of committee. Doderer insisted no connection existed between the two bills and that the Senate had made the right decision.[33]

Other legislators made bargains that had more willing takers. When James Anderson (Republican, Brayton) was offered help getting an appropriation for $15 million to purchase and improve a rail line connection important to his district, he said: "If they marry the two of these together, I don't see how I can vote against it [pari-mutuel betting]."[34] When bargaining did not work, other pressures came to bear, as one legislator described: "They beat us up. There were no deals. This was capitulation." Andrew McKean (Republican, Morley) described the coercion involved: "The amount of energy and the amount of human destruction that has been reaped in this bill is a disgrace."[35] He added that legislators should have two votes: one for the way they felt and another for the way they were told to vote.

After Jack Woods (Democrat, Des Moines) announced that he planned to subvert the committee process by adding pari-mutuel betting as an amendment to an appropriations bill, some opponents reconsidered their positions. House rules allow amendments to bills (first degree), and amendments to amendments (second degree), but not amendments to amending amendments (third degree). If pari-mutuel began as an amendment, it would limit the ways to amend it. Convinced that the bill would be debated in some form, Doderer called a meeting of the House Ways and Means Committee. Betty Jean Clark (Republican, Rockwell), a leader of the group that opposed betting, describes the evening the committee met to pass the bill:

> I never will forget the night that Minnette had to call the Ways and Means Committee back into committee to get some changes in the votes in order to pass that bill out. She didn't want to at all, you know; she had sat on it in the Senate [in an earlier session]. But she knew that they were going to pass another pari-mutuel bill that wasn't going to have any restrictions or anything, and she said, "We've got to have a responsible bill if we're going to have a bill at all so we've got to put this thing out." And I said, "Well, do you have to have my vote changed?" "Oh," she said, "Beje, I hate to see you have to do that." And I said, "Well, I'll talk to my caucus." So I went ahead and talked with them, and I told them Minnette had asked me not to change my vote, but what did they think in light of the necessity of getting something more responsible than the slap-happy thing they were going to put through. They all said, no, Beje, it would be very damaging to you after the leadership you have taken against the thing for you to vote for it, so don't do that. So I didn't. I was relieved when they took that position.[36]

House Ways and Means Committee members Doderer, David Osterberg (Democrat, Mount Vernon) and Tom Fey (Democrat, Davenport) voted to allow it out of committee with no recommendation for passage. These and other opponents continued their campaign against gambling by drafting several amendments to the bill that placed restrictions on the races such as outlawing drugging the horses. The amendments allowed them to repeatedly argue their objections point by point as well as to offer a number of provisions that created safeguards against questionable activities. The strategy, sometimes referred to as papering a bill with amendments, drags out the debate, tries lawmakers' patience, and can stall a bill, an unlikely possibility in this case but one opponents could hope for.[37]

The day the House debated the bill, Jack Woods (Democrat, Des Moines) pointed to the economic development potential of racing horses and dogs: "It [pari-mutuel betting] will create jobs. It will increase tourism. It will increase revenue for the state of Iowa."[38] Doderer countered: "There is scandal after scandal in every state in the nation in which there is horse racing. Why do we want to open ourselves up to this? If horse racing were a clean industry, I would have no objection to it, but there is no state in the nation that has been able to control it."[39] State Representative Betty Hoffman-Bright (Republican, Muscatine) "pounded her desk" and said: "We're peddling hopes and dreams to the poor."[40] But the legislature passed the bill and the governor signed it.

Some women, including Doris Peick (Democrat, Cedar Rapids) supported pari-mutuel betting, feeling that she had her constituents' support.[41] Others did not particularly care whether or not the legislature legalized gambling; it was simply not an important issue to them. But many others opposed it for a number of reasons: concerns about the effects on compulsive gamblers, fears that gambling would take some people into poverty, and belief that state programs should not be financed with gambling proceeds. These arguments were raised by both women and men, including William Dieleman (Democrat, Pella), a senator who steadfastly opposed any form of gambling in the state.

After Iowa approved pari-mutuel betting on horses and dog races, other forms of gambling won acceptance. Republican Governor Terry Branstad twice vetoed bills for a state lottery, but accepted it on the third try. Proponents and opponents of these measures raised many of the same arguments they had used in the pari-mutuel debate. Sue Mullins (Republican, Corwith) called the lottery "a tax on stupidity;" Betty Hoffman-Bright (Republican, Muscatine) characterized it as "breeding a society of gamblers;" and Betty Jean Clark (Republican, Rockwell) predicted that the lottery would "literally rip families apart and starve children."[42] Later riverboat gambling won state approval, justified as a form of economic development.

Like the agricultural and environmental issues previously discussed, women's efforts in the area of revenue policy show the breadth of women's interests. Just as women had ventured into unfamiliar territory when they became candidates and legislators, they also explored new territories when they entered debates on truck licensing fees and pari-mutuel betting. They converted the skills to question and to investigate that they had developed as League of Women Voters and Women's Club members into tools that helped them identify and propose solutions to issues in state government. As they ventured into these areas, some women became the acknowledged experts in areas far different from those traditionally associated with women.

Through their work, women broadened the debate and added new dimensions to the issues. The perspectives they brought as mothers and volunteers, farmers and lawyers, contributed to their ability to seek sometimes novel approaches to solving problems or to become advocates for priorities that might otherwise have not been as clearly articulated or as persistently pursued. The differences between women's and men's occupational backgrounds, their traditional family responsibilities, and the kinds of organizations to which they belong suggest some of the reasons that women and men might seek solutions in separate ways.

Other factors may also be involved in women's approaches to identifying problems and remedies for them. They relate to women's status as outsiders.

Because women do not have the close ties with lobbyists that many of their male colleagues have, women may be more independent of lobbyists' influence. Another explanation could be that because women have not been privy to the deals leadership has brokered, they have little or no investment in them. Or, perhaps leadership and lobbyists have not expected women to have the fortitude to engage in rigorous debate or to pursue their proposals, leading lobbyists and leadership to believe that they could intimidate women into abandoning their ideas. Another factor could be that because women acquire and use power in ways that appear different from men, men have misunderstood the strength of women's power. The stories women have told and that have been reported in newspapers suggest that all of these possibilities may contribute to women's willingness and ability to reframe questions and add to the array of possible answers.

In recent decades, groups like the National Women's Political Caucus and women like Joan Lipsky have encouraged women to become candidates for political office. They have generally pointed to the need for more women's votes in legislatures to enact legislation for women, families, and children. As has been shown, women have made significant contributions to those areas of state policies. Yet, as Lipsky's own legislative career demonstrates, women's influence in state policy transcends gender related issues and extends to every area of it.

Epilogue

In 1985, Vermont Governor Madeleine Kunin told a conference of women legislators that she hoped the increasing number of women in local and state elective offices would create a pool of candidates for higher office.[1] She had good reason to believe in the potential for women to use their legislative experience as a launching place for a continuing political career. After serving in the Vermont legislature, Kunin became governor of that state, a route also followed by Ella Grasso in Connecticut. Several women, like Shirley Chisolm of New York, Olympia Snowe of Maine, Martha Griffiths of Michigan, and others, began their political lives in state legislatures and moved on to congressional seats. The path from the legislature to other political offices has long been travelled by both men and women. The difference between the sexes has been that far more men than women have taken that initial step toward beginning the journey.

While women continue to be a small minority in Congress and among governors, by 1994, women had been elected to statewide offices in forty-three states and women from forty-three states had served in Congress.[2] Nine Iowa women have served in statewide offices, but an Iowa woman has yet to become governor or to serve in Congress. The director of an Iowa public opinion poll believes the reason is that "there still is something of a glass ceiling" for Iowa women seeking those positions.[3]

Several women have attempted to break through the glass ceiling. For most women, however, it has proved impenetrable. For example, in 1970, Minnette Doderer ran for lieutenant governor in the general election, but lost. She tried again in 1978, but lost in the primary. In both of her contests for lieutenant governor, her adamant pro-choice position and her gender became obstacles she could not overcome. In 1986, Republican Joan Lipsky returned to politics to run for lieutenant governor and in the same race Jo Ann Zimmerman ran on the Democratic ticket. Zimmerman won.

In the 1990 elections, the governor and lieutenant governor ran as a team. Zimmerman ran for governor in the Democratic primary in 1990, but when her campaign faltered, she agreed to become Don Avenson's running mate, he for governor, she for lieutenant governor. The Avenson-Zimmerman ticket lost to the Republican ticket which had incumbent Terry Branstad running for a third term as governor and incumbent State Senator Joy Corning as his lieutenant governor. In 1994, Attorney General Bonnie Campbell ran for governor with State Senator Leonard Boswell for lieutenant governor. Branstad and Corning ran again in 1994 and won.

Elaine Baxter served in the House before running for and winning her race for Secretary of State in 1986, which she won again in 1990. Then in 1992, with two years remaining in her second term as Secretary of State she unsuccessfully ran for Congress, an attempt she repeated, again unsuccessfully in 1994. Also in 1992, State Senator Jean Lloyd-Jones unsuccessfully challenged incumbent U.S. Senator Charles Grassley.

More than fifty women have run for statewide offices and for Congress; some of them had served in the legislature before seeking the office but most had not. A few lost in primary races, but most survived to run in the general election. The reasons for these women's successes and failures are as diverse as the women themselves. Some of those who lost made tactical errors in their campaigns, others ran against such entrenched incumbents that any challenge was likely doomed. Without doubt gender contributed to these women's defeats, but the extent of it is uncertain. The kinds of problems these women encountered can be seen in the classic case of sexism that appeared in Democrat Roxanne Conlin's 1982 campaign for governor when the *Des Moines Register* ran several pictures of her showing her changing hairstyles over the years.

In addition to the women who sought higher offices, a few women continued their political lives in other ways. Edna Lawrence became an Ottumwa city commissioner; Elizabeth Shaw became a county attorney; Mary

O'Halloran was appointed to an administrative position in the United States Department of Energy; and Nancy Shimanek Boyd joined Governor Robert Ray's staff. For Lawrence and Shaw some of the appeal of their new positions came from working close to home. O'Halloran wanted the opportunity to influence energy policy on regional and national levels. Shimanek Boyd was later to be appointed to the utilities division of the Iowa Commerce Commission, where she saw possibilities to use her legal and political skills in new ways. Hallie Sargisson became her county's treasurer in 1975, a position which she held for sixteen years. Joyce Lonergan also won a county position as recorder. For these women, legislative service led to other political pursuits. Other women remained active in policy making through appointments to state boards and commissions.

Most of Iowa's women legislators have not chosen to remain in public life but have returned to private endeavors. Helen Crabb became the state president of the Iowa Federation of Women's Clubs; Opal Miller became involved in mission work for her church; and Betty Jean Clark completed the work to become a Methodist lay minister, a goal she had set aside to run for the legislature.

Perhaps more of the women who served in the Iowa General Assembly would have sought higher offices if the political glass ceiling had not appeared so impenetrable. As women continue to present themselves as candidates, without doubt eventually women will win those races for Congress and for governor. The real achievement, however, will be when the novelty is over and women readily seek political lives.

APPENDIXES

APPENDIX A

TEXT OF MINNETTE DODERER'S POINT OF PERSONAL PRIVILEGE

Text of the paper Minnette Doderer distributed to members of the Iowa Senate.

Point of Personal Privilege
Written to Tell Off Gridiron Group, But Not Worth Wasting
Senate Time Giving Orally

Last Week I received an invitation to attend a dinner and show from the Advertising Club of Iowa, and I understand all Senators and Representatives received this same invitation. You know the one wherein we were all graciously invited to come, eat their food and enjoy the performance. I should add at this point that for all this gracious living, the Advertising Club would charge each of us a $15 wining and dining fee. But once in awhile I get carried away with a desire for some gracious living with the wheels who make business and industry tick. They claim to be the generators of this economy through advertising so I mailed them a check for $30—$15 for a ticket for myself and $15 for a ticket for my husband.

Now I am aware that the advertising industry hasn't had a high regard for the American woman for some time as demonstrated by their ads. You know the ones I'm talking about. The little lady can't make a decent cup of coffee and her young grouchy husband tells her so so she runs crying into the street, the kitchen or the nearest bowling alley to find a kindly Mrs. Olson who always tells her the same answer, Get Folgers instant coffee. Or the one which shows the typical housewife squeezing that loveable bathroom tissue—like time after time, her greatest joy is to squeeze the tissue. Or we find the typical woman happily comparing floor waxes to see which makes the best mirror—and so on. The advertisers as a profession long ago convinced me that their idea of the ideal female was one who spent twice as much money as the family earned on white knights, tornado soaps, oleomargarine crowns for their ever-child-disciplining-husbands, but I didn't know the real depth of their animosity to the weaker sex until today.

Today is a black tornado, no oleo crown, dirty floors, no bathroom tissue squeezing day for me. The advertisers discovered that the Senator from Johnson is a woman, and brought my check back, with a sorry you aren't wanted statement. They took away my crown, my tissue, my floor wax, my coffee and carved my name on the list that forever more will not be allowed to pay $15 for the privilege of wining and dining with the image makers.

I am certain that the Gridiron Group, like all other self-righteous organizations, will "ascribe the results of their imprudence to the firmness of their principles."

Next year, gentlemen, please leave me off of your invitation list. Once a year is too often to be singled out for your insult.

Happy dandelion year to you,
/s/ Minnette Doderer

P.S. This senator is happy that she voted NO to the repeal of the 3% tax on advertising.[1]

APPENDIX B

JUNE FRANKLIN'S COMMENTS ON ABORTION

For the past several weeks and months, I have been very busy reading, researching, and contemplating the question before us today.

During all this time I have tried to remain cool, calm, and level-headed; I have also tried to keep an open mind on the subject.

I have listened to all the arguments for and against this measure, and I have come to some conclusions.

Both sides are sincere in their beliefs, but their arguments for the most part are phony and hypocritical and I would like to extend on this for a moment.

Those against legalized abortion say human life is most precious and in the good old American tradition we must protect life. Human life has never been a top priority in this country—we have never valued life or the quality of life. Property has always been top priority ever since the Indian was killed and his land was stolen. An entire race of people were lynched, and one-fifth of our population is slowly starving to death, while we spend billions to send two men to a dead planet to play golf.

Those both for and against argue we need education, yet they storm this building by the thousands, against sex education.

Those who are for legalized abortion say a woman should have control of her body to do with as she pleases, that the decision should be between her and her doctor. But when a young man says he also would like to have control of his body and does not desire to take it to Viet Nam to rot in a ditch someplace, when he says he does not want to kill or be killed, he is considered an outcast, a traitor, and has three choices—either go and take his chances of being killed, go to Canada or go to jail.

Proponents for this bill have argued that this bill is for the Blacks and for the poor who want abortion and can't afford one. This is the phoniest and most preposterous argument of all. Because I represent the inner-city where the majority of the Blacks and poor live, and I challenge anyone here to show me a waiting line of either Blacks or poor whites who are wanting an abortion. They do feel, and there is a fear among them that this bill *is meant for them*. They feel this is the first step down the road to forced sterilization, euthanasia, and genocide. They fear, and I tend to agree with them, that there are a few social workers who, in their zest and zeal to keep cost down, are just sick enough to force poor Blacks and whites to have abortions.

I am ashamed to say, but I also have a fear that there may be those among us here, who feel that this bill would cut down on our welfare costs.

The elderly fear this bill because they feel they may be the next target, in future legislation—the Blacks fear this bill and relate it to genocide and the first step down the road to fascism. I have always fought for everyone to have equal rights, and to be able to have a share in the good things of life.

I am against forcing young men to kill and be killed to satisfy the sick sadistic egos of a few—I have fought to feed the hungry, and save the young and elderly from poverty and neglect. I have also fought to protect those who are defenseless.

I feel we must re-direct our priorities and make human life, instead of our greed for property, the number one priority in this state and this nation. And I would say to the people on both sides of this question—stop being hypocritical—your hypocrisy is destroying the very threads of our civilization.

> No man is an island unto himself,
> I am involved in mankind.
> Ask not for whom the bell tolls.
> It tolls for me, and it tolls for thee.[1]

APPENDIX C

BIOGRAPHICAL NOTES ON WOMEN LEGISLATORS

This information primarily comes from *Iowa Official Registers* published between 1929 and 1993. Other sources include newspapers and interviews from "A Political Dialogue: Iowa's Women Legislators."

Abbreviations:

AAUW	American Association of University Women
ABWA	American Business Women's Association
BPW	Business and Professional Women
DAR	Daughters of the American Revolution
DCC	Democratic Central Committee
DWC	Democratic Women's Club
FWC	Federation of Women's Clubs
IBEW	International Brotherhood of Electrical Workers
ICFS	Iowa Children's and Family Services
ICLU	Iowa Civil Liberties Union
ISEA	Iowa State Education Association
ISTC	Iowa State Teacher's College (now, University of Northern Iowa)
ISU	Iowa State University
IWPC	Iowa Women's Political Caucus
LWV	League of Women Voters
NAACP	National Association for the Advancement of Colored People
NIACC	North Iowa Area Community College
NOW	National Organization for Women
NOWL	National Order of Women Legislators
OES	Order of Eastern Star
RCC	Republican Central Committee
RWC	Republican Women's Club
UNI	University of Northern Iowa
U of I	University of Iowa
UPI	United Press International
WEAL	Women's Equity Action League

Adams, Janet: Democrat from Webster City; b. 30 August 1937 in Webster County; graduate of Buena Vista College, 1954; teacher; president of Iowa LWV, Dubuque

Archdiocese Board of Education; member of Hamilton County DCC, Hamilton County Youth Service Center Board, ISEA, AAUW, BPW, Women of Moose, Catholic Daughters of America, and Roman Catholic Church. Assistant Majority Leader. Married, 7 children.

Baxter, Elaine: Democrat from Burlington; b. 16 January 1933; graduate of Iowa Wesleyan, 1970; MS, University of Iowa, 1978; teacher; Burlington City Council member; board member, League of Iowa Municipalities; senior liaison officer, Office of Legislation and Congressional Relations, Department of Housing and Urban Development; chair, Burlington Steamboat Days; nominating panel, U.S. Court of Appeals, Eighth Circuit; board member, WEAL, Burlington Area Arts Council, Foundation for ICFS. Iowa Secretary of State, 1987- 1995. Married, 3 children.

Beatty, Linda: Democrat from Indianola; b. 13 September 1942 in Boone; graduate of UNI; teacher; member of AAUW, BPW, Carousel Theatre Board, and Presbyterian Church; former Warren County DCC chair. Married, 2 children.

Bloom, Amy: Republican from Dayton; b. 4 April 1889 in Webster County; attended ISTC; teacher; member of OES, Farm Bureau, library board, FWC; Lutheran. Married.

Bock, Lenabelle: Republican from Garner; b. 30 June 1904 in Linden; attended ISTC and ISU; teacher; member, OES, Historical Society of Iowa, Garner Recital Club; delegate, Iowa Council for Community Improvement, Garner Town and County Planning Council; secretary, Hancock County Conservation Board; board member, Garner Chapter of Red Cross; partner, Bock Oil and Transport Company; Methodist. Married, 2 children.

Bogenrief, Mattie: Democrat from Des Moines; b. 26 October 1912 in Duluth, MN; attended Northwest Missouri State Teachers College; married.

Boyd, Nancy Shimanek: Republican from Monticello; b. 1 December 1947 in Monticello; BA, Clarke College, 1970; JD, U of I, 1973; law clerk, Iowa Supreme Court; lawyer; assistant attorney general; member, American Bar Association, Iowa State Bar Association, Jones County Bar Association, IWPC, BPW, American Legion Auxiliary, RWC; Roman Catholic. Utilities Division, Iowa Commerce Commission. Married after legislative service.

Brandt, Diane: Democrat from Cedar Falls; b. 28 August 1938 in Emmett County;

graduate of ISU; president of AAUW-Waterloo branch, LWV-Waterloo-Cedar Falls branch; member of Cedar Falls Planning and Zoning Commission, IWPC, Iowans for Better Justice, National Municipal League, NAACP, Common Cause, ICLU; Presbyterian. Married.

Buhr, Florence: Democrat from Des Moines; b. 7 April 1933 in Mills County; BA, UNI, 1954; teacher; legislative secretary; member, IWPC, Mental Health Association of Central Iowa, NAACP, LWV, Polk County Democratic Central Committee; Presbyterian. Assistant Majority Leader. Married, 3 children.

Carl, Janet: Democrat from Grinnell; b. 24 February 1948 in Atlantic; graduated from U of I, 1970; MA, U of I, 1973; higher education administration; president, Iowa Student Personnel Association; member NOW, LWV. Married, 2 children.

Carpenter, Dorothy: Republican from West Des Moines; b. 13 March 1933 in Ismay, MT; graduated from Grinnell College, 1951; member, LWV, IWPC, TTT, Common Cause; president, Planned Parenthood Mid-Iowa; Episcopalian. Assistant Minority Leader. Married, two children.

Chapman, Kathleen: Democrat from Cedar Rapids; b. 19 January 1937 in Estherville; graduated, U of I, 1959; JD, U of I, 1974; member, AAUW, IWPC, Linn County and Iowa bar associations, Association of Trial Lawyers, Common Cause, Cedar Rapids Board of Adjustment; board member, Children's Home of Cedar Rapids; Roman Catholic. Assistant Majority Leader. Married, 2 children.

Clark, Betty Jean: Republican from Rockwell; b. 18 April 1920 in Kansas City; attended Fort Hays Kansas State College, University of Utah, University of the Pacific, Garrett Evangelical Seminary; director, Student Program, Wesley Foundation, ISU; news editor, Iowa Conference United Methodist Women; publisher-editor, The Periodical Key; member, Farm Bureau, Chamber of Commerce, LWV, IWPC, Common Cause, Federation of Republican Women, PEO, YWCA, Oikoumene Religious Center Board of NIACC, BPW; Methodist. Married, 3 children.

Cohen, Gertrude: Democrat from Waterloo; b. 1 November 1913 in Chicago; graduated, University of Minnesota; attended graduate school, U of I; member, United World Federalists, LWV, NAACP, ICLU, Hadassah, National Women's Committee of Brandeis University; honorary citizen, Boys Town, NE; Jewish. Married, 2 children.

Conklin, Willa Charlene: Republican from Waterloo; b. 10 July 1929 in Pottawattamie County; BA, ISTC; MA, U of I; teacher; speech therapist; member, AAUW, DAR, Waterloo Women's Club, PEO, ABWA, NOWL, Alpha Gamma Delta, National Society of State Legislators, medical auxiliary; board member, YWCA, Iowa Society Preservation of Historic Landmarks; leader, Girl Scouts, Cub Scouts; president, Cedar Valley Historical Society; Presbyterian. Married, 5 children.

Corning, Joy: Republican from Cedar Falls; b. 7 September 1932 in Bridgewater; BA, UNI; member, Iowa Housing Finance Authority, AAUW, PEO, Cedar Arts Forum, LWV, Black Hawk County Family and Children's Council; president, Iowa Talented and Gifted; director, Iowa Association of School Boards; United Church of Christ. Assistant Minority Leader. Lieutenant governor, 1991- . Married, 3 children.

Crabb, Helen: Democrat from Jamaica; b. 11 November 1916 in Lavinia; attended American Institute of Business, Simpson College, University of Colorado; teacher; president, Iowa Federation of Women's Clubs; board member, Iowa Conservation Commission; member, Delta Delta Delta; worthy matron, OES; Jamaica Union Church. Married, 1 child.

Doderer, Minnette: Democrat from Iowa City; b. 16 May 1923 in Grundy County; attended ISTC, graduated U of I; visiting professor, Stephens College, ISU; state secretary, Citizens for a Constitutional Convention; member, Iowa Advisory Council for the Construction of Facilities for Mentally Retarded and Community Mental Health Centers, Family and Children Services Advisory Committee, Iowa Kidney Foundation of Iowa, LWV, United Nations Association, City Manager Association of Iowa, International Platform Association, NOW, IWPC, ICLU, WEAL, BPW; board member, Iowa Center for Education in Politics, University of Iowa School of Religion, United Cerebral Palsy of Iowa, Iowa Health Facilities Commission; Iowa Educational Broadcasting Network Advisory Committee; Governor's Task Force, Early Childhood Development; Education Commission of the States; jury commissioner, Johnson County District Court; vice-chair, Johnson County Democratic Central Committee; Democratic National Committeewoman; national Democratic Policy Council; director, National Society of State Legislators; Methodist. Senate President Pro Tempore. Inducted into Iowa Women's Hall of Fame, 1979. Married, 2 children.

Duitscher, Lucille: Democrat from Clarion; b. 7 March 1922; attended ISU; chair, Wright County Family Living Extension Council; member, Wright County Community Action Program, Federated Women's Clubs; Methodist. Married, 4 children.

Egenes, Sonja: Republican from Story City; b. 19 October 1930 in St. Paul, MN; attended St. Olaf, U of I; BS, ISU; graduate studies, ISU; Fulbright Scholar; taught at ISU; congressional candidate, 1962; member, Federation of Republican Women, Landscape Critics Council, Ames Choral Society, United Nations Association, Ames International Orchestra Festival Association, IWPC, Federated Women's Club, School Reorganization Study Committee, Academy of Political Science, Phi Kappa Phi; commissioner, Education Commission of the States; director, Iowa Metropolitan Opera; UPI "Woman of the Year"; Lutheran. Married, 1 child.

Elliott, Isabel: Democrat from Bronson; b. 20 February 1887 near Hawarden; graduated, St. Clara College, Sinsinawa, WI; teacher; farmer; leader, 4-H; chair, Woodbury County Farm Women's Organization; a director, Woodbury County Fair Board. Married, 3 children.

Franklin, A. June: Democrat from Des Moines; b. 1931; attended Drake University; board member, Urban Affairs Committee of Greater Des Moines Chamber of Commerce, Americans for Democratic Action; secretary, National Conference of Black Elected Officials; member, Puella Legatoes Social Club, Polk County DWC, National Society of State Legislators; Roman Catholic. Assistant Minority Leader. Married, 3 children.

Garman, Teresa: Republican from Ames; b. 29 August 1937 in Webster County; graduated from Fort Dodge High School; Story County Board of Adjustment; Gilbert Community School District School Board Advisory Committee; State Republican Farm Policy Council; secretary, Story County Republican Central Committee; member, RWC, Story County Porkettes, VFW Auxiliary, ABWA, Boone Women's Club, Farm Bureau, chamber of commerce, Story City Greater Community Club, NOWL; Republican National Platform Committee; Republican State Central Committee; Roman Catholic. Assistant Minority Leader. Married, 4 children.

Garner, Ada: Democrat from Shell Rock; b. 6 February 1882 in Shell Rock; teacher; member, Butler County Historical Society, Rebekah Lodge, Women's Relief Corps, school board. Married, 2 children.

Gentleman, Julia: Republican from Des Moines; b. 24 August 1931 in Des Moines; B.S., Northwestern University. Married, 5 children.

Glanton, Willie Stevenson: Democrat from Des Moines; BS, Tennessee A & I State University; LL.B., Robert H. Terrell Law School, Washington, D.C.; assistant Polk

County attorney; board member, Wendell Wilkie House, Polk County Society for Crippled Children, Town and Country, YWCA, Des Moines library, urban renewal committee for Des Moines; participant, Know Your Neighbor; vice-president, Des Moines Board, International Education; member, Delta Sigma Theta, Links, Jack and Jill, county, state, national bar associations, Polk County DWC. Married, one child.

Gregerson, Mary Pat: Democrat from Council Bluffs; b. 25 May 1938 in Cass County; BA, Creighton University, 1960; MA, Creighton University, 1965; teacher; Roman Catholic. Married.

Greiner, Sandra: Republican from Keota; b. 26 October 1945 in Washington; attended Stephens College; member, Pork Producers, Corn and Soybean Growers, Farm Bureau, Keota Unlimited, Iowa Agri-Women, Agricultural Women's Leadership Network, American Feed Industry Association, Keokuk County Republican Women; Roman Catholic. Married, three children.

Gruhn, Josephine: Democrat from Spirit Lake; b. 14 April 1927 in Britt; BA, Morningside College; family farm owner-operator; teacher; member, IWPC, AAUW, BPW, Farm Bureau, OES, American Legion Auxiliary; treasurer, Dickinson County Democrats; Methodist. Married, 3 children.

Grundberg, Betty: Republican from Des Moines; b. 16 February 1938 in Woden; BA, Wartburg College; MA, University of Iowa; Advanced Studies, Drake University; property management and renovation; member, Des Moines School Board, Des Moines Housing Council, PTA, Iowa Children and Family Services board, Civic Center board, Polk County Health Services board, Polk County Medical Auxiliary, League of Women Voters, AAUW, Women's Political Caucus; Lutheran. Married, four children.

Hakes, Frances: Republican from Laurens; b. 13 February 1897 in Laurens; graduate of U of I; teacher; president, Laurens public schools; member, DAR, Progressive Club, State Historical Society of Iowa, FWC; Laurens Library Board, OES; national vice-president, American Legion Auxiliary; Methodist. Father: Congressman Fred C. Gilchrist. Married, 2 children.

Hammond, Johnie: Democrat from Ames; b. 22 August 1932 in Europa, MS; attended University of Texas; BA, University of Minnesota, 1953; BBA, ISU, 1981; manager, adult day care center; board member, Ames Visiting Nurse Service, Agency for Peace and Justice, Iowa Interchurch Forum; member, ICLU, NOW,

LWV, Phi Kappa Phi; advisory board, Iowa Correctional Institution for Women; Baptist. Elected to Story County Board of Supervisors, 1975-1979. Married, 4 children.

Hannon, Beverly: Democrat from Anamosa; b. 30 March 1932 in Manchester; AA, Kirkwood Community College, 1982; BLS, U of I, 1990; member, Jones County Democratic Central Committee, Jones County Historical Society, Jones County Farm Bureau, Jones County Tourism Association, Kirkwood Alumni Board, Commission on Children, Youth, and Families, IWPC. Married, 6 children.

Harper, Mattie: Democrat from West Grove; b. 15 December 1923 in MS; attended Copiah Lincoln Junior College, Mississippi State University; teacher; director, girls state; partner, family agribusiness; state president, American Legion Auxiliary; member, BPW, United Methodist Women, ABWA, IWPC, NOWL, YWCA, Farm Bureau, Eagles Auxiliary, Elks Club, DWC, Legislative Ladies League; Methodist. Married, 1 child.

Harper, Patricia: Democrat from Waterloo; b. 4 December 1932 in Howard County; BA, ISTC, 1954; MA, ISU, 1961; teacher; president, Waterloo Education Association, Hawkeye Uniserve Unit; member, AAUW, Alliance for the Mentally Ill; Roman Catholic. Married, 1 child.

Hester, Joan: Republican from Honey Creek; b. 20 November 1932; graduated from Persia High school; postal clerk; farmer; member, Farm Bureau, Pork Producers, Live and Learn Extension Club; appointed, 4th Judicial Nomination Commission; 4-H leader, West Pottawattamie County Youth Committee; superintendent, Home Economics Projects, Westfair; Republican Party positions; Methodist. Married, 6 children.

Hoffman-Bright, Betty: Republican from Muscatine; b. 1 December 1921; graduated from Indiana State University; teacher; member, Phoenix Federated Club, Farm Bureau, LWV, IWPC, BPW; Methodist. Assistant Majority Leader; Assistant Minority Leader. Married, 3 children.

Jochum, Pam: Democrat from Dubuque; b. 26 September 1954 in Dubuque; AA, Loras College; residence hall director and director of public information and marketing, Loras College; member, Dubuque County Association for Retarded Citizens, Women's Recreation Association, National Catholic Basketball Tournament, Dubuque County Compensation Board, Loras College Arts and Lecture Series,

Dubuque County Democratic Central Committee chair; delegate, Democratic National Convention; Roman Catholic. One child.

Judge, Patty: Democrat from Albia; b. 2 November 1943; Iowa Methodist School of Nursing; attended U of I; livestock farmer, regional coordinator for Iowa Mediation Service; Democratic county chair, district treasurer; member, board of Albia Area Chamber of Commerce, PEO; Roman Catholic. Married, three children.

Kiser, Emma Jean: Republican from Davenport; b. 11 July 1925 in Oskaloosa; graduate of Oskaloosa High School; secretary, Scott County TB and Health Association; president, Scott County RWC; vice-chair, Scott County Young Republicans; committeewoman, Davenport City and Scott County Republican Central Committees (21 years); PTA and Little League offices; Presbyterian deacon. Married, 4 children.

Kramer, Mary E.: Republican from Des Moines; b. 14 June 1935; BA, U of I, 1957; MA, U of I, 1971; insurance company vice-president; president, Iowa Management Association; chair, Iowa Supreme Court's Family Work Life Initiative Committee; member, chamber of commerce, Polk County Child Care Resource Center, YWCA, Des Moines Pastoral Counseling Center, Rotary; recipient, YWCA Woman of Achievement, Iowa Management Association's Manager of the Year Award, Department of Human Services' Distinguished Service Award, *Business Record*'s Community Involvement Award; Presbyterian. Married, 2 children.

Larsen, Sonja: Republican from Ottumwa; b. 1 February 1941; graduated from Elk Horn-Kimballtown High School; realtor; vice-president, Ottumwa Board of Realtors; member, chamber of commerce, area development corporation, LWV, Iowa Junior Miss Development Corporation; Lutheran. Married, 3 children.

Laughlin, Janis Torrence: Republican from Atalissa; b. 13 September 1926 in Montpelier Township; graduate of Wilton High School; Muscatine County Supervisor; chair, Muscatine County Conservation Board, Great River Substance Abuse Board, Wilton American Legion Auxiliary; member, Muscatine Women of Moose, Pilot Club, OES, Social Services County Board, Systems Unlimited of Iowa City, Bistate Planning Commission, Community Health Nurses Board, West Liberty Fair Board. Married, 2 children.

Lawrence, Edna: Republican from Ottumwa; b. 28 April 1906; graduate, ISTC; business college teacher; newspaper advertising sales; president, Ottumwa Board of

Education; secretary, Wapello chapter of American Red Cross; Methodist. Ottumwa City Commissioner. Married, 2 children.

Lipsky, Joan: Republican from Cedar Rapids; b. 9 April 1919 in Cedar Rapids; BS, Northwestern University, 1940; graduate study at U of I; psychologist; lawyer; member, Cedar Rapids Women's Club, Altrusa, Delta Kappa Gamma, AAUW, LWV, Cedar Rapids Art Association, RWC, Hadassah, Sisterhood of Temple Judah, Linn County Mental Health Association; appointed, Mayor's Commission Housing; chair, Mayor's Commission on Alcoholism; chair, Employment Security Advisory Council; chair, Midwest Conference of State Legislators; member, Intergovernmental Relations Committee, National Legislative Conference; awards, Iowa Kidney Foundation, Foster Parents Association, Iowa Association of Developmentally Disabled, Cedar Rapids Woman of the Year; Jewish. Assistant Minority Leader. Republican candidate for lieutenant governor. Married, 3 children.

Lloyd-Jones, Jean: Democrat from Iowa City; b. 14 October 1929 in Washington, D.C.; BS, Northwestern University, 1951; MA, U of I, 1971; president, Iowa LWV; member, Iowa 2000 state planning committee, Governor's Task Force on Governmental Ethics, Iowa Railroad Passengers Association, BPW, ICLU, Common Cause, LWV, NOW, Nature Conservancy, WEAL, United Nations Association, IWPC; board member, Iowa City Library Board, Iowa Commission on the Status of Women; advisory committee, Iowa Natural Heritage Foundation; chair, Iowa Committee for International Women's Year, Iowa Peace Institute; Episcopalian. Assistant Majority Leader. Married, 4 children.

Lonergan, Joyce: Democrat from Boone; b. 5 March 1934 near Belle Plaine; attended Boone Junior College; international affairs chair of Sioux City Diocese Council of Catholic Women; president, Boone County Church Women United, Home-School Association; secretary, Boone County Democratic Central Committee; member, ABWA, Altar Society, IWPC, Boone County Historical Society, Farm Bureau; Roman Catholic. Boone County Recorder. Soroptimists' "Women Helping Women" award. Married, 4 children.

Lundby, Mary: Republican from Marion; b. 2 February 1948 in Carroll County; BA, Upper Iowa University, 1971; staff assistant for U.S. Senator Roger Jepsen; Outstanding Young Woman in America; member, Linn County Republican Central Committee. Assistant Minority Leader; House Speaker Pro Tempore. Married, 1 child.

Lynch, Mae: Democrat from Pocahontas; b. in Osceola County; graduated from ISTC; law degree, U of I, 1932; teacher; principal; lawyer. Married.

Mann, Karen: Republican from Scranton; b. 26 July 1948 in Fairbanks, AK; BA, Dickinson State College, 1971; Pleasant Ridge Community Church. Married, 1 child.

Martin, Mona: Republican from Davenport; b. 22 October 1934; BS, Western Illinois State Teachers College; graduate studies, ISU, U of I; business partner, teacher; member, AAUW, Scott County Republican Women, Northwest Davenport Business Association, Rock Island Historical Society, Davenport Plan and Zoning Commission, Scott County Landfill Recycling Committee, Scott County Mental Health/Developmentally Disabled Advisory Committee, chair of U.S. Department of Education Consumer Affairs Advisory Board; Methodist. Married, two children.

McElroy, Lillian: Republican from Percival; b. 28 April 1917 in Maynard; attended Upper Iowa University; farm owner; member, RWC, IWPC, PEO, Farm Bureau, Community Club; chair, Fremont County Heart Association; board member, State Extension Advisory Board; Methodist. Iowa Master Farm Homemaker; State 4-H Alumni Award. Married, 4 children.

McKee, Vera Shivvers: Republican from Knoxville; b. 16 June 1897 near Melcher; AB with honors, Simpson College, 1920; teacher; member, school board, Farm Bureau, Zoning Commission, Extension Council, Improvement Association, Knoxville Women's Club, Pi Beta Phi, Epsilon Sigma; Christian Church. Iowa Master Farm Homemaker. Married, 3 children.

Mertz, Dolores: Democrat from Ottosen; b. 30 May 1928 in Bancroft; AA, Briar Cliff College; farmer; Kossuth County Supervisor; secretary, Kossuth County Central Committee; regent, Catholic Daughters of America; secretary, Iowa Lakes Coordinating Council; member, Soroptimist International, Drama Club; Roman Catholic. Married, 7 children.

Metcalf, Janet: Republican from Des Moines; b. 31 December 1935 in Des Moines; attended Grinnell College; BS, ISU; retail business owner; member, LWV, IWPC; president, Planned Parenthood Mid-Iowa; Episcopalian. Married, 2 children.

Metz, Katheryn: Republican from Lamoni; b. 20 June 1904 in Lucas; attended Graceland and Penn; teacher; magazine writer; newspaper owner-publisher; worthy matron, OES; member, Iowa Press Women, National Federation of Press Women, FWC, BPW. Married, 2 stepchildren.

Miller, Elizabeth: Republican from Marshalltown; b. 24 August 1905 in Marshalltown; graduated from Marshalltown High School; member, Farm Bureau, RWC, Marshalltown Women's Club, BPW, Iowa Federation of Republican Women, NOWL, American Institute of Parliamentarians, YWCA, International Platform Association, YWCA; Congregational. Republican Woman of the Year, Marshall County, Outstanding Civic Leaders Award, Merit Mother of the Year. Married, 4 children.

Miller, Opal: Democrat from Rockwell City; b. 6 October 1915 in Rockwell City; attended ISTC; farm owner; deputy recorder, Warren and Allamakee counties; member, Legislative Ladies League, IWPC, NOWL, OES, BPW, Federated Women's Club, Calhoun County Historical Society, farm organizations; Presbyterian. Married, 6 children.

Mullins, Sue: Republican from Corwith; b. 18 June 1936 in Denver, CO; BS, ISU; free lance writer for farm publications; member, AAUW, Girl Scouts of America, Kossuth County Farm Bureau, IWPC, Ripon; State Planning Committee, Iowa 2000 Phase II, State Advisory Council for Community Betterment and Continuing Education; Dean's Advisory Council, ISU College of Agriculture; Dean's Advisory Committee, ISU College of Home Economics, State Study Committee, "Politics of Food"; board member, Iowa Freedom Foundation; Methodist. Married, 3 children.

Nelson, Gladys: Republican from Newton; b. 23 April 1895 in Crary, ND; graduate of the University of North Dakota; teacher; principal; president, Newton Women's Club, Iowa LWV; member, YWCA, Jasper county Child Welfare Association, PEO, OES, Delta Kappa Gamma; board member, Red Cross, Community Chest; Worthy High Priestess of White Shrine; secretary, Iowa Child Welfare Committee, Iowa Legislative Council; treasurer, Council for Better Education; Congregational. Married, 2 children.

Nelson, Linda: Democrat from Council Bluffs; b. 27 July 1951; BS, University of Nebraska-Lincoln; teacher; Council Bluffs Education Association president, Southwest Uniserve Unit president, member, national and state education associations, Council Bluffs Education Association, Alpha Delta Kappa, Iowa Reading Association, Iowa Council of Teachers of Mathematics, Council Bluffs Sister City Association, Pottawattamie County DCC, Democratic National Convention delegate; Christian.

Neuhauser, Mary: Democrat from Iowa City; b. 27 August 1934, New York; AB, Radcliffe, 1956; JD, U of I, 1982; lawyer; mayor, Iowa City; president, Iowa League of Municipalities; board member, National League of Cities; member, Iowa Advisory Commission on Intergovernmental Relations, LWV, chamber of commerce, Episcopalian. Assistant Majority Leader. Married, 3 children.

Nielsen, Joyce: Democrat from Cedar Rapids; b. 20 November 1933 in Askov, MN; graduated from high school; president, financial consulting firm; board member, LWV, United Nations Association, Women Unlimited, United Way, YWCA; Peoples Church. Married, 1 child.

O'Halloran, Mary: Democrat from Cedar Falls; b. 1 May 1943 in Norfolk, NE; attended Creighton University; BA, Clark College, 1966; teacher; member, AAUW, IWPC, National Education Association, ISEA, LWV; Roman Catholic. American Legion Outstanding Young Woman Award; Distinguished Service Award, Future Business Leaders of America, Friend of Education Award, Cedar Falls Education Association. U.S. Department of Energy Region IV administrator. Single.

Orr, Jo Ann: Democrat from Grinnell; b. 10 February 1923 in Cedar Rapids; BME, Oberlin College, 1946; later attended Chicago Teachers College, U of I; teacher; board member, Poweshiek County Mental Health Center; member, United Nations Association, Common Cause, IWPC, Farm Bureau; president, LWV of Grinnell; People' Unitarian Church. Married.

Peick, Doris Ann: Democrat from Cedar Rapids; b. 22 September 1933 in Jones County; attended Kirkwood Community College, U of I, University of Wisconsin; employed at Rockwell-Collins; member, Second District Farm-Labor Coalition, Iowa State Historical Society, Linn County Democratic Central Committee, Hawkeye Labor Council Auxiliary, IBEW, Women of the Moose, Fraternal Order of Eagle's Auxiliary, Marion Democratic Club, Fleet Reserve Auxiliary, Eighties Club; Lutheran. Delegate and Arrangements Committee member, 1980 Democratic National Convention. Married, 2 children.

Pendray, Carolyn: Democrat from Maquoketa; b. 9 December 1881 in Mount Pleasant; attended college; teacher; county superintendent of schools; member, PEO, DAR, Outlook Study Club, BPW; chairwoman, Jackson County Democratic Party; chairwoman of Democratic Party, second congressional district; Congregational. Married.

Poffenberger, Virginia: Republican from Perry; b. 12 November 1934 in Perry; BS, ISU, 1957; JD, Drake University, 1978; lawyer; member, American, Iowa, Dallas county bar associations, PEO, BPW, IWPC, State Extension Advisory Committee; president, Perry Day Care, Inc.; Methodist. Married, 3 children.

Sargisson, Hallie: Democrat from Salix; b. 1 January 1907 in Luton; business school; president, Luton Consolidated School Board, Woodbury County Library Board; chair, Iowa Federation of Women's Clubs; district instructor and officer, OES; board member, Woodbury County Red Cross; Methodist. Woodbury County Treasurer. Married, 3 children, and raised another child.

Shaw, Elizabeth: Republican from Davenport; b. 2 October 1923 in Monona; AB, Drake University, 1945; JD, U of I, 1948, Order of the Coif; graduate studies at University of Minnesota; member, Davenport Country Club, Davenport Club, Davenport Outing Club, LWV, RWC, PEO, Kappa Kappa Gamma, Federated Women's Club, ABWA; Congregational. Assistant Minority Leader. Married, 3 children.

Smith, Jo: Republican from Davenport; b. 24 September 1926 in Columbus Junction; attended U of I; president, Davenport Jaycettes, Fairmount Pre-school for Multi-handicapped, Friendly House, River Bend and Mississippi Valley Girl Scout Councils; board member, United Neighborhood Centers of America; Methodist. Married, 3 children.

Svoboda, Jane: Democrat from Clutier; b. 3 November 1944 in Tama County; business school graduate; secretary, Outstanding Young Women of America; recipient, Iowa Porkettes' County Bellringer Award, Iowa Bar Association's American Citizenship Award; Roman Catholic. Married, 4 children.

Svoboda, Linda: Democrat from Amana; b. in Amana; BA, Marquette University; newspaper reporter; researcher, Iowa House; member, IWPC. Single.

Szymoniak, Elaine: Democrat from Des Moines; b. 24 May 1920 in Boscobel, WI; BS, University of Wisconsin; MS, ISU; board member, Civic Center, Westminster House; member, United Way of Central Iowa, IWPC, NEXUS, YWCA, House of Mercy, Coalition for the Homeless, Planned Parenthood, NOW, Girl Scouts, Community Focus; Roman Catholic. Married, 5 children.

Teaford, Jane: Democrat from Cedar Falls; b. 1 July 1935 in Mitchell County, KS; BS, Kansas State University, 1957; president, LWV of Iowa; member, Iowa Professional and Occupational Regulation Commission, Black Hawk County Board of Human Services, Cedar Falls Board of Adjustment, NAACP, IWPC, ICLU, AAUW; Methodist. Married, 2 children.

Thompson, Patricia: Republican from West Des Moines; b. 17 September 1927 in Grant; AA, University of Nebraska, 1947; bank employee; president, West Des Moines Community School District Board of Directors; director, Iowa Association of School Boards; member, Chamber of Commerce, Community Education District-wide Advisory Council, United Way Information and Referral Advisory Council, IWPC, PEO, West Des Moines' Women's Club, BPW, Iowa Autism Center Board, Des Moines District Dental Auxiliary, Brevity Club; Methodist. Assistant Majority Leader. Married, 5 children.

Tinsman, Maggie: Republican from Bettendorf; b. 14 July 1936 in Moline, IL; BA, University of Colorado, Phi Beta Kappa, Pi Gamma Mu; MSW, U of I; Scott County Supervisor; president, Women Officials of National Association of Counties; chair, Iowa Advisory Commission on Intergovernmental Relations, Iowa Federation of Republican Women Special Projects; commissioner, Department of Elder Affairs; secretary/treasurer, Iowa Supervisors' Association; member, chamber of commerce, Farm Bureau, Quad Cities Vision of the Future Steering Committee, Junior League, American Lung Association of Iowa, Information, Referral & Assistance Service of Scott & Rock Island Counties; Episcopalian. Assistant Minority Leader. Married, 3 children.

Trucano, JoAnn: Republican from Des Moines; b. 30 August 1943 in Early; attended ISU; member, Bishop's Steering Committee for Women on Justice; scholarship chair, Des Moines Panhellenic Association; leader, Boy Scouts, Girl Scouts; Roman Catholic. Married, 4 children.

Van Alstine, Percie: Republican from Gilmore City; b. 9 October 1905 in Gilmore City; attended Rockford College; BA, U of I, 1928; employed in commercial home economics; president, Humboldt County Council of Republican Women; Methodist. Iowa Development Commission. Single.

Walter, Marcia: Democrat from Council Bluffs; b. 3 April 1950 in Omaha; attended Iowa Wesleyan Community College; president, DWC; member, BPW, Legislative Ladies League, Historical Society of Pottawattamie County, La Leche League, Southwest Iowa Talented and Gifted; 1981 Outstanding Young Woman of America. Married, 2 children.

Wick, Kathlyn Kirketeg: Republican from Bedford; b. 18 July 1903 near Nashua; attended Grinnell College, BA, U of I; graduate study at University of Wisconsin, University of Colorado; teacher; Grand Esther of the Grand Chapter of OES; member, PEO; board member, State Historical Society of Iowa, Bedford Library; county president, Iowa Children's Home Society, American Legion Auxiliary; state auditor, Iowa Council of Republican Women's Clubs; Presbyterian. Married.

Wolcott, Olga Doran: Democrat from Rockwell; b. 12 August 1904 in Colesburg; graduated from Mason City Junior College; teacher; deanery president, Mason City Council of Catholic Women; vice-president, Dubuque Archdiocesan Council; chair, Cerro Gordo County FWC; member, Farm Bureau, LWV, BPW, Wigwam and Wagon Campers, Rake and Hoe County Garden Club, Catholic Daughters of America, American Legion Auxiliary, Mason City Friends of Libraries; Roman Catholic. Married, 2 children.

Yenger, Sue: Republican from Ottumwa; b. 5 August 1938; graduated from Ottumwa Heights Junior College, 1958; BA, Parsons College, 1961; teacher; director, Headstart Program in Wapello County; manager, Work Incentive Program for Ottumwa area; chair, Advisory Board of Wapello County Alcoholism Program, Ottumwa Day Care Center; board member, Wapello County United Way, Women's Center of Indian Hills Community College, Displaced Homemakers Program of Indian Hills Community College, Iowa Commission on Aging; member, IWPC, RWC; Disciples of Christ. Married, 2 children.

Zastrow, Katherine Mull Falvey: Democrat from Albia; b. 19 March 1904, Muscatine County; BA, U of I; Phi Beta Kappa; teacher; managed lumberyard and farm; director, First Iowa State Bank; member, BPW, Albia Women's Club, American Legion Auxiliary, Council of Interstate Cooperation, Zeta, Tau Alpha, Pi Lambda Theta, Monroe County Farm Bureau, Cancer Society, Polio Foundation, Red Cross; trustee, Albia Library, Arthritis and Rheumatism Foundation; Roman Catholic. Appointed to Iowa Development Commission. Married.

Zimmerman, Jo Ann: Democrat from Waukee; b. 21 December 1936 in Van Buren County; school of nursing, 1958; BA, Drake University, 1973; graduate studies, ISU; nurse; health planner; board member, Iowa League of Nursing, PTA, Dallas County Democratic Central Committee; member, American Nurses Association, LWV, IWPC, NOW; Christian Church. Lieutenant governor, 1987-1990. Married, 5 children.

NOTES

INTRODUCTION

1. "They'll Add Feminine Touch at the Next Assembly," *Des Moines Sunday Register*, 17 November 1946, sec.A, p. 1.

2. Ibid.

3. Patricia Aburdene and John Naisbitt, *Megatrends for Women* (New York: Villard Books, 1992), pp. 1-2.

4. Women in the U.S. Congress 1994, and Women in State Legislatures, Fact Sheets, Center for the American Woman and Politics (CAWP), National Information Bank on Women in Public Office, Eagleton Institute of Politics, Rutgers University.

5. A research note about the stories may be informative for those interested in methodology. The interviews from which the stories have been excerpted ranged in length from about two hours to ten hours. The questions for them were as open ended as the interviewer could make them and still provide some focus and direction for the narrator. In general, the information requested in the interviews included the legislator's natal or adopted family, her childhood, early adulthood, family life, volunteer and professional work, candidacy for the legislature, experiences in the legislature and life after it. In preparation for each interview, local newspapers and the House and Senate Journals were searched for background on the legislator. The interviews were informal. Narrators wanted to tell their stories in their own ways and that was respected. In those cases in which the legislator was deceased, family members or friends were often interviewed. Narrators had the opportunity to examine and edit the transcripts from their interviews. The edited transcripts are available at the Iowa Women's Archives at the University of Iowa and at Special Collections, Parks Library, Iowa State University.

6. Small cracks in the walls surrounding Iowa voting booths emerged in 1894 and 1915. In response to objections of taxation without representation, the 1894 session of the legislature granted women voting rights in school bond elections and in public votes on whether to borrow money or raise the tax levy. In 1897 those voting privileges remained intact, but a Code revision stated women's ineligibility to vote for school board members or officers. Legislation passed in 1915 allowed women who owned land to vote on local drainage district issues. In those elections in which Iowa women could vote, they cast their votes on separate ballots and deposited them in separate ballot boxes. (Segregation of women voters also occurred in other states. For example, until passage of the Nineteenth Amendment, Missouri women voted with pink ballots.)

The next year, 1916, male voters decided the fate of Iowa women's suffrage when they defeated a state constitutional amendment to allow women to vote in general elections. Despite a rigorous campaign, the amendment for woman suffrage failed 162,849 to 172,990. In 1919 the legislature passed a bill allowing women to vote in presidential elections, but the bill had no effect because women gained voting rights through the passage of the Nineteenth Amendment before the next presidential election. Ruth A. Gallaher, *The Legal and Political Status of Iowa Women in Iowa: An Historical Account of the Rights of Women in Iowa from 1838 to 1918* (Iowa City: State Historical Society of Iowa, 1918) pp. 202, 208, 217, 220; John E. Briggs and Jacob Van Ek, "The Legislation of the Fortieth General Assembly of Iowa," *The Iowa Journal of History and Politics* 21 (October 1923): 524; "Legal Decisions for Women Voters," *The Woman Citizen*, 30 October 1920: 598; John E. Briggs, "The Legislation of the Thirty-ninth General Assembly of Iowa," *The Iowa Journal of History and Politics* 19 (October 1921): 507.

7. When the 39th General Assembly met in 1921, legislative leaders anticipated amending the Iowa Constitution to remove the male qualification for legislative service, but other issues complicated the matter. In the years that end with zero, Iowa voters decide whether or not to call a constitutional convention. In 1920, they voted to have a convention. Therefore, the most direct means for allowing women in the legislature would have been through the anticipated new state constitution. Governor Nate Kendall refused to call the convention, and the state lost the opportunity for a speedy change. Another issue unrelated to the amendment also delayed action aimed at revising the state's constitution. In 1921 legislators assumed that Governor Kendall would call a special session which would finish codifying Iowa's laws, a process begun in 1919. In anticipation of the special session, legislators delayed action on an amendment to allow women to serve in the General Assembly until the extraordinary session. Governor Kendall declined to call a special session, however, thus delaying the amendment process for two years.

In 1923 the 40th General Assembly began the process to remove the only prohibition to any public office for women. The resolution passed without dissenting votes. The legislature passed the resolution again in 1925, setting the stage for voters to act on it in the 1926 general election. The amendment generated little interest but a few months before the election the Iowa League of Women Voters campaigned for its passage. Iowans approved the amendment with 239,999 voters supporting it and 133,929 opposing it. Upon passage of the amendment, Iowa became the last state in the nation to remove barriers to women serving in its legislature. New Hampshire continued to have the prohibition until 1956, but women had won elections and served since 1920. Briggs, "The Legislation of the Thirty-ninth General Assembly of Iowa," 507; Briggs, "The Legislation of the Fortieth General Assembly of Iowa," 522, 535; "Iowa Women Win," *The Woman Citizen*, 30 January 1927: 32; State of Iowa, *Iowa Official Register, 1927-1928*, p. 39; Leon Anderson, *New Hampshire Women Legislators: 1921-1971* (Evans Printing, 1971), n.p.

8. In 1917, fifty-four women were county superintendents of schools in Iowa. Gallaher, *Legal and Political Status of Women in Iowa*, pp. 228-230, 232-233.

9. David W. Jordan, "Those Formidable Feminists: Iowa's Early Women Vote-getters," *Iowan* (1 December 1982) 48; Ethel W. Hanft and Paula J. Manley, *Outstanding Iowa Women Past and Present* (Muscatine: River Bend Publishing, 1980), p. 93.

10. "Woman to Run for Senate," *New York Times*, 17 March 1922, p. 8; *Iowa Official Register, 1921-1922*, pp. 450, 478; "Vote League to Ask Women Quit Race for House," *Des Moines Register*, 4 May 1922, p. 14; *Iowa Official Register, 1923-1924*, pp. 399, 507, 510.

11. "Of Interest," *CAWP News and Notes*, Center for the American Woman and Politics, Winter 1991, p. 15; Emmy E. Werner, "Women in the State Legislatures," *The Western Political Quarterly*, 21 (March 1968): 42.

12. Frank J. Stork, *Lawmaking in Iowa: System and Structure* (Des Moines: Iowa Senate, 1980), p. 28.

1. CANDIDACY: THE PIONEERS

1. Malcom E. Jewell and Samuel C. Patterson, *The Legislative Process in the United States*, 2d ed. (New York: Random House, 1973), pp. 73-87; William J. Keefe, *The American Legislative Process* (Englewood Cliffs, New Jersey: Prentice-Hall, Inc., 1985), pp. 109-117.

2. Joanne Varner Hawks, "A Select Few: Alabama's Women Legislators, 1922-1983," *The Alabama Review* 38 no. 3, p. 177; M. Carolyn Ellis and Joanne V. Hawks, "Ladies in the Gentlemen's Club: South Carolina Women Legislators, 1928-1984," in *Proceedings of the 1986 South Carolina Historical Association*: 17; Mary K. Dains, "Forty Years in House: A Composite Portrait of Missouri Women Legislators," typescript; R. Darcy, Susan Welch, and Janet Clark, *Women, Elections, and Representation* (New York: Longman, 1987), p. 33.

3. Darcy, *Women, Elections, and Representation*, pp. 97-105.

4. Gertrude Cohen, interview with author, 1 March 1991; Helen Crabb, interview with author, 18 April 1988; Percie Van Alstine, interview with author, 1 August 1988.

5. The number of candidates is inexact because the *Iowa Official Register* does not identify the candidate's sex. Because some names can be either gender, only those most likely to be female (Barbara, Linda, Mary, etc.) were counted. Undoubtedly, some women were not counted.

6. Eleanor Flexner, *Century of Struggle: the Woman's Rights Movement in the United States*, rev. ed. (Cambridge, Mass.: Harvard University Press, 1975), pp. 339-340.

7. The thirteen women with rural interests discussed here are: Carolyn Pendray, Ada Garner, Isabel Elliott, Mae Lynch, Amy Bloom, Kathlyn Wick, Helen Crabb, Katheryn Metz, Katherine Zastrow, Lenabelle Bock, Frances Hakes, Percie Van Alstine, and Vera McKee. Also elected between 1928 and 1963, but lacking identifiable rural interests are: Edna Lawrence and Gladys Nelson.

8. Deborah Fink, *Open Country Iowa: Rural Women, Tradition and Change* (Albany: State University of New York, 1986), p. 30.

9. Dorothy Schwieder, "Education and Change in the Lives of Iowa Farm Women," *Agricultural History* 60 (Spring 1986): 213-214.

10. The first secretary won her seat in the 1970s and the first nurse in the 1980s. After teaching, Katheryn Metz (Republican, Lamoni) owned a newspaper, Mae Lynch (Democrat, Pocahontas) practiced law, and Katherine Zastrow (Democrat, Monroe) managed a lumberyard. Dains, "Forty Years in the House;" Joan M. Jensen, "Pioneers in Politics," *El Palacio* 92 (Summer/Fall 1986): 15; Ellis, "Ladies in the Gentlemen's Club," 17.

11. Amy Bloom, Mae Lynch, Katheryn Metz, Carolyn Pendray, Percie Van Alstine (never married), Kathlyn Kirketeg Wick, and Katherine Falvey Zastrow had no children.

12. Iowa had 515 newspapers in 1948, 254 Republican, 43 Democrat, and with only a few exceptions, the balance were Independent. As noted, the newspapers were not evenly distributed across the state. Des Moines provides the most outstanding example with its eighteen newspapers, and Polk county had another five newspapers in the communities surrounding Des Moines. *State of Iowa Official Register, 1947-1948* (Des Moines: State of Iowa, 1947), pp. 217-236.

13. "Has Always Lived in Atmosphere of Politics and is Ardent Democrat," *Des Moines Tribune-Capital*, 11 January 1929, p. 8; "Much Platform, Little Performance," *Jackson Sentinel*, 15 January 1929, p. 6.

14. "Vote for Every Republican," *Mt. Pleasant Journal*, 4 November 1910, p. 1; "Vote for Elder," *Mt. Pleasant Free Press*, 24 October 1912, p. 1; "The County Ticket," *Mt. Pleasant Free Press*, 17 October 1912, p. 1; "The County Ticket," *Mt. Pleasant Free Press*, 31 October 1912, p. 1; "Weddings," *Mt. Pleasant Weekly News*, 31 March 1920, p. 2.

15. "Nice Compliment Paid by Des Moines Register," *Jackson Sentinel*, 1 June 1928, p. 1; "Maquoketa Woman Honored," *Jackson Sentinel*, 31 July 1928, p. 1; "Jackson County

Entitled to Able Representation," *Jackson Sentinel*, 5 October 1928, p. 1.

16. The *Maquoketa Excelsior* repeatedly pointed to the need for a man to represent Jackson County. For example, within two paragraphs a reporter wrote "A representative goes from here and mixes with other competent minded men of the state in legislature," "In such places as this there is needed men of good judgment, men who have had experience that show them to be of a weight that they can deal with other men with the assurance of receiving consideration at the hands of those who are helping to frame laws," and "J. L. Kinley, the man who is asking the Republicans to vote their ticket," and "A man of much experience and a man with safe and sound judgment that is what is needed, and this is what you find in the personality of this safe candidate." "Kinley Out for Representative," *The Maquoketa Excelsior*, 2 October 1928, p. 1; "J. L. Kinley for Representative," *Maquoketa Excelsior*, 21 October 1928, p. 1; "J. L. Kinley is a Farmer Plus," *Maquoketa Excelsior*, 16 October 1928, p. 1.

17. "A Condensed Survey of Our Candidates," *Jackson Sentinel*, 26 October 1928, p. 1; "Political Pot Boils Merrily as Battle Nears," *Jackson Sentinel*, 2 November 1928, p. 1.

18. Vernon A. Garner, interview with author, 8 February 1991.

19. Earle D. Ross, *Iowa Agriculture: An Historical Survey* (Iowa City: State Historical Society of Iowa, 1951), pp. 164-165.

20. "Wilford Discusses Present Tariff Evils," *Iowa Recorder*, 12 October 1932, p. 1.

21. "Democratic Rally at Shell Rock," *Iowa Recorder*, 19 October 1932, p. 1; "Meeting Well Attended," *Shell Rock News*, 13 October 1932, p.1.

22. "Democratic Rally at Shell Rock," *Iowa Recorder*, 19 October 1932, p. 1.

23. "Legislative News from Iowa's Capitol Hill," *Iowa Recorder*, 22 February 1933, p. 8; No headline, *Iowa Recorder*, 22 March 1933, p. 2.

24. Helen Vandenburg, interview with author, 23 May 1991.

25. "Mrs. Frank Elliott, Only Woman Member of Iowa Legislature Turns the Tables," *Sioux City Journal*, 13 February 1937, p. 1.

26. Kathlyn Wick, interview with author, 23 May 1988.

27. Helen Margaret Crabb interview.

28. Ibid.

29. "Three Women to Serve in the Iowa House of Representatives Next January," *Des Moines Sunday Register*, 14 November 1948, sec. L, p. 3.

30. Helen Margaret Crabb interview.

31. Advertisement, *Bagley Gazette*, 26 October 1948, p. 7.

32. "Oh! Brother—Guthrie County Goes Democratic," *Bagley Gazette*, 4 November 1948, p. 1; "Jamaica Club Woman Smashes Tradition," *Bagley Gazette*, 4 November 1948, p. 1.

33. "Leader of 'Margarine Bill' also Founder of Newton LWV in 1934," newspaper article, Gladys Nelson scrapbook, in her possession; Phyllis Yuhas, letter to author, 12 December 1988.

34. Phyllis Yuhas, letter to author, 12 December 1988.

35. Another family member had also been a legislator. Lawrence Falvey's father, M.C. Falvey had served in the Iowa House in 1933 and 1935. "Record Number of Women in Legislature," *Cedar Rapids Gazette*, 13 February 1963, sec. B, p. 10; Katherine Zastrow, interview with author, 10 June 1988; Stork, *The Iowa General Assembly*, p. 471.

36. Katherine Zastrow interview.

37. Percie Van Alstine's father, H. S. Van Alstine, served in the 37th, 38th, and 39th General Assemblies (1917-1921). Her mother had devoted her life to suffrage efforts, and later the League of Women Voters. Percie Van Alstine interview.

38. Percie Van Alstine interview.

39. "Corn Bread 'Battle' Won by Legislator," *Des Moines Register*, 29 January 1963, p. 1.

40. "Miss Van Alstine's Caper," *Christian Science Monitor,* 21 March 1963, section C, p. 1.

41. "Record Number of Women in Legislature," *Cedar Rapids Gazette*, 13 February 1963, section B, p. 10; "Look Like a Girl, Think Like a Man, Act Like a Lady and Work Like a Dog," *Ames Daily Tribune*, 19 January 1962, p. 6.

42. "Urge Women in Races for Legislature," *Des Moines Register*, 21 March 1964, p. 1.

43. "420 in Races for Assembly," *Des Moines Register*, 15 April 1964, pp. 1, 7.

44. Sister Mary Ramona, letter to author, 31 May 1991.

45. Mary Pat Gregerson, interview with author, 26 July 1989.

46. Gertrude Cohen interview.

47. Minnette Doderer also ran in 1964, but as an incumbent.

48. Frances Hakes did not run in 1964 because reapportionment placed her in the same district as Percie Van Alstine. Hakes decided to retire. Minnette Doderer was elected in a special election in 1964 and re-elected in that year's special election. Katherine Zastrow had remarried and moved to another part of the state. A sidebar to Zastrow's story is that she had remarried shortly after the end of the 1963 session. When Governor Harold Hughes called a special session early in 1964, the attorney general decided that Zastrow could not serve in it because she had moved out of the district. Even though Zastrow maintained a residence in her former district and continued to own businesses there, the attorney general wrote that a woman's residence was her husband's and since Zastrow's husband lived outside the district, Zastrow no longer lived in the legislative district she had been elected to serve. *Iowa Official Register, 1965-1966*, p. 73.

49. "Mrs. Blair Chides Adams," *New York Times*, 29 June 1923, p. 20. For an example of Blair's advocacy, see Emily Newell Blair, "Women in the Political Parties," *Annals of the American Academy of Political and Social Science*, 143 (May 1929): 217-229.

2. CANDIDACY: THE MID-1960S AND AFTER

1. Betty Friedan, *The Feminine Mystique* (New York: W.W. Norton & Company, Inc., 1963), pp. 15-32; Margaret Mead and Frances Balgley Kaplan, eds., *American Women: The Report of the President's Commission on the Status of Women and Other Publications of the Commission* (New York: Charles Scribner's Sons, 1965).

2. Sara M. Evans, *Born for Liberty: A History of Women in America* (New York: The Free Press, 1989), pp. 276-277.

3. This paragraph has been liberally excerpted from Louise Noun, *More Strong-Minded Women: Iowa Feminists Tell Their Stories* (Ames: Iowa State University Press, 1992), pp. xiv-xvi.

4. Fact Sheet, Women in State Legislatures 1987, Center for the American Woman and Politics, National Information Bank on Women in Public Office, Eagleton Institute of Politics, Rutgers University; Sharon Sherman, "Women Legislators Seek 'Critical Mass,'" *State Legislatures* 10 (January 1984) 26.

5. Diane Brandt, interview with author, 26 June 1989; Dorothy Carpenter, interview with author, 4 October 1992; Julia Gentleman, interview with author, 29 June 1989; Johnie Hammond, interview with author, 17 October 1991; Sonja Larsen, interview with author, 26 June 1989; Jean Lloyd-Jones, interview with author, 27 July 1989; Mary Neuhauser, interview with author, 21 May 1991; Mary O'Halloran, interview with author, 5 August 1989; JaneTeaford, interview with author, 23 May 1991; Susan M. Hartman, *From Margin to Mainstream: American Women and Politics Since 1960* (New York: Alfred A. Knopf, 1989), p. 92; Ethel Klein, *Gender Politics: From Consciousness to Mass Politics* (Cambridge, Massachusetts: Harvard University Press, 1984), p. 31; Ruth B. Mandel, *In the Running: The New Woman Candidate* (New Haven: Ticknor & Fields, 1981), p. 233.

6. Minnette Doderer, interview with author, 27 June 1989.

7. "Reapportionment Plea is Made to 'First Class' Iowa Citizens," *Chariton Leader*, 3 May

1960, p. 1.

8. Minnette Doderer interview, 1989.

9. Ibid.

10. "Swisher Sentenced to Six-Month Term in Income Tax Case," undated newspaper article, Minnette Doderer Papers, MsC 457, Box 11, Iowa Women's Archives, University of Iowa Libraries, Iowa City, Iowa.

11. Minnette Doderer interview, 1989.

12. Ibid.

13. Mandel, *In the Running*, pp. 84-91.

14. Minnette Doderer interview, 1989.

15. Some examples: Mary Neuhauser was Iowa City mayor; Jo Ann Zimmerman served on the Waukee Community School Board; Elaine Baxter served on the Burlington City Council; Johnie Hammond served on the Story County Board of Supervisors; Patricia Thompson served on the West Des Moines Community School Board; and Janis Torrence Laughlin served on the Muscatine County Board of Supervisors. Virginia Poffenberger, interview with author, 2 August 1989.

16. Poffenberger relates that if she ever writes a book, the title will be *Women Don't Understand Sewers*. Ibid.

17. Ibid.

18. Ibid.

19. "Politics for Dinner," *Redbook*, August 1978, 144.

20. Betty Jean Clark, interview with author, 13 July 1989.

21. Ibid.

22. Ibid.

23. Mandel, *In the Running*, pp. 148-150, 248-249; Sherman, "Women in State Legislatures Seek 'Critical Mass,'" 26.

24. Pat Thompson, interview with author, 16 September 1989.

25. In addition, Thompson had participated in Republican Party activities for several years. Sonja Egenes's (Republican, Story City) candidacy for Congress also played a role in Thompson's political activities. Egenes's campaign was the first in which Thompson had been active, working in the campaign headquarters and hosting a fundraiser for her. Thompson remembers that "I was interested in electing a woman to Congress and trying to unseat the Democrat to get a Republican elected." Ibid.

26. Dorothy Carpenter interview.

27. Janet Metcalf, interview with author, 7 October 1991.

28. Ibid.

29. Ibid.

30. Janet Carl, interview with author, 15 June 1990.

31. Ibid.

32. In addition to working together on Carl's campaign, Johnson and Carl continued their relationship and married. Leland L. Sage, *A History of Iowa* (Ames: Iowa State University Press, 1974), p. 324; Janet Carl interview.

33. Janet Carl interview.

34. "Jesse's Challenger Hits His Record of Absences," *Des Moines Register*, 29 October 1980, sec. A, p. 14.

35. "Jesse Says Victor Trucano 'Dumber than a Post,'" *Des Moines Register*, 6 November 1980, sec. B, p. 6.

36. "Political Notes by Ken Sullivan," *Cedar Rapids Gazette*, 18 January 1981, sec. A, p. 20.

37. Joan Hester declined to be interviewed, a regrettable loss. Her insights into serving with her spouse would have contributed another dimension of women's legislative experiences. At

least one other married couple has served together in a state legislature, she in the Mississippi Senate and he in the House in the 1950s. "Two Incumbents Find Residency Doubts Harmful," *Des Moines Register*, 6 June 1984, sec. M, p. 1; "Capitol Couple Calling It Quits," *Des Moines Register*, 23 January 1994, sec. B, p. 2; Joanne V. Hawks, M. Carolyn Ellis, and J. Byron Morris, "Women in the Mississippi Legislature (1924-1981)," *Journal of Mississippi History* 43 (November 1981): 268.

38. Mandel, *In the Running*, pp. 186-190; Susan J. Carroll, *Women as Candidates in American Politics* (Bloomington: Indiana University Press, 1985), p. 56; Darcy, *Women, Elections, and Representation*, pp. 59-62.

39. Lenabelle Bock, interview with author, 31 May 1988; "A Report on Campaign Finance in Iowa, 1988," Common Cause of Iowa, 1989, n.p.; "A Report on Legislative Election

40. Beverly Hannon, interview with author, 25 February 1991.

41. "A Report on Campaign Finance in Iowa, 1988," Common Cause of Iowa, 1989, n.p.; "A Report on Legislative Election Campaign Finance in Iowa, 1992," Common Cause/Iowa, pp. 18-19.

42. Jean Lloyd-Jones, Florence Buhr, Jane Svoboda, Joan Hester, and Linda Beatty worked as floor clerks before running for their seats. Linda Svoboda, interview with author, 20 June 1989.

43. Mary O'Halloran, interview with author, 5 August 1989.

44. Mary Lundby, interview with author, 1 October 1991.

45. Lenabelle Bock interview.

46. Incumbent senators bring the total number of women serving in 1973 and 1993 to the totals found in Table 1.1.

3. WOMEN IN A MEN'S CLUB

1. Jeane J. Kirkpatrick, *Political Woman* (New York: Basic Books, 1974), p. 106-107.

2. "Ladies of the House (and Senate)," *Boston Phoenix*, 30 June 1981, n.p., photocopy in author's possession.

3. Madeleine Kunin, "Keynote Address," in "Women in Legislative Leadership: Report from a Conference, November 14-17, 1985," Center for the American Woman and Politics, Eagleton Institute of Politics, Rutgers-The State University of New Jersey, p. 7; Mandel, *In the Running*, p. 98.

4. Dorothy W. Cantor and Toni Bernay with Jean Stoess, *Women in Power: The Secrets of Leadership* (Boston: Houghton Mifflin Company, 1992), p. 35.

5. Ibid., pp. 36-37.

6. Kirkpatrick, *Political Woman*, p. 42.

7. Cantor, *Women in Power: The Secrets of Leadership*, p. 48.

8. "Gossip about Iowa's Legislators," *Des Moines Register*, 15 January 1929, p. 6.

9. "Smoking O.K., Says Lady," *Des Moines Register*, 15 January 1929, p. 30.

10. Helen Crabb interview.

11. Gertrude Cohen interview.

12. "An Outstanding Legislator," *Des Moines Register*, 1 July 1956, section G, p. 12.

13. "Fine Record," *Newton Daily News*, 28 June 1956, no page number, Gladys Nelson scrapbook, in her possession.

14. "Leader of 'Margarine Bill' also Founder of Newton LWV in 1934," newspaper article, Gladys Nelson scrapbook, in her possession.

15. Joan Lipsky, interview with author, 7 July 1989.

16. Sonja Larsen interview; Janet Adams, interview with author, 13 February 1992.

17. Kirkpatrick, *Political Woman*, pp. 122-123; Jo Ann Orr, interview with author, 22 June

1989; Jo Ann Orr, letter to author, 29 November 1991.

18. Kirkpatrick, *Political Woman*, p. 109.

19. Hawks, "Women in the Mississippi Legislature (1924-1981)," p. 288; Arvone S. Fraser and Sue E. Holbert, "Women in the Minnesota Legislature," in Barbara Stuhler and Gretchen Kreuter, eds., *Women of Minnesota: Selected Biographical Essays* (St. Paul: Minnesota Historical Society Press, 1977), p. 268.

20. "A Pretty Tribute," *Jackson Sentinel*, 17 February 1931, p. 1.

21. Journal of the House, 1945, pp. 394-395.

22. "4 Women Legislators Honor Males," *Garner Leader*, 10 May 1961, p. 1.

23. "Mrs. Smith, as Senator, Not 'Talkative,' She Says," *New York Times*, 17 October 1949, p. 10.

24. Hawks, "A Select Few," 182; Ellis, "Ladies in the Gentlemen's Club: South Carolina Women Legislators, 1928-1984," 26.

25. Jean Lloyd-Jones interview.

26. Ibid.

27. Helen Margaret Crabb interview.

28. Lillian McElroy, interview with author, 5 June 1989.

29. "'Status on Women' Program Looks at Society Sex Roles," *Cedar Rapids Gazette*, 20 March 1972, p. 8.

30. Janet Metcalf interview; Josephine Gruhn, interview with author, 23 October 1989.

31. Betty Jean Clark interview.

32. Lenabelle Bock interview; "One 'Politician' in Legislature; Most Farmers," *Des Moines Tribune*, 8 January 1965, p. 4.

33. The minority party that Pendray attempted to organize in 1929 had not been in the majority in either chamber since 1892 when Senate Democrats had held a twenty-five to twenty-four majority membership over the Republicans. "Hammill Postpones Appointments for a Week," *Des Moines Register*, 15 January 1929, pp. 1, 3; "Lone Woman in Assembly Gets Democrats Lined Up," *Des Moines Tribune-Capital*, 19 January 1929, p. 21.

34. "White Wash for Liquor Probe is Voted by Senate," undated newspaper article in author's possession.

35. "Downs Public Hearing Move," *Des Moines Tribune*, 13 February 1935, p. 1.

36. "Blue Opposed on Abolishing Interim Board," *Des Moines Register*, 17 January 1947, p. 1.

37. "Attacks 'Gag' On Board of Control Bills," *Des Moines Register*, 28 March 1947, p. 1.

38. "Denies 'Gag Rule' Used on Board Bills," *Des Moines Tribune* 28 March 1947, p. 8.

39. The legislature did conduct a school the Friday before the session began in 1949. "First Termers Form '52' Club," *Des Moines Register* 10 April 1947, p. 9; "Kuester Denies Withdrawing," *Des Moines Tribune* 7 January 1949, p. 7.

40. Susan and Martin Tolchin, *Clout: Womanpower and Politics* (New York: Coward, McCann & Geoghan, Inc., 1974), p. 63; June Franklin, interview with author, 17 April 1991; Gertrude Cohen interview.

41. Gertrude Cohen interview.

42. Newspaper clipping in Gertrude Cohen's possession.

43. Gertrude Cohen interview.

44. "Day Parole Bill Passes House," *Cedar Rapids Gazette*, 13 April 1965, p. 3; Frank T. Nye, "The 61st General Assembly of Iowa," *The Palimpsest* 44 (September 1965): 464.

45. Gertrude Cohen interview.

46. Iowa Official Register, 1969-1970, pp. 345, 367.

47. Irene Diamond, *Sex Roles in the State House* (New Haven: Yale University Press, 1977), p. 105.

48. Lenabelle Bock interview.
49. Gertrude Cohen interview.
50. Joyce Lonergan, interview with author, 23 June 1989.
51. Jean Lloyd-Jones interview.
52. Josephine Gruhn interview.
53. "Woman Legislator Lures Committee with Cigars," *Des Moines Register*, 25 February 1949, p. 6.
54. Betty Jean Clark interview.
55. Ibid.
56. Ibid.
57. Vera McKee (Republican, Marion and Monroe) expressed a similar sentiment: "The male members of the legislature were very courteous and gallant towards me. I don't think that they thought I knew enough to be in on some of the private maneuverings of the Senate, but I had no complaint about the way they treated me." "Vera Shivvers McKee Spends Life Giving," *Knoxville Journal*, 17 October 1983, p. 1; Lenabelle Bock interview.
58. Joan Lipsky interview.
59. "Mary O'Halloran—'A Bit of a Rebel,'" *Des Moines Sunday Register*, 24 June 1973, Parade Section, p. 6.
60. Elizabeth Shaw, interview with author, 26 October 1989.
61. "2 State Senators Snap Male Barrier," *Washington Post*, 8 March 1972, sec. C, p. 2; Diamond, *Sex Roles in the Sate House*, pp. 157-159; Kirkpatrick, *Political Woman*, p. 128.
62. Sherman, "Women Legislators Seek 'Critical Mass,'" 26; Kirkpatrick, *Political Woman*, pp. 222-223.
63. Betty Hoffman-Bright, interview with author, 27 July 1989.
64. Dorothy Carpenter interview.
65. Florence Buhr, interview with author, 28 June 1990; Kathleen Chapman, interview with author, 21 May 1991.
66. Judy Ann Miller, "The Representative is a Lady," *Black Politician*, 1, (Fall 1969): 17.
67. Hazel C. Smalley, "Black Women Legislators Answer Questions," *Black Politician*, 2 (1971): 41.
68. A. June Franklin interview.
69. Minnette Doderer Collection, MsC 457, Box 10, Iowa Women's Archives, University of Iowa Libraries, Iowa City, Iowa.
70. The Senate President Pro Tempore becomes governor if neither the governor nor the lieutenant governor can fulfill the duties of office. Within the Senate, the President Pro Tempore only has the power allotted to the position by the Senate rules. Minnette Doderer interview, 1989.
71. Ibid.
72. "Majority Leader Accused of Sex Bias by Doderer," *Des Moines Register*, 8 January 1975, p. 5.
73. "Doderer Drops Bombshell into Demo Ranks," *Cedar Rapids Gazette*, 14 January 1975, p. 1.
74. "Shaky Peace in Legislature after Doderer Power Move," *Des Moines Register*, 15 January 1975, p. 7; "Senate Democrats Regain Majority," *Cedar Rapids Gazette*, 15 January 1975, sec. A, pp. 1-2.
75. Minnette Doderer interview, 1989; "Shaky Peace in Legislature after Doderer Power Move," *Des Moines Register*, 15 January 1975, p. 7; "Democrats End 2 Days Infighting; Unanimously Defeat Rules Change," *Des Moines Register*, 16 January 1975, p. 3.
76. The Senate president pro tempore becomes governor upon the resignation or death of the governor and lieutenant governor. "Demos Unite, Give Post to Doderer," *Cedar Rapids Gazette*, 16 January 1975, p. 1.

77. Ibid.

78. "Republican Leader Heaps High Praise on Doderer," *Cedar Rapids Gazette*, 20 January 1975, p. 4.

79. "Women Legislators Cheer Doderer in Power Tiff," *Cedar Rapids Gazette*, 26 January 1975, sec. B, pp. 1-2.

80. Ibid.

81. Minnette Doderer interview, 1989.

82. Mary Lundby interview.

83. "Two GOP Leaders Seek Key House Job," *Des Moines Register*, 12 November 1992, sec. A, pp. 1-2.

84. Until 1991, the lieutenant governor served as the presiding officer of the Senate, but a constitutional amendment removed the lieutenant governor from that position, and the Senate now elects its president from the body.

85. "Day Care Ignored: Lipsky Miffed," *Cedar Rapids Gazette*, 24 April 1974, sec. C, p. 2.

86. Kathy A. Stanwick, "Women's Legislative Caucuses: Altering State Policy and Politics," *News & Notes* 5 (May 1987): 5-6, Center for the American Woman and Politics, Rutgers University; Norma Paulus, "Women Find Political Power in Unity," *Journal of State Government* 60 (September/October 1987): 228; Katherine E. Kleeman, "Women in State Government: Looking Back, Looking Ahead," *Journal of State Government* 60 (September/October 1987): 202.

87. Elaine S. Knapp, "A Woman's Place in the Capitol," *State Government News* (September 1984), 6; Ellis, "Ladies in the Gentlemen's Club: South Carolina Women Legislators, 1928-1984," 27-29.

88. Don Avenson's aversion to legislators fraternizing with pages and his direct approach in chastising legislators who attempt it has been recorded by David Yepsen in "Avenson to Bid Farewell to Iowa House," *Des Moines Register*, 6 April 1990, sec. A, p. 2; "It's a Big Joke at Statehouse," *Des Moines Register*, 27 April 1992, sec. A, p. 13; Sonja Larsen interview.

89. Several state legislators have women's caucuses, some more formal than others. Massachusetts has an office and a paid staff; Maryland also has an office and uses student interns for staff. Iowa's women caucus has been classified as an informal one because it has neither staff nor office space. Carol Mueller, "A Scholar's Perspective," in "Women State Legislators: Report from a Conference, June 17-20, 1982," Center for the American Woman and Politics, Eagleton Institute of Politics, Rutgers, The State University of New Jersey, pp. 72-88; Jo Ann Zimmerman, interview with author, 18 February 1991.

90. The importance of women asserting themselves by asking for what they want also emerged in a conference of female state legislators. One woman said that she intended to go "back home and I'm going to push" for more power in the legislature. "Bipartisan Caucus Wants Focus on Bills Important to Women," *Cedar Rapids Gazette*, 16 January 1983, sec. A, pp. 1, 13; "Women State Legislators: Report from a Conference May 18-12, 1972," Center for the American Woman in Politics, Eagleton Institute of Politics, Rutgers, The State University, p. 12.

91. In the House, women served on 16 of the 17 standing committees in 1991, but only Doderer chaired one, Small Business, Development and Trade. Of the appropriations subcommittees, women served on 6 of the 11, but chaired 5 of them: Josephine Gruhn chaired Claims; Kathleen Chapman, Education; Jane Teaford, Health, Human Rights; Johnie Hammond, Human Services; and Linda Beatty, Regulation. In the Senate, women served on 12 of the 16 standing committees, and women chaired 2: Jean Lloyd-Jones, Ethics; and Beverly Hannon, Human Resources. Of the 10 appropriations subcommittees, women served on 3, and chaired 2: Florence Buhr, Health and Human Rights; and Elaine Szymoniak, Human Services.

92. "Women State Legislators: Report from a Conference, June 17-20, 1982," Center for

the American Woman and Politics, Eagleton Institute of Politics, Rutgers, The State University of New Jersey, p. 74.

93. "'Stereotyping' Blamed in Putting off Improvements to ISU Home Ec Building," *Cedar Rapids Gazette*, 30 March 1983, sec. B, p. 11.

94. Jean Lloyd-Jones interview.

95. Ibid.

96. Diamond, *Sex Roles in the State House*, pp. 104-106.

97. Irene Diamond observed that women in her study tended to serve on health and welfare committees and that those areas do not have lobbyists with the financial resources often commanded by business and industry groups. Linda Beatty, interview with author, 26 September 1991; Johnie Hammond interview; Diamond, *Sex Roles in the State House*, p. 107.

98. "Woman Protests Against 'Third Degree Lobbying' in House," *Des Moines Tribune-Capital*, 19 February 1931, p. 1; "Drivers Bill Passed; Fee is Lowered," *Des Moines Tribune-Capital*, 15 April 1931, p. 12.

99. "More Hell-Raising Needed," newspaper article, undated, in author's possession.

100. "Rope to Keep Lobbyists off Senate Floor," *Des Moines Tribune*, 28 January 1935, p. 1.

101. "Woman May Seek Office," *Des Moines Tribune*, 1 February 1935, p. 8.

102. One lobbyist recalled that it could be comical trying to signal the votes. During the debate on liquor by the drink in 1965, the lobbyist described a lawmaker whose sight was poor and who called to the back of the chamber, saying he could not see the signal. Finally, the embarrassed lobbyist tried a stage whisper, but the lawmaker's hearing had also diminished. The lobbyist described his discomfort resulting from trying to find a dignified way to respond to the lawmaker's insistent demands for directions on how to vote.

103. "Women State Legislators: Report from a Conference, May 18-12, 1972," Center for the American Woman in Politics, Eagleton Institute of Politics, Rutgers-The State University, p. 10; Diane Brandt interview; Jo Ann Orr interview.

104. Kathlyn Wick interview.

105. Elizabeth Shaw interview.

106. Joan Lipsky interview.

107. "Little 'Night-Life' Lobbying for 7 Women Legislators," *Des Moines Tribune*, 12 March 1970, pp. 1, 12; Helen Crabb interview; Minnette Doderer interview, 1991; Kathleen Chapman interview.

108. Beverly Hannon interview.

109. Jean Lloyd-Jones interview.

110. "Women in Politics Study Their Impact," *St. Louis Dispatch*, 22 November 1987, reprinted by the Center for the American Woman and Politics, Rutgers University; Ellis, "Ladies in the Gentleman's Club: South Carolina Women Legislators, 1928-1984,", p. 27; Mandel, *In the Running: The New Woman Candidate*, p. 65; Kirkpatrick, *Political Woman*, p. 118.

111. "Ladies of the House (and Senate)," *Boston Phoenix*, 30 June 1981, n.p., photocopy in author's possession.

112. Lenabelle Bock interview; Frank Nye, "Political Notes, *Cedar Rapids Gazette*, 9 February 1969, sec. B, p. 4, and 25 January 1971, p. 5.

113. "At One Ad Club, She is Welcome," *Des Moines Tribune*, 23 April 1969, p. 41.

114. "Nude Poster 'Demeaning,' Woman Senator Charges," *Des Moines Register*, 20 April 1970, p. 3.

115. "Gals Invited to Gridiron Fest, Or Are They?" *Cedar Rapids Gazette*, 26 March 1971, p. 7.

116. The irony in Jepsen's comments is that women senators used his private restroom because the Senate did not have a women's restroom, as it did for men. "Political Notes by

Frank Nye," *Cedar Rapids Gazette*, 18 April 1971, sec. B, p. 7.

117. "Women Legislators' Plea to Boycott Gridiron Dinner Fails to Move Ray," *Des Moines Tribune*, 8 April 1971, pp. 1, 19.

118. "Some Firsts at Ad Club's '75 Gridiron," *Des Moines Register*, 9 April 1975, p. 11.

119. Cantor, *Women in Power: The Secrets of Leadership*, p. 58.

4. WOMEN'S ISSUES

1. Kirkpatrick, *Political Woman*, pp. 99-101; "Women State Legislators: Report from a Conference, May 18-21, 1972," p. 19.

2. "Women State Legislators: Report from a Conference, May 18-21, 1972," pp. 17-18.

3. Pendray has been credited with passing bills giving women property rights and making women legal heads of households. Research does not support that view. Women's property rights in Iowa began their development in the *Iowa Code of 1851*, gradually increasing over the years. Researchers in the Legislative Service Bureau have also attempted to identify the connection between Pendray, property rights, and women as legal heads of households, but could not find more than is described here. Gallaher, *Legal and Political Status of Women in Iowa*, pp. 86-143; Jacob A. Swisher, "The Legislation of the Forty-third General Assembly of Iowa," Iowa Monograph Series, no. 1 (Iowa City: State Historical Society of Iowa, 1929), p. 24.

4. "Women's Lib Victorious in Voting Bill," *Cedar Rapids Gazette*, 11 February 1972, p. 10.

5. "House Hears Women's Lib 'Assailed'; Yields on Names," *Des Moines Register*, 11 February 1972, p. 4.

6. Ibid.

7. "Women's Lib Victorious in Voting Bill," *Cedar Rapids Gazette*, 11 February 1972, p. 10.

8. "House Hears Women's Lib 'Assailed'; Yields on Names," *Des Moines Register*, 11 February 1972, p. 4.

9. "Women's Lib Victorious in Voting Bill," *Cedar Rapids Gazette*, 11 February 1972, p. 10.

10. "Bill on 'Equal Treatment' of Men, Women Offered," *Des Moines Register*, 5 February 1974, p. 7; "Bill Would Equalize Code Words," *Cedar Rapids Gazette*, 9 February 1982, sec. A, p. 9.

11. 50 States Committee of the Iowa Commission on the Status of Women, "Iowa '50 States Project: A Review of the 1983 Iowa Code for Sex Discrimination'" (Des Moines: Iowa Commission on the Status of Women, 1984), p. 5; "Branstad Panel Finds Sexism in Iowa Laws," *Cedar Rapids Gazette*, 3 February 1984, sec. A, p. 6.

12. "Farm Slogan's Male Slant Riles Female Iowa Lawmaker," *Cedar Rapids Gazette*, 15 February 1983, sec. A, p. 2; "Mullins Still Unhappy with Booklet, Accused of 'Discrediting' Ag Agency," *Cedar Rapids Gazette*, 25 February 1983, sec. C, p. 9.

13. "Doderer Expresses Concern on Ray's Selection of Women," *Cedar Rapids Gazette*, 7 April 1973, p. 2.

14. "House Approves Gender Balance on Local Boards," *Des Moines Register*, sec. A, p. 1; Dorothy Carpenter interview; Minnette Doderer interview, 1991.

15. "Will Honor First Governor," *Cedar Rapids Gazette*, 7 June 1975, p. 8.

16. "New Battle Brewing over Building Name," *Cedar Rapids Gazette*, 18 February 1976, sec. C, p. 2.

17. "New Options for Naming State Office Building," *Cedar Rapids Gazette*, 13 June 1975, p. 4.

18. "Norpel Jousts Doderer in Long Truck Debate," *Cedar Rapids Gazette*, 15 March 1976, pp. 1, 3.

19. "Avenson Won't Trade Volga Lake for Votes," *Cedar Rapids Gazette*, 22 January 1977, pp. 1, 3; "New Options for Naming State Office Building," *Cedar Rapids Gazette* 13 June 1975, p. 4; "Political Notes by Frank Nye," *Cedar Rapids Gazette*, 8 February 1976, sec. B, p. 4; "New Battle Brewing over Building Name," *Cedar Rapids Gazette*, 18 February 1976, sec. C, p. 2.

20. Evans, *Born for Liberty: A History of Women in America*, pp. 99, 103.

21. Ibid., pp. 275, 291.

22. "House Boosts Ray $5,000; Cuts Aero Chief $1,428," *Cedar Rapids Gazette*, 17 June 1971, p. 5.

23. "House Gives Clerk Raise Despite Spending, Discrimination Charges," *Des Moines Register*, 13 January 1983, sec. A, p. 3.

24. "Bargaining Bill Faces Uncertain Fate in House," *Cedar Rapids Gazette*, 17 May 1973, sec A, p. 4; "Pay Formula is Criticized," *Cedar Rapids Gazette*, 30 April 1974, p. 4; "IHEA Claims Inequity in Area School Pay," *Cedar Rapids Gazette*, 26 April 1974, p. 8.

25. Evans, *Born for Liberty: A History of Women in America*, pp. 230-231, 310.

26. "Female Legislators Make Equal Pay Issue a Priority," *Des Moines Register*, 27 January 1983, sec. A, p. 3.

27. "Branstad Names Task Force to Study Equal State Pay," *Cedar Rapids Gazette*, 2 February 1983, sec. A, p. 2; "Unequal-pay Studies Asked," *Des Moines Register*, 24 February 1983, sec. A, p. 3; "State Task Force Urges 'Equal Pay' Study," *Cedar Rapids Gazette*, 24 February 1983, sec. A, p. 2.

28. "'Mini' Liquor Store Legislation Sent to Branstad," *Cedar Rapids Gazette*, 11 May 1983, sec. A, p. 4.

29. "Survey Finds Bias on Pay," *Cedar Rapids Gazette*, 7 February 1984, sec. A, p. 3.

30. "Workers Get Lesson on Comparable Worth," *Cedar Rapids Gazette*, 9 March 1983, sec. A, p. 11.

31. "As Senate Nears Close, Democrats Clash over Female Pay Issue," *Des Moines Register*, 18 April 1984, sec. A, p. 2.

32. "'Comparable Worth' Bill Wins Approval," *Des Moines Register*, 21 April 1984, sec. A, p. 2; "House Mulls Appeals on Comparable Worth," *Des Moines Register*, 5 April 1985, sec. A, p. 2; "House Votes Appeal System for Comparable Pay Disputes," *Des Moines Register*, 12 April 1985, sec. A, p. 2; "Legislature Enters its Final Week," *Des Moines Register*, 28 April 1985, sec. B, pp. 1, 6; "Group Sues Branstad over Pay Equity," *Des Moines Register*, 8 January 1986, sec. M, p. 1.

33. Winifred D. Wandersee, *On the Move: American Woman in the 1970s* (Boston: Twayne Publishers, 1988), pp. 91-95.

34. Mary O'Halloran interview.

35. "Doderer Vows to Remove Iowa Rape Law Inequities," *Cedar Rapids Gazette*, 3 March 1974, sec. B, p. 11.

36. Ibid.

37. "Senate Strikes out Rape Corroboration," *Cedar Rapids Gazette*, 2 April 1974, sec. C, p. 2.

38. "Corroboration Rule Cut from Rape Bill," *Cedar Rapids Gazette*, 1 May 1974, sec. C, p. 2.

39. Mary O'Halloran interview.

40. "Get Tough Measures are Approved by Senate," *Cedar Rapids Gazette*, 27 February 1975, p. 4.

41. "House Adopts Major Revision to Rape Law," *Cedar Rapids Gazette*, 16 March 1976, p. 3.

42. "Senate Rejects Need to Prove Rape Resisted," *Cedar Rapids Gazette*, 7 May 1976, p. 1.

43. "Sexual Abuse Proposal Gets House Approval," *Cedar Rapids Gazette*, 16 March 1976, p. 4.

44. "Senate Permits Abuse Charges by Spouses," *Cedar Rapids Gazette*, 6 May 1976, pp. 1, 3.

45. "Criminal Code," *Cedar Rapids Gazette*, 8 May 1976, p. 3.

46. Ibid.

47. "'No-knock', Massage Regulations Removed," *Cedar Rapids Gazette*, 25 May 1976, p. 5.

48. "Sexual Abuse Issue Unresolved," *Cedar Rapids Gazette*, 18 May 1976, p. 4.

49. "'No-Knock,' Massage Regulations Removed," *Cedar Rapids Gazette*, 25 May 1976, p. 5.

50. Joan Lipsky interview.

51. "Marital Rape Bill is Passed in Iowa House," *Des Moines Register*, 19 March 1986, sec. A, pp. 1, 2.

52. "Senate OKs Bill Outlawing Marital Rape," *Des Moines Register*, 4 April 1989, sec. A, p. 2; "Statehouse Briefing," *Des Moines Register*, 18 April 1989, sec. A, p. 2; Dorothy Carpenter interview.

53. Minnette Doderer interview, 1989.

54. "'Terror of Rape Attack' Touches Senate," *Cedar Rapids Gazette*, 27 March 1978, p. 8.

55. Joan Lipsky interview.

56. Josephine Gittler, "Hospital Cost Containment in Iowa: A Guide for State Public Policymakers," *Iowa Law Review* 69 (July 1984): 1273.

57. "New Indigent Medical Care System Eyed," *Des Moines Sunday Register*, 16 March 1986, sec. B, pp. 1, 4.

58. "Indigents Would get Health Care Nearer to Home under House Bill," *Des Moines Register*, 26 February 1986, sec. A, p. 2.

59. Jo Ann Zimmerman, News Release, 25 April 1986; News Release, 14 May 1986.

60. "New Indigent Medical Care System Eyed," *Des Moines Sunday Register*, 16 March 1986, sec. B, pp. 1, 4.

5. CHILDREN

1. Susan Welch and Sue Thomas, "Do Women in Public Office Make a Difference?" in Debra Dodson, ed., *Gender and Policymaking: Studies of Women in Office* (New Brunswick, New Jersey: State University of New Jersey, 1991), pp. 17-19; Aburdene, *Megatrends for Women*, pp. 22-23.

2. Journal of the House, 1933-1934 Extraordinary Session, p. 22.

3. William H. Chafe, *The American Woman: Her Changing Social, Economic, and Political Roles, 1920-1970* (London: Oxford University Press, 1972), p. 28; J. Stanley Lemmons, *The Woman Citizen: Social Feminism in the 1920s* (Urbana: University of Illinois Press, 1973), p. 147.

4. "Battle Slated on Child Labor," *Des Moines Register*, 18 November 1933, pp. 1, 2.

5. "House to Act on Child Labor," *Des Moines Register*, 3 December 1933, sec. L, p. 3; "Mrs. Garner Speeds Bill for Local Firm," *Iowa Recorder*, 20 December 1933, p. 1; *Journal of the Iowa House of Representatives, 1933*, p. 1606; *Journal of the Iowa Senate, 1933*, p. 424; *Journal of the Iowa Senate, 1933-1934 Extraordinary Session*, p. 166; J Lemmons, *The Woman Citizen*, p. 147.

6. "Iowa Fight over Shots for Children," *Des Moines Register*, 3 April 1977, sec. A, p. 1.

7. Ibid.

8. "House Votes to Require Immunization," *Des Moines Register*, 13 April 1977, sec. A, p. 1.

9. "Child Immunization Bill Clears Iowa Legislature," *Des Moines Register*, 7 May 1977, sec. A, p. 1.

10. "Iowa Measles Cases Drop from 4,333 to 76 in a Year," *Des Moines Register* 12 May 1979, sec. B, p. 2; Minnette Doderer interview, 1989.

11. "House Backs Tot Restraint in Cars, 81-17," *Des Moines Register*, 15 February 1983, sec. A, pp. 1, 2.

12. "Senator Coleman Vows He'll Block Child-Restraint Bill," *Des Moines Register*, 23 February 1983, sec. A, p. 3.

13. Ibid.

14. "Child Restraint Measure OK'd by Iowa House," *Cedar Rapids Gazette*, 25 February 1984, sec. A, pp. 1, 15.

15. "Subject Not Mentioned in Care-Center Debate: Child," *Des Moines Register*, 22 February 1984, sec. A, p. 9.

16. "Day Care Measure Loses in Iowa House," *Des Moines Register*, 28 February 1981, sec. A, p. 10.

17. "Child Abuse Report Bill Passed by Senate, 46-0," *Cedar Rapids Gazette*, 2 April 1965, p. 8; *Laws of the Sixty-First General Assembly* (Des Moines: State of Iowa, 1965), pp. 352-354.

18. Minnette Doderer interview, 1989.

19. "Seek to Break Cycle of Battered Children," *Cedar Rapids Gazette*, 2 April 1974, p. 5.

20. "Child Abuse Legislation Is Proposed," *Cedar Rapids Gazette* 23 January 1974, sec. C, p. 3.

21. "Seek To Break Cycle of Battered Children," *Cedar Rapids Gazette*, 2 April 1974, p. 5.

22. Joan Lipsky interview.

23. "Foster Homes for Orphans Bill Filed," *Cedar Rapids Gazette*, 12 February 1967, sec. A, p. 14.

24. Joan Lipsky interview.

25. Ibid.

26. Ibid.

27. Ibid.

28. Ibid.

29. Ibid.

30. "Sweeping Revision of Adoption Laws is Charted," *Cedar Rapids Gazette*, 15 March 1974, p. 9; "Child Abuse Bill Filed," *Cedar Rapids Gazette*, 27 March 1974, sec. C, p. 3.

31. "House Defeats Adoption Plan," *Cedar Rapids Gazette*, 11 April 1974, p. 5.

32. "Senate Bill Allows Natural Parent to Reclaim Child After Adoption," *Des Moines Register*, 6 April 1976, sec. A, p. 3.

33. "Lawmakers Grapple with Adoption Bill," *Des Moines Register*, 17 March 1986, pp. 1, 8.

34. Ibid.

35. Ibid.

36. "Senate Committee Kills Adoption Bill for this Year," *Des Moines Register*, 27 March 1986, sec. A, p. 2.

37. "Rep. Cohen Sees Danger in Plan for Juveniles," newspaper article, in Gertrude Cohen's possession.

38. "Would Blackout Juvenile Cases," *Cedar Rapids Gazette*, 14 February 1967, p. 4; "See Fight in Juvenile Law Area," *Cedar Rapids Gazette*, 6 March 1967, p. 5; "Lipsky Raps Juvenile Bills," *Cedar Rapids Gazette*, 12 March 1969, sec. C, p. 3.

39. "Status Offenders Need Aid, not Trips to Criminality's Classroom," *Cedar Rapids Gazette*, 1 March 1978, sec. A, p. 9.

40. Joan Lipsky interview.

41. "Criticism of Juvenile Bill is Answered," *Cedar Rapids Gazette*, 9 March 1977, pp. 1, 3; "Problems Seen in Juvenile Law," *Cedar Rapids Gazette*, 23 February 1977, sec. C, p. 2.

42. "'Status Offenses' Taken from Juvenile Court," *Cedar Rapids Gazette*, 3 May 1977, p. 3.

43. Minnette Doderer interview, 1989.

44. "Rights at 18 Passed by Senate," *Cedar Rapids Gazette*, 5 February 1973, pp. 1, 2.

45. "Fate of Adult Rights at 18 Bill Uncertain," *Cedar Rapids Gazette*, 3 February 1972, pp. 1, 10.

46. Ibid.

47. "'Not Much to Vote for' in Drinking Age Bill," *Cedar Rapids Gazette*, 15 March 1976, p. 4.

48. "Political Notes by Frank Nye," *Cedar Rapids Gazette*, 23 May 1976, sec. B, p. 2.

49. "Drinking Age Bill Proposed," *Cedar Rapids Gazette*, 12 January 1977, sec. A, p. 2; "Legislation's Fate," *Cedar Rapids Gazette*, 13 May 1978, sec. A, p. 4.

50. "Vote to Curb 'Pregnancy Marriages,'" *Des Moines Tribune*, 11 April 1973, sec. S, p. 3.

51. "Bar to Young Marriages Eyed," *Cedar Rapids Gazette*, 11 April 1973, sec. C, p. 4.

52. Minnette Doderer interview, 1989.

6. RIGHTS: EXPANSION AND DEFINITION

1. Katherine Zastrow interview.

2. "Votes to Abolish Gallows," *Cedar Rapids Gazette*, 4 February 1963, pp. 1, 3.

3. Katherine Zastrow interview.

4. "Urges Death Penalty Foe to Visit Family of Victim," *Des Moines Register*, 11 December 1962, p. 1.

5. "Votes to Abolish Gallows," *Cedar Rapids Gazette*, 5 February 1963, p. 1.

6. Katherine Zastrow interview.

7. "End Death Penalty, She Argues," *Des Moines Tribune*, 4 February 1963, p. 1.

8. "Votes to Abolish Gallows," *Cedar Rapids Gazette*, 5 February 1963, p. 1.

9. "End Death Penalty, She Argues," *Des Moines Tribune*, 4 February 1963, p. 1.

10. "The Death Penalty," *Des Moines Sunday Register*, 10 February 1963, section F, p. 6.

11. "Votes to Abolish Gallows," *Cedar Rapids Gazette*, 5 February 1963, p. 1.

12. Katherine Zastrow interview.

13. Ibid.

14. Edward S. Allen, *Freedom in Iowa: The Role of the Iowa Civil Liberties Union* (Ames: Iowa State University Press, 1977), pp. 99-104.

15. "Long Wait Just to See King Pass," *Des Moines Tribune*, 23 March 1965, p. 1; "Glanton, His Wife Fasting in Sympathy," *Des Moines Register*, 24 March 1965, p. 1; "Iowa Bill on Rights Advances," *Des Moines Tribune*, 23 March 1965, pp. 1, 9.

16. "House Studies Special Civil Rights Commission," undated newspaper article, in Gertrude Cohen's possession.

17. "Iowa House Approves Rights Bill," undated newspaper article, in Gertrude Cohen's possession.

18. "Low-rent Plan Support Asked," *Des Moines Register*, 19 October 1966, p. 20; "'Fair Housing' Bill Planned," *Des Moines Sunday Register*, 12 February 1967, sec. L, p. 5.

19. June Franklin interview.

20. Ibid; "Fair Housing Bill Okay Called Tribute to Reps. Reed, Franklin," *Cedar Rapids Gazette*, 18 April 1967, p. 5.

21. Cecil A. Reed with Priscilla Donovan, *Fly in the Buttermilk* (Iowa City: University of Iowa Press, 1993), p. 131.

22. "Fair Housing Bill Sent to Governor," *Cedar Rapids Gazette*, 20 April 1967, pp. 1, 3.

23. "Fair Housing Bond Assailed," *Des Moines Register*, 6 November 1967, p. 17.

24. "Seeks Fire Union Stand," *Des Moines Tribune*, 28 April 1967, p. 15.

25. "Asks City Council to Sue Board Here on 'Separate but Equal' School Plan," *Des Moines Register*, 29 February 1968, p. 3.

26. "Will Oppose I.S.U. Funds, Cites Racism," *Des Moines Register*, 3 August 1968, p. 3.

27. "Legislative Probe at Waterloo Asked," *Cedar Rapids Gazette*, 12 March 1969, sec. A, p. 5.

28. "Says Legislators Shun Racial Plea," *Cedar Rapids Gazette*, 27 March 1969, p. 8.

29. "Pay Tribute in March to Statehouse," *Des Moines Register*, 8 April 1968, sec. A, pp. 1, 6.

30. "Private Discrimination," *Cedar Rapids Gazette*, 2 March 1984, sec. A, p. 4.

31. "Lawmakers Work to Keep Legislation Alive," *Des Moines Register*, 2 March 1984, sec. A, p. 2.

32. "Branstad Signs Bill on Bias at Private Clubs," *Cedar Rapids Gazette*, 18 April 1984, sec. A, p. 4.

33. Barbara Sinclair Decker, *The Women's Movement: Political, Socioeconomic, and Psychological Issues*, 3rd ed. (Cambridge: Harper & Row, 1983), pp. 442-447.

34. "'Instant' Lobby: Women Swing Rights Vote," *Des Moines Tribune*, 25 March 1972, pp. 1, 5.

35. Minnette Doderer interview, 1989.

36. "'Instant' Lobby: Women Swing Rights Vote," *Des Moines Tribune*, 25 March 1972, pp. 1, 5.

37. "Iowa is Fourth State to Ratify Rights for Women," *Des Moines Register*, 25 March 1972, pp. 1, 2.

38. Ibid.

39. Ibid.

40. Ibid.

41. Ibid.

42. Ibid.

43. "Victory and Defeat on Last Day," *Cedar Rapids Gazette*, 25 March 1972, pp. 1, 3.

44. "Iowa is Fourth State to Ratify Rights for Women," *Des Moines Register*, 25 March 1972, pp. 1, 2.

45. Ibid.

46. "'Instant' Lobby: Women Swing Rights Vote," *Des Moines Tribune*, 25 March 1972, pp. 1, 5.

47. "Flurry of Senators Speak Out on ERA," *Cedar Rapids Gazette*, 12 March 1975, sec. C, p. 1.

48. "Iowa ERA is Proposed," *Cedar Rapids Gazette*, 15 February 1977, p. 4.

49. The loaves of bread created a lasting impression. In 1982, Doderer's clerk baked bread at home and shared some of the bread with friends in the House. The clerk left a loaf for her boss and went on to other tasks. When Doderer saw a loaf of bread on her desk, she began questioning everyone around her about the source of the bread. Doderer thought that anti-ERA

or anti-abortion activists had left the bread and that it announced some impending action. "Anti-ERA Move Launched in Iowa," *Cedar Rapids Gazette*, 2 March 1977 pp. 1, 3.

50. "Opponents Angry as ERA Hearing Delayed," *Cedar Rapids Gazette*, 11 May 1977, pp. 1, 3.

51. "Verbal Warfare at ERA Rallies," *Cedar Rapids Gazette*, 17 May 1977, pp. 1, 11.

52. Ibid.

53. Ibid.

54. Ibid.

55. "Stromer Rails Against 'Covert' Action on ERA," *Des Moines Register*, 11 January 1978, sec. A, p. 3; "House Amends ERA, then Halts Debate," *Cedar Rapids Gazette*, 16 January 1978, p. 3; "Legislative Notes," *Cedar Rapids Gazette*, 17 January 1978, p. 11.

56. Interestingly, in a story thirty column inches long, the *Des Moines Register* did not quote one woman or refer to any women legislators' presence. "Iowa ERA Approved by House, 70-25," *Des Moines Register*, 1 February 1978, sec. A, p. 1.

57. "ERA Backers Ecstatic," *Cedar Rapids Gazette*, 1 February 1978, p. 16.

58. "Legislative Notes," *Cedar Rapids Gazette*, 8 February 1978, sec. A, p. 6.

59. "Political Notes by Frank Nye," *Cedar Rapids Gazette*, 5 March 1978, sec. B, p. 4.

60. "Senate Unit Adds ERA 'Intent' Section," *Cedar Rapids Gazette*, 8 March 1978, sec. C, p. 8.

61. "He's Got a Fist Full of Amendments to Fight ERA," *Cedar Rapids Gazette*, 17 March 1978, p. 8; "Senate Beats Back ERA Amendments," *Cedar Rapids Gazette*, 20 March 1978, p. 3.

62. "Tempers Flare on ERA 'Intent' Action," *Cedar Rapids Gazette*, 21 March 1978, pp. 1, 9; "ERA Amendment Gets Final First-Round OK," *Cedar Rapids Gazette*, 31 March 1978, p. 10.

63. "Abortion Bill Foes Absent," *Des Moines Register*, 28 April 1967, p. 15.

64. Ibid.

65. Minnette Doderer interview, 1989.

66. "Abortion Proposal Too Broad, Most Women Legislators Fear," *Marshalltown Times-Republican*, 18 January 1969, p. 1.

67. Ibid.; "Rep. Lipsky Ask Abortion Law Delay," *Cedar Rapids Gazette*, 23 January 1969, p. 4; "Women Legislators' Abortion Law Views," *Des Moines Tribune*, 18 January 1969, p. 14.

68. "Abortion Proposal Too Broad, Most Women Legislators Fear," *Marshalltown Times-Republican*, 18 January 1969, p. 1.

69. Minnette Doderer interview, 1989.

70. Doderer's papers are housed in a collection at the Iowa Women's Archives at the University of Iowa Libraries, the letters regarding abortion have been separated and are not available to researchers. Doderer explained that the stories included in the letters tell such personal stories that she wanted them closed until the writers are deceased. "Her Battle on Law on Abortions," *Des Moines Tribune*, 17 March 1969, p. 18; "She Will Not Quit Fight," *Cedar Rapids Gazette*, 17 March 1969, pp. 1, 5; "Delay Action on Abortion Law Change," *Cedar Rapids Gazette*, 18 February 1969, p. 2; W. Charlene Conklin, interview with author, 2 November 1989.

71. "Emotion High in Debate on Abortion Law," *Cedar Rapids Gazette*, 21 February 1969, pp. 1, 3.

72. "Ties Abortion Bill Defeat to Remarks by Valbracht," *Des Moines Tribune*, 22 February 1969, pp. 1, 4.

73. "Defeat Abortion Bill; Revival Chances Slim," *Cedar Rapids Gazette*, 22 February 1969, pp. 1, 2.

74. Ibid.

75. "Ties Abortion Bill Defeat to Remarks by Valbracht," *Des Moines Tribune*, 22 February 1969, pp. 1, 4; "Abolishing Abortion Law," *Des Moines Register* 20 November 1969, p. 16.

76. "Abortion Reform," *Des Moines Tribune*, 27 January 1970, p. 8.

77. "Abortion Should be Matter Between Woman, Physician," *Council Bluffs Nonpareil*, 15 February 1970, p. 1.

78. "Pros and Cons Even at Abortion Law Hearing," *Cedar Rapids Gazette*, 3 April 1970, p. 8.

79. "Abortion Bill Action Told," *Cedar Rapids Gazette*, 7 April 1970, pp. 1, 3.

80. "Abortion Bill is Filed in Iowa Senate," *Cedar Rapids Gazette*, 28 January 1971, p. 17; "She'd Alter Abortion Law, *Waterloo Daily Courier*, 25 January 1971, p. 8; "Disagree on Ill. Ruling's Effect on Iowa Abortion Legislation," *Cedar Rapids Gazette*, 31 January 1971, sec. A, p. 8.

81. Franklin's perceptions of inherent racism in abortion debates has its roots in the racism of early birth control advocates. "Abortion has been associated with sterilization and racist population control and labeled a form of genocide," in Wendy Kaminer, *A Fearful Freedom: Women's Flight from Equality* (New York: Addison-Wesley Publishing Company, 1990), pp. 166-167. "Liberalized Abortion Bill Approved by House Unit," *Cedar Rapids Gazette*, 3 February 1971, sec. A, p. 5; "Woman's Words Defeat Abortion Bill," *Cedar Rapids Gazette*, 12 February 1971, pp. 1, 15.

82. "Woman's Words Defeat Abortion Bill," *Cedar Rapids Gazette*, 12 February 1971, pp. 1, 15.

83. "Sen. Doderer Helps Delay Abortion Bill," *Cedar Rapids Gazette*, 16 February 1973, p. 12.

84. "Iowa Senate Crackdown on Feticide," *Des Moines Tribune*, 2 February 1975, pp. 1, 3.

85. "Sexual Abuse Proposal Gets House Approval," *Cedar Rapids Gazette*, 16 March 1976, p. 4.

86. "Senate Unit to Study Bill on Abortions," *Cedar Rapids Gazette*, 8 February 1974, p. 4; "Sen. Doderer Hits Abortion Proposal," *Cedar Rapids Gazette*, 18 March 1973, p. 4.

87. "Senate Passes Abortion 'Conscience' Bill 42-5," *Cedar Rapids Gazette*, 30 April 1975, sec. C, p. 3.

88. "Women Legislators Seek Abortion Bill Change," *Des Moines Register*, 29 January 1975, sec. A, p. 3.

89. "Iowa House Amends, Passes 'Conscience Clause' Abortion Bill," *Cedar Rapids Gazette*, 6 February 1976, pp. 1, 3; "'Conscience' Bill Approved," *Cedar Rapids Gazette*, 5 March 1976, pp. 1, 3.

90. "Ray: State is Obligated in Abortions for Poor," *Cedar Rapids Gazette*, 12 January 1978, p. 12.

91. "Senate Votes End to Medicaid Abortions," *Cedar Rapids Gazette*, 2 March 1978, p. 8.

92. Ibid.

93. "'String' added to Social Services Bill," *Cedar Rapids Gazette*, 3 March 1978, p. 8.

94. "Anti-Abortionists Dealt Legislative Surprise," *Cedar Rapids Gazette*, 31 March 1979, sec. A, p. 5.

95. "Senate Backtracks on U of I Abortions," *Cedar Rapids Gazette*, 21 May 1981, sec. A, p. 1.

96. "House Modifies Abortion Funds Ban," *Cedar Rapids Gazette*, 16 May 1981, sec. A, pp. 1, 2; "Iowa House Reverses Abortion Vote," *Des Moines Register*, 16 May 1981, sec. A, pp. 1, 3.

97. "House Modifies Abortion Funds Ban," *Cedar Rapids Gazette*, 16 May 1981, sec. A, p. 1.

98. "Iowa House Reverses Abortion Vote," *Des Moines Register*, 16 May 1981, sec. A, pp. 1, 3.

99. "House Modifies Abortion Funds Ban," *Cedar Rapids Gazette*, 16 May 1981, sec. A, p. 1.

100. In 1991, all states and the District of Columbia provided public funds to save the life of the mother; twenty states for rape or incest, fifteen for fetal deformity; and twelve states provided public funds for abortions in all or most circumstances. "House Won't Relax Limitations on Medicaid Abortion Funding," *Cedar Rapids Gazette*, 19 May 1981, sec. A, p. 9. National Abortion Rights Action League, "Who Decides? A State-by-State Review of Abortion Rights," NARAL Foundation, 3rd Edition, January, 1992, p. 148.

101. "Abortion Bill Debated into Night," *Des Moines Register*, 4 February 1994, sec. A, p. 1.

102. Ibid.

103. "Abortion Measure Passed by House," *Des Moines Register* 5 February 1994, sec. M, p. 1.

104. "Legislative Committee Kills Abortion Reporting Bill," *Cedar Rapids Gazette*, 2 March 1982, sec. A, p. 3; "House Rejects Plan to Collect Abortion Data," *Des Moines Register*, 24 February 1990, sec. A, pp. 1, 3.

7. AGRICULTURAL AND ENVIRONMENTAL ISSUES

1. Robert Hogan, "Oleo's Case Against Butter," *The Iowan*, February/March 1953, 10.

2. The five states were Iowa, Montana, Minnesota, Wisconsin, and South Dakota. "Political Ringside," *Newton Daily News*, 5 February 1953, p. 4; "Housewives, Farmers Debate Sale of Yellow Oleo," *Des Moines Register*, 30 January 1953; "Political Ringside," *Newton Daily News*, 30 January 1953, p. 4; "Only Five States Bar Colored Oleo," *Newton Daily News*, 10 February 1953, p. 8.

3. "Leader of 'Margarine Bill' also Founder of Newton LWV in 1934," newspaper article, Gladys Nelson scrapbook, in her possession.

4. "Political Ringside," *Newton Daily News*, 5 February 1953, p. 4.

5. Iowa State Department of Agriculture, *51st Annual Iowa Year Book of Agriculture* (Des Moines: State of Iowa, 1951), p. 21.

6. Ibid., pp. unnumbered, 23, 27, 28.

7. Geo. M. Strayer, Secretary of American Soybean Association, to Gladys Nelson, 9 January 1953, in Nelson's possession.

8. "Housewives, Farmers Debate Sale of Yellow Oleo," *Des Moines Register*, 30 January 1953, p. 1.

9. Frank T. Nye, "Organization of the Assembly," *Palimpsest* 35 (January 1954), p. 10; "Names Iowa House Standing Committees," *Newton Daily News*, 19 January 1953, p. 1.

10. "Housewives, Farmers Debate Sale of Yellow Oleo," *Des Moines Register*, 30 January 1953, p. 1.

11. Typewritten statement, Gladys Nelson scrapbook, in her possession.

12. Ibid.

13. Ibid.

14. Edris H. Owens to Gladys Nelson, telegram, 7 April 1953, Gladys Nelson scrapbook, in her possession.

15. References to angry citizens and constituents appear in telegrams and letters in Nelson's scrapbooks. Gladys Nelson scrapbooks, in her possession.

16. Mary O'Halloran interview.

17. Ibid.

18. Ibid.
19. Ibid.
20. Ibid.
21. Ibid.
22. Ibid.
23. "Aerosol Ban Support Seen," *Cedar Rapids Gazette*, 16 March 1976, p. 4; "Push is on for Solar, Wind Power Bill in the Legislature," *Cedar Rapids Gazette*, 15 April 1978, sec. A, p. 4; "Set Energy Efficiency Standards: EPC Report," *Cedar Rapids Gazette*, 1 March 1978, p. 4; "House Unit: ISCC Should Fix Plant Sites," *Cedar Rapids Gazette*, 26 February 1976, p. 4; "State 'Lax' on Safeguards," *Cedar Rapids Gazette*, 25 April 1975, p. 9; "House Clears Hazardous Waste Authority Measure," *Cedar Rapids Gazette*, 22 February 1978, sec. C, p. 2; "Utilities Bill Remains Aglow in Iowa House," *Des Moines Register*, 15 March 1978, sec. A, p. 4; "Amendments Offered on Land Use Bill," *Cedar Rapids Gazette*, 18 April 1975, p. 9; "Land Use Bill Gains Slim House Passage," *Cedar Rapids Gazette*, 12 April 1975, pp. 1, 3; "Glimmer of Life in State Land Use Policy Bill," *Cedar Rapids Gazette*, 22 March 1974, p. 4; "Sides Aired on Land Use Plan," *Cedar Rapids Gazette*, 20 February 1975, p. 4.
24. Mary O'Halloran interview.
25. "Cans to be Banned?" *Cedar Rapids Gazette*, 26 April 1977, p. 15; "Home Bill Surprise in Iowa House," *Cedar Rapids Gazette*, 1 May 1973, p. 9.
26. "'Ban the Can' Battle Threatened in House," *Cedar Rapids Gazette*, 25 February 1974, p. 4.
27. Mary O'Halloran interview.
28. Ibid.
29. "Bottle, Can Bill to House," *Des Moines Register*, 17 April 1975, p. 7.
30. Mary O'Halloran interview.
31. "Labor, Manufacturer Fight Can Deposits," *Cedar Rapids Gazette*, 13 January 1977, p. 4; "Consumer Revolt is Predicted over Deposit on Beverage Containers," *Cedar Rapids Gazette*, 21 March 1977, p. 4.
32. "Cans to be Banned?" *Cedar Rapids Gazette*, 26 April 1977, p. 15.
33. Ibid.
34. "Bottle Bill Back to Senate," *Cedar Rapids Gazette*, 2 March 1978, p. 10.
35. "'Ban-the-Can' Forces Lose First Showdown," *Cedar Rapids Gazette*, 6 April 1977, sec. C, p. 2; "Iowa Ready for 'Ban the Can' Law?" *Cedar Rapids Gazette*, 20 January 1977, p. 5.
36. "Iowa Legislators Resist her Attempt to be a 'member of the club.'" *Des Moines Register*, 11 April 1977, sec. A, p. 6.
37. Ibid.
38. Mary O'Halloran interview.
39. "Ban-the-Can Talks Wednesday," *Cedar Rapids Gazette*, 22 April 1977, p. 2.
40. "Ray Urges House Bottle Deposit OK," *Cedar Rapids Gazette*, 10 February 1978, pp. 1, 3.
41. Ray has said that he is proudest of that bill's passage of all the legislation he worked on during his fourteen years in office. Jon Bowermaster, *Governor: An Oral Biography of Robert D. Ray* (Ames: Iowa State University Press, 1987) pp. 168-173.
42. "Bottle Bill Back to Senate," *Cedar Rapids Gazette*, 2 March 1978, p. 10.
43. "Bottle-can Bill Ready for Ray's Signature," *Cedar Rapids Gazette*, 12 April 1978, sec. C, p. 2.
44. "45,000 Help to Clean Up Iowa Litter," *Des Moines Register*, 6 May 1979, sec. B, p. 1.
45. Jean Lloyd-Jones interview.
46. Ibid.

47. "1993 Annual Report of the Iowa Railway Finance Authority," prepared by the Rail and Water Division, Iowa Department of Transportation, February 1994, p. 1.

48. "$100 Million Railroad Plan Endorsed by Ray," *Des Moines Register*, 6 April 1980.

49. "Ray-endorsed Plan to Sell State Rail Bonds 'Monstrous,' says Rigler," *Des Moines Register* 16 April 1980, sec. A, p. 3.

50. "Rigler: Rail Bill 'Monster,'" *Cedar Rapids Gazette*, 16 April 1980, sec. B, p. 5.

51. "Ray Signs Bill Setting up New Rail Authority," *Des Moines Register* 21 May 1980, sec. B, p. 5.

52. "No Quick Response Seen for Rail Needs," *Cedar Rapids Gazette* 5 February 1981, sec. A, p. 15.

53. "House OK's Measure to Keep Rail Line Open," *Cedar Rapids Gazette*, 10 March 1981, sec. A, p. 5.

54. "1993 Annual Report of the Iowa Railway Finance Authority," prepared by the Rail and Water Division, Iowa Department of Transportation, February 1994, pp. 7-10.

55. Jean Lloyd-Jones interview.

8. REVENUE ISSUES

1. For a discussion of Iowa's economic problems in the 1980s, see Steffen W. Schmidt, "Challenges for the Future," in Lee Ann Osbun and Steffen W. Schmidt, eds., *Issues in Iowa Politics* (Ames: Iowa State University Press, 1990), pp. 229-254.

2. Joan Lipsky interview.

3. "Would Tap Trucks to Aid Roads," *Cedar Rapids Gazette*, 7 April 1969, p. 1.

4. "Ray Backs Lipsky Truck Fee Bid," *Cedar Rapids Gazette* 10 April 1969, p. 8.

5. Joan Lipsky interview.

6. Lipsky prefaced her comments about rude truck drivers with statements crediting many truck drivers as safe and courteous operators. Joan Lipsky interview.

7. "Truck Bill Deadlock Forecast," *Cedar Rapids Gazette*, 17 May 1969, p. 5.

8. Joan Lipsky interview; "Truck Bill Deadlock Forecast," *Cedar Rapids Gazette*, 17 May 1969, p. 5; "Truckers Protest Lipsky Proposal to Raise Fees," *Cedar Rapids Gazette*, 17 April 1969, p. 3.

9. "Legislative Notes by Frank Nye," *Cedar Rapids Gazette*, 14 April 1969, p. 5.

10. "Statehouse Notebook," *Des Moines Tribune*, 23 April 1969, p. 31.

11. "Legislative Notes by Frank Nye," *Cedar Rapids Gazette*, 14 April 1969, p. 5.

12. "Truck Fee Battle in House Set," *Cedar Rapids Gazette*, 20 April 1969, sec. B, p. 11; "Solons Go Home 'Til Next Year," *Cedar Rapids Gazette*, 24 May 1969, pp. 1, 5.

13. Amendments pass with a majority vote; bills require 51 votes in the House and 26 in the Senate. "Tax-Rich Plan may Derail Bill," *Cedar Rapids Gazette*, 4 February 1982, sec. A, pp. 1, 14.

14. "Taxing Rich Amendment a Move 'Toward Fairness,'" *Cedar Rapids Gazette*, 5 February 1982, sec. A, p. 11.

15. "Tax-Rich Plan May Derail Bill," *Cedar Rapids Gazette*, 4 February 1982, sec. A, pp. 1, 14.

16. Ibid.

17. Ibid.

18. Ibid.

19. Ibid.

20. "Ray Tax Bill Still Bogged Down," *Cedar Rapids Gazette*, 5 February 1982, sec. A, pp. 1, 10.

21. "'Tax the Rich' Plan Ok'd by Iowa House," *Cedar Rapids Gazette*, 19 March 1983,

sec. A, pp. 1, 11.

22. "Repeal of Tax on Food Aired," *Cedar Rapids Gazette*, 1 February 1973, sec. C, p. 1.

23. "Sales Tax Idea Pre-empted: 'Love It,' Says Senator Orr," *Des Moines Register*, 18 January 1974, p. 22; "Ray: Repeal Food Sales Tax," *Cedar Rapids Gazette*, 15 January 1974, pp. 1, 3; "How Ray Grabbed Sales Tax Issue," *Des Moines Sunday Register*, 20 January 1974, sec. A, pp. 1, 3.

24. "Pari-Mutuel Income for Welfare Urged," *Cedar Rapids Gazette*, 12 January 1970, sec. A, p. 3.

25. "East Iowans Urge Pari-Mutuel Bill to Aid Welfare," *Cedar Rapids Gazette*, 3 March 1970, p. 4.

26. "Pari-Mutuel Betting Passes Committee Hurdle," *Cedar Rapids Gazette*, 16 April 1971, pp. 1, 2.

27. "Pari-Mutuel's Odds Are Even," *Cedar Rapids Gazette*, 6 April 1975, sec. B, pp. 1, 7.

28. "Parimutuel Betting Comes up Again," *Cedar Rapids Gazette*, 18 January 1980, sec. A, p. 9.

29. "Parimutuel Betting Faces Rough Road after Panel OK," *Cedar Rapids Gazette*, 9 March 1983, sec. A, p. 3.

30. "Who's in Charge: Branstad or Bureaucrats?" *Cedar Rapids Gazette*, 28 March 1983, sec. A, p. 13.

31. "Backers of Pari-mutuel Betting Turn to Last-ditch Bargaining," *Des Moines Register*, 5 May 1983, sec. A, p. 3.

32. Ibid.

33. "Parimutuel Bill may yet Beat the Odds," *Cedar Rapids Gazette*, 10 May 1983 sec. A, pp. 1, 11.

34. "Backers of Pari-mutuel Betting Turn to Last-ditch Bargaining," *Des Moines Register*, 5 May 1983, sec. A, p. 3.

35. "Parimutuel Bill to House Floor," *Cedar Rapids Gazette*, 12 May 1983, sec. A, pp. 1, 13.

36. Betty Jean Clark interview.

37. "Pari-mutuel Bill Clears Toughest Hurdle," *Cedar Rapids Gazette*, 12 May 1983, sec. A, p. 3.

38. "Horse, Dog Betting OK'd by Iowa House," *Cedar Rapids Gazette*, 13 May 1983, pp. 1, 13.

39. Ibid.

40. Ibid.

41. "Mondale the Front-runner for Linn County Demos," *Cedar Rapids Gazette*, 1 March 1983, sec. A, p. 9.

42. "Iowa Lottery Plan Passes House, 54-43," *Des Moines Register*, 4 May 1983, sec. A, pp. 1, 3; "House Approves Setting up State Lottery," *Cedar Rapids Gazette*, 4 May 1983, sec. A, pp. 1, 15; "House OK Moves Lottery Showdown Closer," *Cedar Rapids Gazette*, 17 February 1984, sec. A, pp. 1, 13; "Hard Choices Expected for State Agenda," *Des Moines Sunday Register*, 21 April 1985, sec. A, pp. 1, 7.

EPILOGUE

1. Madeleine Kunin, "Keynote Address," in "Report from a Conference: Women in Legislative Leadership, November 14-17, 1985," Center for the American Woman in Politics, Eagleton Institute of Politics, Rutgers State University of New Jersey.

2. Women in the U.S. House of Representatives 1994, and Statewide Elective Executive Women 1994, Fact Sheets, Center for the American Woman and Politics (CAWP), National Information Bank on Women in Public Office, Eagleton Institute of Politics, Rutgers University.

3. "Much Still to Be Done by Women in Politics, Say Ames Speakers," *Des Moines Register*, 21 March 1993, sec. B, p. 3.

APPENDIX A

1. "Point of Personal Privilege," Minnette Doderer Collection, MsC 457, Box 7, University of Iowa Libraries, Iowa City, Iowa.

APPENDIX B

1. Quoted in Susan Jane Kennell, "The Politics of Abortion: The Case of Iowa," Master's thesis, Iowa State University, 1971, pp. 99-102.

BIBLIOGRAPHY

INTERVIEWS IN AUTHOR'S POSSESSION

Adams, Janet. 13 February 1992.
Anderson, Helen. 11 March 1991.
Baxter, Elaine. 26 June 1990.
Beatty, Linda. 26 September 1991.
Bock, Lenabelle. 31 May 1988.
Boyd, Nancy Shimanek. 5 July 1989.
Brandt, Diane. 26 June 1989.
Buhr, Florence. 28 June 1990.
Canovan, Casey. 21 February 1991.
Carl, Janet. 15 June 1990.
Carpenter, Dorothy. 4 October 1991.
Chapman, Kathleen. 21 May 1991.
Clark, Betty Jean. 13 July 1989.
Cohen, Gertrude. 1 March 1991.
Conklin, W. Charlene. 2 November 1989.
Corning, Joy. October 31, 1991.
Crabb, Helen Margaret. 18 April 1988.
Doderer, Minnette. 27 June 1989.
Doderer, Minnette. 23 May 1991.
Duitscher, Lucille. 16 June 1989.
Franklin, A. June. 17 April 1991.
Garman, Teresa. 29 October 1991.
Garner, Vernon A. 8 February 1991.
Gentleman, Julia. 29 June 1989.
Glanton, Willie. 14 June 1990.
Gregerson, Mary Pat. 26 July 1989.
Gruhn, Josephine. 23 October 1989.
Hammond, Johnie. 17 October 1991.
Hannon, Beverly. 25 February 1991.
Harper, Deverre. 15 April 1991.
Harper, Patricia. 30 January 1991.
Harper, Rick C. 15 April 1991.
Hoffman-Bright, Betty. 27 July 1989.
Kiser, E. Jean. 1 September 1989.
Larsen, Sonja. 26 June 1989.
Laughlin, Janis Torrence. 16 April 1991.
Lipsky, Joan. 7 July 1989.
Lloyd-Jones, Jean. 27 July 1989.
Lonergan, Joyce. 23 June 1989.
Lundby, Mary. 1 October 1991.
McElroy, Lillian. 5 June 1989.
McKee, Vera. 20 May 1988.
Metcalf, Janet. 7 October 1991.
Mullins, Cora A. 19 February 1991.
Mullins, Sue B. 13 July 1989.
Neuhauser, Mary. 21 May 1991.
O'Halloran, Mary. 5 August 1989.
Orr, Jo Ann. 22 June 1989.
Peick, Doris. 29 January 1991.
Poffenberger, Virginia. 2 August 1989.
Sargisson, Hallie. 4 June 1989.
Shaw, Elizabeth. 26 October 1989.

Smith, Jo. 20 May 1991.
Speas, Mary Lou. 12 April 1991.
Svoboda, Jane. 29 October 1989.
Svoboda, Linda. 20 June, 1989.
Teaford, Jane. 23 May 1991.
Thompson, Patricia. 16 September 1989.
Van Alstine, Percie. 1 August 1988.
Vandenburg, Helen. 23 May 1991.
Wick, Kathlyn. 23 May 1988.
Yenger, Sue. 18 February 1991.
Zastrow, Katherine. 10 June 1988.
Zimmerman, Jo Ann. 18 February 1991.

NEWSPAPERS

Bagley Gazette
Cedar Rapids Gazette
Christian Science Monitor
Council Bluffs Nonpareil
Des Moines Register
Des Moines Sunday Register
Des Moines Tribune
Des Moines Tribune-Capital
Garner Leader
Iowa Recorder
Jackson Sentinel
Knoxville Journal
Maquoketa Excelsior
Marshalltown Times-Republican
Mt. Pleasant Free Press
Mt. Pleasant Journal
Mt. Pleasant Weekly News
New York Times
Newton Daily News
Shell Rock News
Sioux City Journal
Waterloo Daily Courier

STATE DOCUMENTS

Code of Iowa
Iowa Official Register
Journal of the Iowa House of Representatives
Journal of the Iowa Senate
Session Laws

BOOKS AND ARTICLES

Aburdene, Patricia, and John Naisbitt. *Megratrends for Women.* New York: Villard Books, 1992.

Allen, Edward S. *Freedom in Iowa: The Role of the Iowa Civil Liberties Union.* Ames: Iowa State University Press, 1977.

Anderson, Leon. *New Hampshire Women Legislators: 1921-1971.* Evans Printing Company, 1971.

Bowermaster, Jon. *Governor: An Oral Biography of Robert D. Ray.* Ames: Iowa State University Press, 1987.

Breckinridge, Sophonisba P. *Women in the Twentieth Century: A Study of Their Political, Social and Economic Activities.* New York: McGraw-Hill Book Company, 1933.

Briggs, John E. "The Legislation of the Thirty-eighth General Assembly of Iowa,"

Iowa Journal of History and Politics 17 (October 1919): 471-612.

_____. "The Legislation of the Thirty-ninth General Assembly of Iowa," *The Iowa Journal of History and Politics* 19 (October 1921): 489-666.

Briggs, John E., and Jacob Van Ek. "The Legislation of the Fortieth General Assembly of Iowa," *Iowa Journal of History and Politics* 21 (October 1923): 507-676.

Caldeira, Gregory A. and Samuel C. Patterson, "Political Friendship in the Legislature," *Journal of Politics* 49 no. 4, November 1987, pp. 953-975.

Cantor, Dorothy W., and Toni Bernay with Jean Stoess. *Women in Power: The Secrets of Leadership*. Boston: Houghton Mifflin Company, 1992.

Carroll, Susan J. *Women as Candidates in American Politics*. Bloomington: Indiana University Press, 1985.

Carroll, Susan J. "Political Elites and Sex Differences in Political Ambition: A Reconsideration," *Journal of Politics* 47 (November 1985): 1231-1243.

Center for the American Woman and Politics. Fact Sheet: Women in State Legislatures 1987. National Information Bank on Women in Public Office. Eagleton Institute of Politics, Rutgers, The State University of New Jersey.

_____. "Of Interest." *CAWP News and Notes*, (Winter 1991). Center for the American Woman and Politics, Eagleton Institute of Politics, Rutgers, The State University of New Jersey.

_____. "Of Interest." *CAWP News and Notes* (Winter 1992). Center for the American Woman and Politics, Eagleton Institute of Politics, Rutgers, The State University of New Jersey.

_____. "Report from a Conference: Women in Legislative Leadership, May 18-21, 1972." Center for the American Woman and Politics, Eagleton Institute of Politics, Rutgers, The State University of New Jersey.

_____. "Report from a Conference: Women in Legislative Leadership, June 17-20, 1982." Center for the American Woman and Politics, Eagleton Institute of Politics, Rutgers, The State University of New Jersey.

_____. "Report from a Conference: Women in Legislative Leadership, November 14-17, 1985." Center for the American Woman and Politics, Eagleton Institute of Politics, Rutgers, The State University of New Jersey.

_____Women in the U.S. Congress 1994, and Women in State Legislatures, Fact Sheets, Center for the American Woman and Politics (CAWP), National Information Bank on Women in Public Office, Eagleton Institute of Politics, Rutgers, The State University of New Jersey.

Chafe, William H. *The American Woman: Her Changing Social, Economic, and Political Roles, 1920-1970*. London: Oxford University Press, 1972.

Common Cause of Iowa. "A Report on Campaign Finance in Iowa, 1988." Des Moines, Iowa.

_____. "A Report on Legislative Election Campaign Finance in Iowa, 1992." Des Moines, Iowa.

Dains, Mary K. Forty Years in the House: A Composite of Portrait of Missouri Women Legislators. Typescript.

Darcy, R., Susan Welch, and Janet Clark. *Women, Elections, and Representation*. New York: Longman, 1987.

Decker, Barbara Sinclair. *The Women's Movement: Political, Socioeconomic, and Psychological Issues*. 3rd ed. Cambridge: Harper and Row, 1983.

Diamond, Irene. *Sex Roles in the State House*. New Haven: Yale University Press, 1977.

Ellis, M. Carolyn, and Joanne V. Hawks. "Ladies in the Gentlemen's Club," *Proceedings of the 1986 South Carolina Historical Association*: 17-32.

Ellis, Mary Carolyn and Joanne V. Hawks. "Creating a Different Pattern: Florida's Women Legislators, 1928-1986," *Florida Historical Quarterly*, 66 (July 1987): 68-83.

Evans, Sara M. *Born for Liberty: A History of Women in America*. New York: Free Press, 1989.

50 States Commission of the Iowa Commission on the Status of Women. "Iowa '50 State Project: A Review of the 1983 Iowa Code for Sex Discrimination.'" Des Moines: Iowa Commission on the Status of Women.

Fink, Deborah. *Open Country Iowa: Rural Women, Tradition and Change*. Albany: State University of New York, 1986.

Flexner, Eleanor. *Century of Struggle*. Cambridge, Massachusetts: Harvard University Press, 1975.

Fraser, Arvonne S. and Sue E. Holbert. "Women in the Minnesota Legislature." In *Women of Minnesota: Selected Biographical Essays*, edited by Barbara Stuhler and Gretchen Kreuter. St. Paul: Minnesota Historical Society Press, 1977.

Friedan, Betty. *The Feminine Mystique*. New York: W.W. Norton & Company, Inc., 1963.

Gallaher, Ruth A. *Legal and Political Status of Women in Iowa: An Historical Account of the Rights of Women in Iowa from 1838 to 1918*. Iowa City: The State Historical Society of Iowa, 1918.

Gittler, Josephine. "Hospital Cost Containment in Iowa: A Guide for State Public Policymakers," *Iowa Law Review* 69 (July 1984): 1269-1343.

Hahn, Harlan. *Urban-Rural Conflict: The Politics of Change*. Beverly Hills: Sage Publications, 1971.

Hanft, Ethel W., and Paula J. Manley. *Outstanding Iowa Women: Past and Present*. Muscatine: River Bend Publishing, 1980.

Harris, Corra. "Practical Politics for Gentlewomen," *Ladies Home Journal*, September 1921, 16, 170.

Hartman, Susan M. *From Margin to Mainstream: American Women and Politics Since 1960*. New York: Alfred A. Knopf, 1989.

Hawks, Joanne Varner. "A Select Few: Alabama's Women Legislators, 1922-1983," *The Alabama Review* 38 (July 1985): 175-201.

Hawks, Joanne V., M. Carolyn Ellis, and J. Byron Morris, "Women in the Mississippi Legislature (1924-1981)," *Journal of Mississippi History* 63 (November 1981): 266-293.

Hogan, Robert. "Oleo's Case Against Butter." *The Iowan*. February/March 1953, 9-10, 42.

Iowa Department of Agriculture. *51st Annual Year Book of Agriculture*. Des Moines: State of Iowa, 1951.

Iowa Department of Transportation. "1993 Annual Report of the Iowa Railway

Finance Authority." Rail and Water Division, 1994. Des Moines, Iowa.
Jensen, Joan M. "Pioneers in Politics," *El Palacio* 92 (Summer/Fall 1986): 12-19.
Jewell, Malcom E., and Samuel C. Patterson. *The Legislative Process in the United States*. 2d ed. New York: Random House, 1973.
Jordan, David W. "Those Formidable Feminists: Iowa's Early Vote-getters," *The Iowan* 1 December 1982, 46-52.
Kaminer, Wendy. *A Fearful Freedom: Women's Flight from Equality*. New York: Addison-Wesley Publishing Company, 1990.
Keefe, William J. *The American Legislative Process*. Englewood Cliffs, New Jersey: Prentice-Hall, Inc., 1985.
Kennell, Susan Jane. "The Politics of Abortion: The Case of Iowa," Master's thesis, Iowa State University, 1971.
Kirkpatrick, Jeane J. *Political Woman*. New York: Basic Books, 1974.
Kleeman, Katherine E. "Women in State Government: Looking Back, Looking Ahead." *Journal of State Government* 60 (September/October 1987): 201-205.
Klein, Ethel. *Gender Politics: From Consciousness to Mass Politics*. Cambridge, Massachusetts: Harvard University Press, 1984.
Knapp, Elaine S. "A Woman's Place is in the Capitol," *State Government News* September 1984, 4-9.
Kunin, Madeleine. "Keynote Address." In "Women in Legislative Leadership: Report from a Conference, November 14-17, 1985." Center for the American Woman in Politics, Eagleton Institute of Politics, Rutgers, The State University of New Jersey.
Larew, James C. *A Party Reborn: The Democrats of Iowa, 1950-1974*. Iowa City: Iowa State Historical Society, 1980.
Lemmons, J. Stanley. *The Woman Citizen: Social Feminism in the 1920s*. Urbana: University of Illinois Press, 1973.
Mandel, Ruth B. *In the Running: The New Woman Candidate*. New Haven: Ticknor & Fields, 1981.
Mead, Margaret, and Frances Balgley Kaplan, eds. *American Women: The Report of the President's Commission on the Status of Women and Other Publications of the Commission*. New York: Charles Scribner's Sons, 1965.
Mezey, Susan Gluck. "Women and Representation: the Case of Hawaii," *Journal of Politics* 40 (May 1978): 369-385.
Moncure, Dorothy Ashby. "Women in Political Life," *Current History* 29 (January 1929): 639-643.
Miller, Judy Ann. "The Representative is a Lady," *Black Politician* 1 (Fall 1969): 17-18.
Mills, George. "1884-1984 Legislative Highlights," Typescript.
Mueller, Carol. "A Scholar's Perspective." In "Women in State Legislatures: Report from a Conference, June 17-20, 1982." Center for the American Woman and Politics, Eagleton Institute of Politics, Rutgers, The State University of New Jersey.
National Abortion Rights Action League. "Who Decides? A State-by-State Review of Abortion Rights." NARAL Foundation, 3rd ed. January 1992.
Noun, Louise. *More Strong-Minded Women: Iowa Feminists Tell Their Stories*. Ames:

Iowa State University Press, 1992.

_____. *Strong-Minded Women: The Emergence of the Woman-Suffrage Movement in Iowa*. Ames: Iowa State University Press, 1969.

Nye, Frank T. "Organization of the Assembly." *The Palimpsest* 35 (January 1954): 9-15.

_____. "The 61st General Assembly of Iowa," *The Palimpsest* 44 (September 1965): 425-488.

Osbun, Lee Ann, and Steffen W. Schmidt, eds. *Issues in Iowa Politics*. Ames: Iowa State University Press, 1990.

Paulus, Norma. "Women Find Political Power in Unity." *Journal of State Government* 60 (September/October 1987): 225-228.

Pinchot, Gifford. "The Influence of Women in Politics," *Ladies Home Journal*, September 1922, 12, 116.

Reed, Cecil A., with Priscilla Donovan. *Fly in the Buttermilk*. Iowa City: University of Iowa Press, 1993.

Riley, Glenda. *Inventing the American Woman: A Perspective on Women's History*. Arlington Heights: Harlan Davidson, Inc., 1986.

Ross, Earle D. *Iowa Agriculture: An Historical Survey*. Iowa City: State Historical Society of Iowa, 1951.

Rothman, Sheila M. *Woman's Proper Place: A History of Changing Ideals and Practices, 1870 to the Present*. New York: Basic Books, Inc., 1978.

Sage, Leland. *A History of Iowa*. Ames: Iowa State University Press, 1974.

Saloutos, Theodore, and John D. Hicks. "The Farm Strike." In *Patterns and Perspectives in Iowa History*, edited by Dorothy Schwieder. Ames: Iowa State University Press, 1973.

Schwieder, Dorothy. "Education and Change in the Lives of Iowa Farm Women," *Agricultural History* 60 (Spring 1986): 200-215.

Sherman, Sharon. "Women Legislators Seek 'Critical Mass,'" *State Legislatures* 10 (January 1984): 26-27.

Shover, John L. *Cornbelt Rebellion: The Farmer's Holiday Association*. Urbana: University of Illinois Press, 1965.

Smalley, Hazel C. "Black Women Legislators Answer Questions," *Black Politician* 2 (Summer 1971): 40-44.

Smith, Richard N. *Development of the Iowa Department of Public Instruction, 1900-1965*. State of Iowa: Department of Public Instruction, 1969.

Stanwick, Kathy A. "Women's Legislative Caucuses: Altering State Policy and Politics." *News and Notes* 5 (May 1987): 5-6. Center for the American Woman and Politics, The Eagleton Institute, Rutgers, The State University of New Jersey.

Stork, Frank J. *Lawmaking in Iowa: System and Structure*. Des Moines: Iowa Senate, 1980.

Stork, Frank J. and Cynthia A. Clingan. *The Iowa General Assembly: Our Legislative Heritage, 1846-1980*. Des Moines: Iowa Senate, 1980.

Swisher, Jacob A. "The Legislation of the Forty-first General Assembly of Iowa," *Iowa Journal of History and Politics* 23 (October 1925): 507-625.

____, "The Legislation of the Forty-third General Assembly of Iowa," Iowa Monograph Series, no. 1. Iowa City: Iowa State Historical Society, 1929.

____, "The Legislation of the Forty-fourth General Assembly of Iowa," *Iowa Journal of History and Politics* 30 (January 1932): 3-114.

____, "The Legislation of the Forty-fifth General Assembly of Iowa: Extra Session," Iowa Monograph Series, no. 7. Iowa City: Iowa State Historical Society, 1934.

____, "The Legislation of the Forty-sixth General Assembly of Iowa," *Iowa Journal of History and Politics* 34 (January 1936): 3-97.

Swisher, Jacob A., and Ruth A. Gallaher. "The Legislation of the Forty-fifth General Assembly of Iowa," Iowa Monograph Series, no. 5. Iowa City: The State Historical Society of Iowa, 1933.

Swisher, Jacob A., and Jack T. Johnson. "The Legislation of the Forty-seventh General Assembly," *The Iowa Journal of History and Politics* 35 (October 1937): 347-470.

Tolchin, Susan, and Martin Tolchin. *Clout: Womanpower and Politics*. New York: Coward, McCann & Geoghan, Inc., 1974.

Upton, Harriet Taylor. "The Machine and the Woman," *Ladies Home Journal*, October 1922, 13, 159.

Wandersee, Winifred D. *On the Move: American Women in the 1970s*. Boston: Twayne Publishers, 1988.

Welch, Susan, and Sue Thomas. "Do Women in Public Office Make a Difference?" In *Gender and Policymaking: Studies of Women in Office*, edited by Debra Dodson. New Brunswick, New Jersey: State University of New Jersey, 1991.

Werner, Emmy E. "Women in the State Legislatures," *Western Political Quarterly* 21 (March 1968): 40-50.

Wilson, Margaret Woodrow. "Where Women in Politics Fail," *Ladies Home Journal*, September 1921, pp. 10, 70.

Winter, Alice Ames. "The Club Citizenship Program," *Ladies Homes Journal,* December 1922, pp. 28, 125, 156, 128.

INDEX

Women members of the Iowa General Assembly are listed in **boldface** type along with their political affiliation.